PASTA

THE **COMPLETE** COOKBOOK

PASTA

TASTY RECIPES FOR EVERY DAY

Edited by Helen Aitkin

METRO BOOKS
NEW YORK

Contents

You will find the following cookery ratings on the recipes in this book:

A single pot symbol indicates a recipe that is simple and generally straightforward to make—perfect for beginners.

Two symbols indicate the need for just a little more care and a little more time.

Three symbols indicate special recipes that need more investment in time, care and patience—but the results are worth it.

A Guide to Pasta

Even though there are 300 different shapes available today, there is nothing very complicated about pasta; it is one of the simplest foods to cook and also one of the most versatile. Nevertheless, here are a few tips on how best to prepare and serve pasta, and even instructions for making your own.

FRESH OR DRIED?

Basic dried pasta is made with durum wheat semolina and water, which is passed through a die to make shaped pastas or long pasta such as spaghetti. In the recipes in this book, when the ingredient list simply states 'pasta' we are referring to dried pasta.

Fresh pasta is made either with a soft wheat or durum wheat semolina and water. When fresh pasta is more appropriate to a recipe we will state 'fresh pasta' in the ingredient list.

Many people assume that fresh pasta must be 'better' than dried. This is not the case—some sauces are better teamed with fresh pasta and some are best with dried. Fresh pasta works well with rich sauces made from cream, butter and cheese, because its soft texture absorbs the sauce. Alfredo is one of the nicest sauces to serve on fresh pasta, as is plain butter and Parmesan. Dried pasta is more robust if you're serving a hearty tomato-based sauce. If your sauce has olives, anchovies, chillies, meat or seafood, you'll almost certainly be better using dried pasta.

STORING PASTA

Dried pasta can be stored in a cool dry place for months. However, dried wholewheat pasta will only last for one month before turning rancid. Fresh pasta must be refrigerated and won't keep for as long, so buy it as you need it. Filled pasta is best bought a day or so before you need it, but some vacuum-packed filled pastas can be kept for up to three weeks (check the use-by date). It can also be frozen in a single layer between sheets of plastic wrap for up to three months but creamy fillings don't freeze well.

MATCHING THE SAUCE TO THE PASTA

With up to 300 different pasta shapes, it can be confusing knowing which sauce to serve with which pasta. A basic rule to remember is that a chunky pasta is best with a chunky sauce and a thin pasta is best with a thin sauce. Chunky pasta shapes enable you to pick up the sauce with the pasta. Smooth, slender pasta shapes will not hold a chunky sauce but will suit an olive oil or fresh tomato sauce. Tubular shapes such as penne capture thick sauces, while flat or long pastas are traditionally served with thin smooth sauces. Some pastas are ridged specifically so that they can capture more sauce. Tiny pasta such as ditalini or stelline are usually smooth and used in soups; larger pastas would absorb too much of the liquid. Many of the different pasta shapes are shown over the following pages.

HOW MUCH PASTA?

Pasta varies so much in shape, size and type, it is hard to be specific about how much pasta you need per serve. As a general guide, use about 90 g (3 oz) of dried pasta per person for a starter and 150 g (5 oz) for a main course. With fresh pasta (which weighs a little more because it contains more water) use approximately 60 g (2 oz) for a starter and 125 g (4 oz) for a main course.

How much sauce is obviously a matter of personal taste, but it should be pointed out that in Italy pasta is served with only enough sauce to just coat the pasta. Once the pasta and sauce are tossed together, there should be no sauce left sitting in the bottom of the bowl.

COOKING PASTA

Pasta should be cooked in a large deep saucepan of water to prevent the pasta pieces from sticking to each other. Allow about 6 litres of water for every 500 g (1 lb) pasta, but never use less than 4 litres even for a small amount of pasta. Filled pasta and large pasta such as lasagne will need more water, between 9 and 12 litres, because they are more likely to stick.

If you need to cook large amounts of pasta, only cook up to 1 kg (2 lb) in one saucepan.

Always bring the water to the boil before adding salt (purely to add flavor and a matter of personal preference) and then stirring in the pasta. When the water comes back to the boil, begin timing, stirring often once the pasta softens a little. Test the pasta just prior to the final cooking time on the packet.

Generally, the fresher the pasta, the shorter the cooking time. Fresh pasta from a delicatessen or pasta shop usually only needs 1–2 minutes. Vacuum-packed fresh pasta from the supermarket requires a little longer—about 6 minutes. Dried pasta varies depending on the size and shape but, because it needs rehydrating as well as cooking, it usually takes longer than fresh pasta. For the most accurate times for all pasta, follow the instructions on the packet.

The best way to ensure pasta is cooked is to taste it. The pasta should be just tender and still retain a slight bite—this is referred to in Italian as al dente which literally means 'to the tooth'.

Adding oil to the cooking water contributes very little and can make the pasta too slippery to hold sauce.

Once the pasta is cooked, it is important to drain it in a colander and then turn it either back into the cooking pan to keep warm, into a heated dish or into a pan or dish with the sauce.

Don't overdrain the pasta: it needs to be a little wet for the sauce to coat it well. Never leave pasta sitting in the colander or it will clump together. If you have mistimed your cooking and the sauce isn't ready, put the pasta back into the hot pan and toss with a small amount of olive oil or butter to prevent it from sticking together. Alternatively, lightly spray the drained pasta with some boiling water and toss it gently (it is always a good idea to keep a little of the cooking water for this, in case you overdrain).

Never rinse the pasta unless stated in the recipe: it is usually only rinsed if used in a baked dish or served cold in a salad because the starches released in cooking help the pasta to meld with the sauce.

Timing can make all the difference between a good pasta meal and a great one. Always read the recipe through first and then coordinate your cooking times. Try to have the sauce ready to dress the pasta as soon as it is cooked, especially if the pasta is fresh (it will continue to cook if you leave it to sit around).

MAKING YOUR OWN PASTA

To make pasta to serve four as a main course, you will need 300 g (10 oz) of plain flour, 3 large (60 g/2 oz) eggs, 30 ml (1 fl oz) of olive oil, optional, and a pinch of salt.

All the ingredients should be brought to room temperature before you start. The proportion of flour to eggs depends on the weather, the quality of the flour and the age and size of the eggs. Oil makes it easier to work with but you don't have to use it.

Use plain or unbleached flour, which gives a well-textured, light dough with good manageability. A percentage of durum wheat semolina is favored by some pasta makers as it improves flavor, color and texture. However, its hard-wheat qualities sometimes make it difficult to work, particularly on a hand-cranked machine and any proportion greater than equal parts durum wheat semolina to plain flour can cause problems.

1 To mix the dough by hand, mound the plain flour on a work surface or in a bowl and make a well in the centre.

2 Break the eggs into the well and add the oil, if using, and a large pinch of salt. Begin to whisk the eggs and oil together with a fork, incorporating a little of the flour as you do so.

3 Gradually blend the flour with the eggs, working from the centre out. Use your free hand to hold the mound in place and stop leakage if any of the egg escapes.

4 Knead the dough on a lightly floured surface with smooth, light strokes, turning it as you fold and press. It should be soft and pliable, but dry to the touch. If it is sticky, knead in a little flour.

5 It will take at least 6 minutes kneading to achieve a smooth and elastic texture with a slightly glossy appearance. If durum wheat semolina is used, the kneading will take a little longer, at least 8 minutes. Put the dough in a plastic bag without sealing, or cover with a tea towel or an upturned bowl. Allow to rest for 30 minutes.

ROLLING AND CUTTING

1 Divide the dough into three or four manageable portions and cover with plastic wrap to prevent drying out.

2 Dust the work surface with semolina (flour will make the pasta heavier). Flatten the first piece of dough so that it is easier to roll through the machine.

3 On the widest setting, feed the dough through the rollers. Fold the flattened dough in half or thirds so it fits across the rollers. Repeat three times to create a velvety texture. As each sheet is completed, place it on a dry tea towel. Leave uncovered to surface dry for 10 minutes if the sheets are to be cut, but cover them if they are to be used for filled pasta.

4 Attach the cutting blades to your machine, the wide one for tagliatelle and the narrower one for linguine.

5 Feed a sheet of pasta into the machine and carefully collect the pasta as it comes out the other end.

6 Either hang up the pasta to dry over a wooden

Feed the pasta through the rollers on the widest setting. Repeat this three times.

Attach the cutting blades to the machine, the wide for tagliatelle and the narrow for linguine.

Feed a sheet of pasta into the machine and collect the pasta as it comes out of the end.

Either hang the pasta up to dry or coil it into nests and toss with semolina.

spoon or on a pasta dryer or coil it into nests. To keep the nests from sticking, toss in a little semolina.

Dried Pasta

Dried pasta is best suited to stronger flavored sauces, such as those containing tomato, chilli or seafood. Some shapes work well with thin sauces and some are better with a chunky topping. Here is a rough guide to suitable sauces but, of course, everyone will have their own favorites.

1 **Penne** (best with thick or chunky sauces)
2 **Tagliatelle** (best with thin coating sauces)
3 **Tomato tagliatelle** (tagliatelle flavored and colored with tomato, best with thin coating sauces)
4 **Lasagne sheets** (best layered with sauces and baked, or rolled up to make cannelloni tubes)
5 **Rigatoni** (best with thick sauces)
6 **Conchiglie or shells** (best with thick sauces that get trapped inside the shells)
7 **Risoni** (best added to soups and casseroles)
8 **Fettucine** (best with thin coating sauces)
9 **Linguine** (best with thin coating sauces)
10 **Fusilli** (best with thick sauces that get trapped in the ridges)
11 **Orecchiette** (best with thick sauces that get trapped in the ridges)
12 **Spaghetti** (best with thin coating sauces or bolognese)
13 **Spiral pasta** (best with thick sauces that get trapped in the ridges)
14 **Spinach tagliatelle** (tagliatelle flavored and colored with spinach, best with thin coating sauces)
15 **Macaroni** (best in baked dishes and soups)
16 **Farfalle or butterflies** (best with thick sauces that get trapped in the ridges)
17 **Tortellini shapes** (best with thick sauces that get trapped in the ridges)
18 **Cannelloni** (best stuffed with filling and baked in a sauce)
19 **Ziti** (suitable for thick or thin sauces)
20 **Miniature star-shaped pasta** (best in soups)
21 **Macaroni elbows** (best in baked dishes and soups)

Fresh Pasta

Most supermarkets and delicatessens stock fresh pasta in their chill cabinets. Some are flavored with herbs and spices or colored with vegetables. Fresh pasta cooks a lot more quickly than dried pasta and is usually suitable for delicately flavored sauces. We have suggested types of sauces for each pasta shape.

1

2

3

4

5

6

1 Lasagne sheets (best layered with sauces and baked)
2 Ravioli (best with mild flavored thin sauces)
3 Tortellini (best with mild flavored thin sauces)
4 Pumpkin gnocchi (best with thin sauces)
5 Gnocchi (best with thin sauces)
6 Cracked pepper tagliatelle (tagliatelle flavored and colored with cracked black pepper, best with thin coating sauces)
7 Pumpkin ravioli (best with mild flavored thin sauces)
8 Spinach gnocchi (best with thin coating sauces)
9 Tomato tagliatelle (best with thin coating sauces)
10 Spinach tagliatelle (best with thin coating sauces)
11 Spaghetti (best with thin coating sauces or bolognese)
12 Spinach tortellini (best with thin sauces)
13 Pappardelle (suitable for thick, thin or chunky sauces)

Classic Sauces

PASTA PUTTANESCA

Preparation time: 15 minutes
Total cooking time: 20 minutes
Serves 4–6

500 g (1 lb) spaghetti or fettucine
2 tablespoons olive oil
3 cloves garlic, crushed
2 tablespoons chopped fresh parsley
$^1/_4$–$^1/_2$ teaspoon chilli flakes or chilli powder
2 x 425 g (14 oz) cans crushed tomatoes
1 tablespoon capers
3 anchovy fillets, chopped
3 tablespoons black olives

1 Cook the spaghetti or fettuccine in a large pan of rapidly boiling salted water until al dente. Drain and return to the pan to keep warm.
2 Meanwhile, heat the oil in a heavy-based frying pan. Add the garlic, parsley and chilli flakes and cook, stirring, for 1 minute over medium heat.
3 Add the crushed tomatoes and stir to combine. Reduce the heat and simmer, covered, for 5 minutes.
4 Add the capers, anchovies and olives and cook, stirring, for 5 minutes. Season with black pepper. Add the sauce to the pasta and toss together gently. Serve immediately.

NUTRITION PER SERVE (6)
Protein 11 g; Fat 7 g; Carbohydrate 63 g; Dietary Fibre 6 g; Cholesterol 0 mg; 1549 kJ (370 Cal)

HINT: If you can't find cans of crushed tomatoes, used canned whole tomatoes— simply chop in the can with a pair of kitchen scissors.

Cook the pasta in boiling water, then drain and return to the pan to keep warm.

Add the crushed tomatoes to the garlic, parsley and chilli flakes.

Add the capers, anchovies and olives and stir for 5 minutes.

Process the pine nuts, basil leaves, garlic, salt and cheeses for about 20 seconds.

With the motor running, add the olive oil in a thin steady stream, until a paste is formed.

PASTA WITH PESTO

Preparation time: 10–15 minutes
Total cooking time: 15 minutes
Serves 4–6

500 g (1 lb) pasta
3 tablespoons pine nuts
2 cups (100 g/3½ oz) fresh basil leaves
2 cloves garlic, peeled
½ teaspoon salt
3 tablespoons grated Parmesan
2 tablespoons grated Pecorino cheese, optional
½ cup (125 ml/4 fl oz) olive oil

1 Cook the pasta in a large pan of rapidly boiling salted water until al dente. Drain well and return to the pan to keep warm.

2 Meanwhile, toast the pine nuts in a dry heavy-based pan over low heat for 2–3 minutes, or until golden. Allow to cool. Process the pine nuts, basil leaves, garlic, salt and cheeses in a food processor for 20 seconds, or until finely chopped.

3 With the motor running, gradually add the oil in a thin steady stream until a paste is formed. Add freshly ground black pepper, to taste. Toss the sauce with the warm pasta until the pasta is well coated.

NUTRITION PER SERVE (6)
Protein 15 g; Fat 30 g; Carbohydrate 60 g; Dietary Fibre 5 g; Cholesterol 8 mg; 2280 kJ (540 cal)

NOTE: Traditionally, linguine, as shown, is used with pesto but you can serve it with any pasta of your choice. Pesto sauce can be made up to one week in advance and refrigerated in an airtight container. Ensure the pesto is tightly packed and seal the surface with some plastic wrap or pour a little extra oil over the top to prevent the pesto turning black. Each time you use the pesto reseal the surface with a little oil.

Remove the tomatoes from the cold water and peel the skin down from the cross.

Halve the tomatoes and scrape out the seeds with a teaspoon.

PASTA AMATRICIANA

Preparation time: 45 minutes
Total cooking time: 20 minutes
Serves 4–6

6 thin slices pancetta or 3 bacon rashers
1 kg (2 lb) very ripe tomatoes
500 g (1 lb) pasta
1 tablespoon olive oil
1 small onion, very finely chopped
2 teaspoons very finely chopped fresh chilli
Parmesan shavings, for serving

1 Finely chop the pancetta or bacon. Score a cross in the base of each tomato. Soak in boiling water for 1 minute, then drain and plunge into cold water briefly. Peel the skin away from the cross. Halve the tomatoes, remove the seeds and chop the flesh.
2 Cook the pasta in a large pan of rapidly boiling salted water until al dente. Drain well and return to the pan to keep warm.
3 Meanwhile, heat the oil in a heavy-based frying pan. Add the pancetta or bacon, onion and chilli and stir over medium heat for 3 minutes. Add the tomato and season to taste. Reduce the heat and simmer for 3 minutes. Add the sauce to the pasta and toss until well combined. Serve garnished with shavings of Parmesan.

NUTRITION PER SERVE (6)
Protein 15 g; Fat 9 g; Carbohydrate 60 g; Dietary Fibre 6 g; Cholesterol 15 mg; 1640 kJ (390 cal)

NOTES: It is believed this dish originated in the town of Amatrice, where bacon is a prized local product. For a change from ordinary tomatoes, you can try Roma (egg or plum) tomatoes in this recipe. They are firm-fleshed with few seeds and have a rich flavor when cooked. Traditionally, bucatini, as shown, is served with this sauce, but you can use any pasta you prefer.

Trim the baby onions, leaving only a small section of green stem.

Add the onions and the bacon and stir over low heat until golden.

PASTA WITH PEAS AND BABY ONIONS

Preparation time: 10 minutes
Total cooking time: 15–20 minutes
Serves 4–6

500 g (1 lb) spaghetti or vermicelli
2 bunches baby onions
1 tablespoon olive oil
4 rashers bacon, chopped
2 teaspoons plain flour
1 cup (250 ml/8 fl oz) light chicken or
    vegetable stock
1/2 cup (125 ml/4 fl oz) white wine
1 cup (150 g/5 oz) shelled fresh peas

1 Cook the pasta in a large pan of rapidly boiling salted water until al dente. Drain well and return to the pan to keep warm.
2 Meanwhile, trim the outer skins and ends from the baby onions, leaving only a small section of the green stem attached. Heat the oil in a large heavy-based deep pan. Add the bacon and the trimmed onions and stir over low heat for 4 minutes, or until golden. Sprinkle the flour lightly over the top and stir for 1 minute.
3 Combine the stock and wine and add to the pan. Increase the heat and bring to the boil. Add the peas and cook for 5 minutes, or until the onions and peas are just tender.
4 Grind black pepper onto the sauce, then toss gently with the pasta.

NUTRITION PER SERVE (6)
Protein 16 g; Fat 6 g; Carbohydrate 65 g; Dietary Fibre 7 g; Cholesterol 10 mg; 1635 kJ (390 cal)

NOTE: Fresh peas are authentic and have the best flavor for this recipe, but you can use frozen if fresh are not available.

Use a large sharp knife to finely chop the speck or bacon.

Slice the chicken livers, then chop them finely and set aside.

PASTA RAGU

Preparation time: 25 minutes
Total cooking time: at least 3 hours
Serves 4–6

180 g (6 oz) speck, or thick bacon rashers
    with rind removed
150 g (5 oz) chicken livers
60 g (2 oz) butter
1 large onion, finely chopped
1 carrot, finely chopped
1 celery stalk, finely chopped
400 g (13 oz) minced topside
2 cups (500 ml/16 fl oz) beef stock
250 g (8 oz) can crushed tomatoes
$1/2$ cup (125 ml/4 fl oz) red wine
$1/4$ teaspoon grated nutmeg
500 g (1 lb) pasta
grated Parmesan, for serving

1 Chop the speck finely. Slice and finely chop the chicken livers. Heat about half the butter in a heavy-based frying pan. Add the speck and cook until golden brown. Add the onion, carrot and celery and cook over low heat for about 8 minutes, stirring occasionally.
2 Increase the heat, add the remaining butter and, when the pan is quite hot, add the mince. Break up any lumps with a fork and stir until brown. Add the livers and cook, stirring, until they change color. Add the stock, tomatoes, wine and nutmeg. Season, bring to the boil and simmer, covered, over very low heat for 2–5 hours, adding a little more stock if the sauce becomes too dry. The longer you cook the sauce the more flavor it will have.
3 Cook the pasta in a large pan of rapidly boiling salted water until al dente. Drain well and return to the pan. Add half the sauce and toss to combine. Serve the rest of the sauce over the top, with grated Parmesan.

NUTRITION PER SERVE (6)
Protein 38 g; Fat 25 g; Carbohydrate 62 g; Dietary Fibre 5 g; Cholesterol 207 mg; 2644 kJ (632 cal)

VARIATION: For a creamier sauce, add 200 ml ($6^{1}/_{2}$ fl oz) cream just before serving.

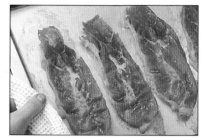

Slowly heat the oil, chilli and garlic over low heat to infuse the oil with the flavors.

Grill the prosciutto until it is crispy, then cool and break into pieces.

SPAGHETTI WITH HERB, GARLIC AND CHILLI OIL

Preparation time: 15 minutes
Total cooking time: 15 minutes
Serves 4–6

1 cup (250 ml/8 fl oz) olive oil
2 bird's eye chillies, seeded and thinly sliced
5–6 large cloves garlic, crushed
500 g (1 lb) spaghetti
100 g (3¹/₂ oz) thinly sliced prosciutto
¹/₂ cup (30 g/1 oz) chopped fresh flat-leaf parsley
2 tablespoons chopped fresh basil
2 tablespoons chopped fresh oregano
³/₄ cup (75 g/2¹/₂ oz) grated Parmesan

1 Pour the oil into a small saucepan with the chilli and garlic. Slowly heat the oil over low heat for about 12 minutes to infuse the oil with the garlic and chilli. Don't allow the oil to reach smoking point or the garlic will burn and taste bitter.

2 Meanwhile, cook the pasta in a large pan of rapidly boiling salted water until al dente. Drain well and return to the pan to keep warm. Cook the prosciutto under a hot grill for 2 minutes each side, or until crispy. Cool and break into pieces.

3 Pour the hot oil mixture over the spaghetti and toss well with the prosciutto, fresh herbs and Parmesan. Season to taste.

NUTRITION PER SERVE (6)
Protein 18 g; Fat 44 g; Carbohydrate 60 g; Dietary Fibre 6 g; Cholesterol 21 mg; 2945 kJ (705 cal)

NOTE: This sauce is traditionally served with spaghetti. It is simple but relies on good-quality ingredients.

Gently squeeze out any excess milk from the soaked bread.

With floured hands, roll teaspoons of the mixture into dumplings.

SPINACH AND RICOTTA GNOCCHI

Preparation time: 45 minutes + 1 hour refrigeration
Total cooking time: 15 minutes
Serves 4–6

4 slices white bread
1/2 cup (125 ml/4 fl oz) milk
500 g (1 lb) frozen spinach, thawed
250 g (8 oz) ricotta
2 eggs
1/2 cup (60 g/2 oz) grated Parmesan
1/4 cup (30 g/1 oz) plain flour
Parmesan shavings, for serving

GARLIC BUTTER SAUCE
100 g (3 1/2 oz) butter
2 cloves garlic, crushed
3 tablespoons chopped fresh basil
1 ripe tomato, diced

1 Remove the crusts from the bread and soak in milk in a shallow dish for 10 minutes. Squeeze out any excess milk from the bread. Squeeze out any excess liquid from the spinach.
2 Place the bread, spinach, ricotta, eggs and Parmesan in a bowl and mix thoroughly. Refrigerate, covered, for 1 hour. Fold the flour in well.
3 Lightly dust your hands in flour and roll heaped teaspoons of the mixture into dumplings. Lower batches of the gnocchi into a large saucepan of boiling salted water. Cook for about 2 minutes, or until the gnocchi rise to the surface. Transfer to a serving plate and keep warm.
4 To make the sauce, combine all the ingredients in a small saucepan and cook over medium heat for 3 minutes, or until the butter is nutty brown. Drizzle over the gnocchi and sprinkle with the Parmesan.

NUTRITION PER SERVE (6)
Protein 17 g; Fat 26 g; Carbohydrate 16 g; Dietary Fibre 5 g; Cholesterol 137 mg; 1504 kJ (360 cal)

Remove the stalks and slice the chillies in half. Wear rubber gloves to protect your skin.

The chilli seeds and membrane are left in as this is a fiery sauce, but remove them if you prefer.

PASTA ARRABBIATA

Preparation time: 30 minutes
Total cooking time: 50 minutes
Serves 4

¹/₂ cup (75 g/2¹/₂ oz) bacon fat
2–3 fresh red chillies
2 tablespoons olive oil
1 large onion, finely chopped
1 clove garlic, finely chopped
500 g (1 lb) very ripe tomatoes, finely
    chopped
500 g (1 lb) pasta
2 tablespoons chopped fresh parsley
grated Parmesan or Pecorino cheese, for
    serving

1 Use a large knife to finely chop the bacon fat. Chop the chillies, taking care to avoid skin irritation—wearing rubber gloves will help. Heat the oil in a heavy-based pan and add the bacon fat, chilli, onion and garlic. Fry for 8 minutes, stirring occasionally.
2 Add the chopped tomato to the pan with ¹/₂ cup (125 ml/4 fl oz) of water and season to taste. Cover and simmer for about 40 minutes, or until the sauce is thick and rich.
3 When the sauce is almost cooked, cook the pasta in a large pan of rapidly boiling water until al dente. Drain well and return to the pan.
4 Add the parsley to the sauce and toss gently with the pasta. Serve with the Parmesan or Pecorino cheese sprinkled over the top.

NUTRITION PER SERVE
Protein 20 g; Fat 25 g; Carbohydrate 95 g; Dietary Fibre 9 g; Cholesterol 20 mg; 2880 kJ (685 cal)

NOTE: Penne rigate, as shown, is traditionally served with this sauce.

Scrub the mussels and pull away their beards. Discard any open mussels.

Remove the quills from inside the calamari tubes and slice the tubes into thin rings.

PASTA MARINARA

Preparation time: 50 minutes
Total cooking time: 30 minutes
Serves 4

1 tablespoon olive oil
1 onion, chopped
2 cloves garlic, crushed
1/2 cup (125 ml/4 fl oz) red wine
2 tablespoons tomato paste
425 g (14 oz) can crushed tomatoes
1 cup (250 ml/8 fl oz) bottled tomato pasta
    sauce
1 tablespoon each of chopped fresh basil
    and oregano
12 mussels, scrubbed and beards removed
    (discard any which are open and don't
    close if tapped)
30 g (1 oz) butter
125 g (4 oz) small calamari tubes, sliced
125 g (4 oz) boneless white fish fillets, cubed

200 g (6 1/2 oz) raw prawns, peeled and
    deveined, tails intact
500 g (1 lb) pasta

1 Heat the olive oil in a large pan. Add the onion and garlic and cook over low heat for 2–3 minutes. Increase the heat to medium and add the wine, tomato paste, tomato and pasta sauce. Simmer, stirring occasionally, for 5–10 minutes or until the sauce thickens slightly. Stir in the herbs and season. Keep warm.
2 Heat 1/2 cup (125 ml/4 fl oz) water in a pan. Add the mussels, cover the pan tightly and steam for 3–5 minutes, or until the mussels have opened. Discard any that don't open in this time. Set the mussels aside and stir the cooking liquid into the tomato sauce.
3 Heat the butter in a pan and sauté the calamari, fish and prawns, in batches, for 1–2 minutes, or until cooked. Add the seafood, including the mussels, to the warm tomato sauce and stir gently.

4 Cook the pasta in a large pan of rapidly boiling salted water until al dente. Drain well and toss gently with the seafood sauce.

NUTRITION PER SERVE
Protein 40 g; Fat 10 g; Carbohydrate 100 g; Dietary Fibre 10 g; Cholesterol 205 mg; 2840 kJ (675 cal)

Chop the vegetables into small, evenly sized pieces before adding to the hot oil.

Dice the tomatoes into small pieces, before adding with the parsley, sugar and water.

PASTA NAPOLITANA

Preparation time: 20 minutes
Total cooking time: 1 hour
Serves 4–6

2 tablespoons olive oil
1 onion, finely chopped
1 carrot, finely chopped
1 celery stick, finely chopped
500 g (1 lb) very ripe tomatoes, chopped
2 tablespoons chopped fresh parsley
2 teaspoons sugar
500 g (1 lb) pasta

1 Heat the oil in a heavy-based pan. Add the onion, carrot and celery. Cover and cook for 10 minutes over low heat, stirring occasionally.
2 Add the tomato to the pan with the parsley, sugar and ½ cup (125 ml/4 fl oz) of water. Bring to the boil, reduce the heat to low, cover and simmer for 45 minutes, stirring occasionally. Season to taste. If necessary, add up to ¾ cup (185 ml/6 fl oz) more water if the sauce needs thinning.
3 Cook the pasta in a large pan of rapidly boiling salted water until al dente. Drain well and return to the pan. Toss gently with the sauce.

NUTRITION PER SERVE (6)
Protein 10 g; Fat 7 g; Carbohydrate 65 g; Dietary Fibre 6 g; Cholesterol 0 mg; 1540 kJ (365 cal)

NOTE: Traditionally, spaghetti is served with this sauce but we have shown penne rigate. The sauce can be concentrated by cooking it for longer. Store in the fridge and add water or stock to thin it when reheating.

Cook the bacon strips, stirring, until they are crisp, being careful not to let them burn.

After beating together the eggs, cream and Parmesan, stir in the cooked bacon.

PASTA CARBONARA

Preparation time: 15 minutes
Total cooking time: 25 minutes
Serves 4–6

8 bacon rashers
500 g (1 lb) pasta
4 eggs
1¹/₄ cups (315 ml/10 fl oz) cream
¹/₂ cup (60 g/2 oz) grated Parmesan

1 Remove the bacon rind and cut the bacon into thin strips. Cook over medium heat until crisp. Drain on paper towels. Meanwhile, cook the pasta in a large pan of rapidly boiling salted water until al dente. Drain well and return to the pan.
2 Beat the eggs, cream and Parmesan together and season well. Stir in the bacon. Pour over the hot pasta in the saucepan and toss gently until the sauce coats the pasta. Return to very low heat and cook for about 1 minute, or until the sauce has thickened slightly. Don't increase the heat or the eggs will scramble. Season with black pepper and serve immediately with extra grated Parmesan.

NUTRITION PER SERVE (6)
Protein 22 g; Fat 36 g; Carbohydrate 60 g; Dietary Fibre 4 g; Cholesterol 213.5 mg; 2700 kJ (645 cal)

NOTE: Traditionally, spaghetti or fettucine is served with this sauce but we have shown tagliatelle.

Cut the capsicum in half to remove the seeds and membrane, then slice into thin strips.

Add the capsicum, tomatoes, water, zucchini, anchovies, capers and olives.

PASTA SIRACUSANI

Preparation time: 15 minutes
Total cooking time: 25 minutes
Serves 4–6

2 tablespoons olive oil
2 cloves garlic, crushed
1 large green capsicum, thinly sliced
2 x 425 g (14 oz) cans crushed tomatoes
2 zucchini, chopped
2 anchovy fillets, chopped
1 tablespoon capers, chopped
3 tablespoons black olives, pitted and halved
2 tablespoons chopped fresh basil leaves
500 g (1 lb) spaghetti or linguine
1/2 cup (60 g/2 oz) grated Parmesan, for
    serving

1 Heat the oil in a large deep pan and fry the garlic for 30 seconds over low heat. Add the capsicum, tomatoes, zucchini, anchovies, capers, olives and 125 ml (4 fl oz) water. Cook for 20 minutes, stirring occasionally.

2 Add the basil to the pan and stir well. Season to taste. Meanwhile, cook the pasta in a large pan of rapidly boiling water until al dente and drain well. Serve the pasta topped with the sauce and grated Parmesan.

NUTRITION PER SERVE (6)
Protein 16 g; Fat 11 g; Carbohydrate 65 g; Dietary Fibre 7 g; Cholesterol 10 mg; 1795 kJ (430 cal)

STORAGE: This sauce will keep in the fridge for up to a day.

While the pasta is cooking, chop the Gorgonzola into cubes.

Cook the celery for 2 minutes before adding the cream, ricotta and Gorgonzola.

PASTA WITH GORGONZOLA SAUCE

Preparation time: 10 minutes
Total cooking time: 20 minutes
Serves 4–6

375 g (12 oz) spaghetti or bucatini
200 g (6½ oz) Gorgonzola cheese
250 g (8 oz) fresh ricotta cheese
1 tablespoon butter
1 celery stalk, finely chopped
1¼ cups (300 ml/10 fl oz) cream

1 Cook the pasta in a large pan of rapidly boiling salted water until al dente. Drain well and return to the pan to keep warm. Meanwhile, chop the Gorgonzola into small cubes and beat the ricotta until it is smooth.
2 Heat the butter in a pan, add the celery and stir for 2 minutes. Add the cream, ricotta and Gorgonzola cheeses and season to taste.
3 Bring to the boil over low heat, stirring constantly. Reduce the heat and simmer for 1 minute. Toss well with the pasta.

NUTRITION PER SERVE (6)
Protein 20 g; Fat 40 g; Carbohydrate 46 g; Dietary Fibre 3 g; Cholesterol 126 mg; 2614 kJ (624 cal)

NOTE: Gorgonzola is a rich strong Italian blue-veined cheese.

If using canned clams, rinse them thoroughly and then drain well.

Add the clams to the sauce and season with ground black pepper.

SPAGHETTI VONGOLE

Preparation time: 25 minutes + soaking
Total cooking time: 35 minutes
Serves 4

1 kg (2 lb) small fresh clams in shells,
　cleaned (see NOTE) or 750 g (1½ lb)
　canned clams in brine
1 tablespoon lemon juice
⅓ cup (80 ml/2¾ fl oz) olive oil
3 cloves garlic, crushed
2 x 425 g (14 oz) cans crushed tomatoes
250 g (8 oz) spaghetti
4 tablespoons chopped fresh parsley

1 Place the cleaned clams in a large pan with the lemon juice. Cover the pan tightly and shake over medium heat for 7–8 minutes until the shells open (discard any clams that do not open in this time). Remove the clams from their shells. If using canned clams, rinse well, drain and set aside.

2 Heat the oil in a large pan. Add the garlic and cook over low heat for 5 minutes. Add the tomatoes and stir well. Bring to the boil and simmer, covered, for 20 minutes. Add the clams to the sauce and season with black pepper. Stir until heated through.

3 Meanwhile, cook the pasta in a large pan of rapidly boiling salted water until al dente. Drain well and return to the pan. Add the sauce and chopped parsley and toss gently.

NUTRITION PER SERVE
Protein 35 g; Fat 25 g; Carbohydrate 55 g; Dietary Fibre 7 g; Cholesterol 355 mg; 2420 kJ (580 cal)

NOTE: To clean the clams, any sand and grit needs to be drawn out of the shells. Combine 2 tablespoons each of salt and plain flour with enough water to make a paste. Add to a large bucket or bowl of cold water and soak the clams in this mixture overnight. Drain and scrub the shells well, then rinse thoroughly and drain again.

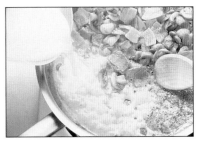

Add a little of the cream and scrape the bottom of the pan with a wooden spoon.

Cook the sauce over high heat until it is thick enough to coat the back of a wooden spoon.

PASTA BOSCAIOLA

Preparation time: 15 minutes
Total cooking time: 25 minutes
Serves 4

500 g (1 lb) pasta
1 tablespoon olive oil
6 bacon rashers, chopped
200 g (6½ oz) button mushrooms, sliced
2½ cups (625 ml/21 fl oz) cream
2 spring onions, sliced
1 tablespoon chopped fresh parsley

1 Cook the pasta in a large pan of rapidly boiling salted water until al dente. Drain well and return to the pan to keep warm.
2 Meanwhile, heat the oil in a large frying pan, add the bacon and mushrooms and cook, stirring, for 5 minutes, or until golden brown.
3 Add a little of the cream and stir well with a wooden spoon.
4 Add the remaining cream, bring to the boil and cook over high heat for 15 minutes, or until thick enough to coat the back of a spoon. Add the spring onion. Pour the sauce over the pasta and toss well. Serve sprinkled with the parsley.

NUTRITION PER SERVE
Protein 30 g; Fat 60 g; Carbohydrate 95 g; Dietary Fibre 8 g; Cholesterol 200 mg; 4310 kJ (1025 cal)

NOTE: This sauce is normally served with spaghetti, but you can use any pasta. We have shown it with casereccie. If you are short on time and don't have 15 minutes to reduce the sauce, it can be thickened with 2 teaspoons of cornflour mixed with 1 tablespoon of water. Stir until the mixture boils and thickens.

'Boscaiola' means woodcutter—collecting mushrooms is part of the heritage of the woodcutters.

If the beans will not slip out of their skins easily, gently slit or break the ends first.

Trim the stalks from the sugar snap peas. Snap the woody ends from the asparagus.

PASTA PRIMAVERA

Preparation time: 25 minutes
Total cooking time: 20 minutes
Serves 4

500 g (1 lb) pasta
1 cup (150 g/5 oz) frozen broad beans
200 g (6½ oz) sugar snap peas
150 g (5 oz) aparagus spears
30 g (1 oz) butter
1 cup (250 ml/8 fl oz) cream
60 g (2 oz) grated Parmesan

1 Cook the pasta in a large pan of rapidly boiling salted water until al dente. Drain well and return to the pan to keep warm.
2 Cook the beans in boiling water for 2 minutes, then refresh in iced water and drain. Remove the skins from the broad beans—you can usually just squeeze them out, otherwise carefully slit the skins first.
3 Trim the stalks from the peas and snap the tough woody ends from the asparagus spears. Cut the asparagus into short lengths.
4 Melt the butter in a frying pan. Add the vegetables, cream and Parmesan. Simmer gently for 3–4 minutes, or until the peas and asparagus are just tender. Season to taste. Pour the sauce over the warm pasta and toss gently. Serve immediately.

NUTRITION PER SERVE
Protein 30 g; Fat 35 g; Carbohydrate 95 g; Dietary Fibre 12 g; Cholesterol 105 mg; 3420 kJ (815 cal)

NOTE: Traditionally, primavera sauce is served with spaghetti. We have shown it with spaghettini.

To finely chop an onion, cut it in half, then thinly slice, without cutting all the way through.

Then slice finely in one direction and then the opposite, to make fine cubes.

PASTA POMODORO

Preparation time: 15 minutes
Total cooking time: 15 minutes
Serves 4

500 g (1 lb) pasta
1½ tablespoons olive oil
1 onion, very finely chopped
2 x 400 g (13 oz) cans crushed tomatoes
¼ cup (7 g/¼ oz) fresh basil leaves

1 Cook the pasta in a large pan of rapidly boiling salted water until al dente. Drain well and return to the pan to keep warm.
2 Heat the oil in a large frying pan. Add the onion and cook over medium heat until softened. Stir in the tomato and simmer for 5–6 minutes, or until the sauce has reduced slightly and thickened. Season to taste. Stir in the basil leaves and cook for another minute. Gently toss through the pasta and serve immediately.

NUTRITION PER SERVE
Protein 20 g; Fat 10 g; Carbohydrate 95 g; Dietary Fibre 10 g; Cholesterol 5 mg; 2295 kJ (545 cal)

NOTE: Traditionally, pomodoro is served with tagliatelle. It is shown here with fettucine.

Soups

BEAN SOUP WITH SAUSAGE

Preparation time: 25 minutes
Total cooking time: 25 minutes
Serves 4–6

2 teaspoons olive oil
4 Italian sausages, diced
2 leeks, sliced
1 clove garlic, crushed
1 large carrot, chopped into small cubes
2 celery stalks, sliced
2 tablespoons plain flour
2 beef stock cubes, crumbled
1/2 cup (125 ml/4 fl oz) white wine
125 g (4 oz) small pasta shells
440 g (14 oz) can three-bean mix, drained
1 teaspoon chopped chilli (optional)

1 Heat the oil in a large heavy-based pan and add the sausage. Cook over medium heat for 5 minutes or until golden, stirring regularly. Drain on paper towels.
2 Add the leek, garlic, carrot and celery to the pan and cook, stirring occasionally, for 2–3 minutes or until soft.
3 Add the flour and cook, stirring, for 1 minute. Add the stock cube and wine and gradually stir in 2 litres of water. Bring to the boil, then reduce the heat and simmer for 10 minutes.
4 Add the pasta, beans and chilli to the pan. Increase the heat and cook for 8–10 minutes, or until the pasta is al dente. Return the sausage to the soup and season to taste.

NUTRITION PER SERVE (6)
Protein 10 g; Fat 4 g; Carbohydrate 30 g; Dietary Fibre 8 g; Cholesterol 7 mg; 888 kJ (212 cal)

VARIATION: Use dried beans, if preferred. Place in a bowl; cover with water; soak overnight. Drain; add to large pan with water to come about 3 cm above beans; simmer 1 hour. Drain well before adding to soup.

Cook the sausage pieces over medium heat for 5 minutes, or until golden.

Add the leek, garlic, carrot and celery and cook until soft.

Cook the onion and celery in the oil until they have softened.

Peel the tomatoes by plunging in boiling water, then scoop out the seeds.

TOMATO DITALINI SOUP

Preparation time: 15 minutes
Total cooking time: 20 minutes
Serves 4

2 tablespoons olive oil
1 large onion, finely chopped
2 celery stalks, finely chopped
3 vine-ripened tomatoes
1.5 litres chicken or vegetable stock
$\frac{1}{2}$ cup (90 g/3 oz) ditalini
2 tablespoons chopped fresh parsley

1 Heat the oil in a large saucepan over medium heat. Add the onion and celery and cook for 5 minutes, or until they have softened.
2 Score a cross in the base of each tomato, then place in a bowl of boiling water for 1 minute. Plunge into cold water and peel the skin away from the cross. Halve the tomatoes and scoop out the seeds with a teaspoon. Roughly chop the flesh.
3 Add the stock and tomato to the pan and bring to the boil. Add the pasta and cook for 10 minutes, or until al dente. Season and sprinkle with parsley. Serve with crusty bread.

NUTRITION PER SERVE
Protein 8 g; Fat 11 g; Carbohydrate 23 g; Dietary Fibre 3.5 g; Cholesterol 0 mg; 925 kJ (220 cal)

Add the beans and chicken stock, cover the pan and bring to the boil.

HEARTY ITALIAN BEAN AND PASTA SOUP

Preparation time: 15 minutes
Total cooking time: 20 minutes
Serves 4

1 tablespoon olive oil
1 onion, finely chopped
3 cloves garlic, crushed
2 x 300 g (10 oz) cans mixed beans, drained
1.75 litres chicken stock (see Note)
100 g (3¹/₂ oz) conchigliette
1 tablespoon chopped fresh tarragon

1 Heat the oil in a saucepan over low heat. Add the onion and cook for 5 minutes, then add the garlic and cook for a further 1 minute, stirring frequently. Add the beans and chicken stock and then cover the pan with a lid.
2 Increase the heat and bring to the boil. Add the pasta and cook until al dente. Stir in the tarragon, then season with salt and cracked black pepper. Serve with crusty bread.

NUTRITION PER SERVE
Protein 12 g; Fat 6.5 g; Carbohydrate 34 g; Dietary Fibre 8 g; Cholesterol 0 mg; 1015 kJ (240 cal)

NOTE: The flavor of this soup is really enhanced by using a good-quality stock. Either make your own or use the tetra packs of liquid stock that are available at the supermarket.

Cook the processed onion, garlic, parsley and pancetta mixture.

Simmer until the pasta and vegetables are al dente.

MINESTRONE WITH PESTO

Preparation time: 25 minutes + overnight soaking
Total cooking time: 2 hours
Serves 6

125 g (4 oz) dried borlotti beans
1 large onion, roughly chopped
2 cloves garlic
3 tablespoons chopped fresh parsley
60 g (2 oz) pancetta, chopped
3 tablespoons olive oil
1 celery stick, halved lengthways, then cut into 1 cm ($1/2$ inch) slices
1 carrot, halved lengthways, then cut into 1 cm ($1/2$ inch) slices
1 potato, diced
2 teaspoons tomato paste
400 g (12 oz) can crushed tomatoes
6 fresh basil leaves, roughly torn
2 litres chicken or vegetable stock
2 thin zucchini, cut into thick slices

$3/4$ cup (120 g/4 oz) shelled fresh peas
60 g (2 oz) green beans, cut into short lengths
90 g (3 oz) silverbeet leaves, shredded
75 g ($2^1/2$ oz) ditalini or other small pasta

PESTO
1 cup (30 g/1 oz) loosely packed fresh basil leaves
1 tablespoon lightly toasted pine nuts
2 cloves garlic
100 ml ($3^1/2$ fl oz) olive oil
$1/4$ cup (30 g/2 oz) grated Parmesan

1 Put the beans in a large bowl, cover with water and soak overnight. Drain and rinse under cold water.
2 Put the onion, garlic, parsley and pancetta in a food processor and process until fine. Heat the oil in a saucepan, add the pancetta mixture and cook over low heat, stirring occasionally, for 8–10 minutes.
3 Add the celery, carrot and potato, and cook for 5 minutes, then stir in the tomato paste,

tomato, basil and borlotti beans. Season with freshly ground black pepper. Add the stock and bring slowly to the boil. Cover and simmer, stirring occasionally, for 1 hour 30 minutes.
4 Season and add the zucchini, peas, green beans, silverbeet and pasta. Simmer for 8–10 minutes, or until the vegetables and pasta are al dente.
5 To make the pesto, combine the basil, pine nuts and garlic with a pinch of salt in a food processor. Process until finely chopped. With the motor running, slowly add the olive oil. Transfer to a bowl and stir in the Parmesan and freshly ground black pepper to taste. Serve the soup in bowls with the pesto on top.

NUTRITION PER SERVE
Protein 9 g; Fat 30 g; Carbohydrate 20 g; Dietary Fibre 5.3 g; Cholesterol 9 mg; 1593 kJ (380 cal)

Using a sharp knife, cut the pancetta into strips, then chop finely.

Chop the zucchini and finely shred the savoy cabbage.

MINESTRONE PRIMAVERA

Preparation time: 15 minutes
Total cooking time: 40 minutes
Serves 4–6

¹/₄ cup (60 ml/2 fl oz) olive oil
45 g (1¹/₂ oz) pancetta, finely chopped
2 onions, chopped
2 cloves garlic, thinly sliced
2 small celery stalks, sliced
2 litres chicken stock
¹/₃ cup (50 g/1³/₄ oz) macaroni
2 zucchini, chopped
2 cups (150 g/5 oz) shredded savoy
    cabbage
1¹/₂ cups (185 g/6 oz) green beans, chopped
1 cup (155 g/5 oz) frozen peas
1 cup (40 g/1¹/₄ oz) shredded English
    spinach leaves
¹/₄ cup (15 g/¹/₂ oz) chopped fresh basil
grated Parmesan, for serving

1 Put the oil, pancetta, onion, garlic and celery in a large pan and stir occasionally over low heat for 8 minutes, or until the vegetables are soft but not brown. Add the stock and bring to the boil. Simmer, covered, for 10 minutes.
2 Add the macaroni and boil for 12 minutes, or until almost al dente. Stir in the zucchini, cabbage, beans and peas and simmer for 5 minutes. Add the spinach and basil and simmer for 2 minutes. Season to taste and serve with the grated Parmesan.

NUTRITION PER SERVE (6)
Protein 7 g; Fat 20 g; Carbohydrate 15 g;
Dietary Fibre 6 g; Cholesterol 40 mg; 1030 kJ
(250 cal)

Cook the leek and carrot until they are soft, then add the chicken and cook until it changes color.

Add the pasta to the soup and simmer for 10 min-utss, or until it is tender.

CHUNKY CHICKEN AND VEGETABLE SOUP

Preparation time: 15 minutes
Total cooking time: 20 minutes
Serves 4

1 tablespoon oil
1 carrot, sliced
1 leek, chopped
2 chicken thigh fillets, cut into bite-sized
   pieces
¼ cup (35 g/1 oz) ditalini or other small
   pasta
1 litre vegetable stock
2 ripe tomatoes, diced

1 Heat the oil in a saucepan and cook the carrot and leek over medium heat for 4 minutes, or until soft. Add the chicken and cook for a further 2 minutes, or until the chicken has changed color.

2 Add the pasta and the vegetable stock, cover and bring to the boil. Reduce the heat and simmer for 10 minutes, or until the pasta is cooked. Add the tomato halfway through the cooking. Season to taste with salt and pepper. Serve with fresh crusty bread.

NUTRITION PER SERVE
Protein 20 g; Fat 7 g; Carbohydrate 9 g; Dietary Fibre 2 g; Cholesterol 40 mg; 725 kJ (173 cal)

Cook the lamb in batches so that it browns without stewing.

Add the carrot and celery, tomatoes and beef stock to the pan.

LAMB AND PASTA SOUP

Preparation time: 10 minutes
Total cooking time: 40 minutes
Serves 6–8

2 tablespoons oil
500 g (1 lb) lean lamb meat, cut into bite-sized cubes
2 onions, finely chopped
2 carrots, chopped
4 celery stalks, chopped
425 g (14 oz) can crushed tomatoes
2 litres beef stock
300 g (10 oz) spiral pasta
chopped fresh parsley, for serving

1 Heat the oil in a large pan and cook the lamb in batches until golden brown. Remove each batch as it is cooked and drain on paper towels. Add the onion to the pan and cook for 2 minutes or until softened. Return all the meat to the pan.
2 Add the carrot, celery, tomato and beef stock. Stir to combine and bring to the boil. Reduce the heat to low and simmer, covered, for 15 minutes.
3 Add the spiral pasta to the soup. Stir briefly to prevent the pasta sticking to the pan. Simmer, uncovered, for another 15 minutes or until the lamb and pasta are tender. Sprinkle with chopped parsley before serving.

NUTRITION PER SERVE (8):
Protein 20 g; Fat 8 g; Carbohydrate 34 g; Dietary Fibre 4 g; Cholesterol 41 mg; 1195 kJ (285 cal)

STORAGE: This soup can be kept, covered, in the fridge for up to 3 days.

HINT: The pasta can be cooked separately, drained and added to the soup just before serving.

VARIATIONS: For a lighter flavor, use half stock and half water. Vegetable stock can be used instead of beef.

SPICY CHICKEN BROTH WITH CORIANDER PASTA

Preparation time: 40 minutes
Total cooking time: 50 minutes
Serves 4

350 g (11 oz) chicken thighs or wings, skin
   removed
2 carrots, finely chopped
2 celery stalks, finely chopped
2 small leeks, finely chopped
3 egg whites
6 cups chicken stock
Tabasco sauce

CORIANDER PASTA
1/2 cup (60 g/2 oz) plain flour
1 egg
1/2 teaspoon sesame oil
small bunch fresh coriander leaves

1 Put the chicken pieces, carrot, celery and leek in a large heavy-based pan. Push the chicken to one side and add the egg whites to the vegetables. Using a wire whisk, beat for a minute or so until frothy (take care not to use a pan that can be scratched by the whisk).

2 Warm the stock in another pan, then add gradually to the first pan, whisking continuously to froth the egg whites. Continue whisking while slowly bringing to the boil. Make a hole in the froth on top with a spoon and leave to simmer, uncovered, for 30 minutes without stirring.

3 Line a large strainer with a damp tea towel or double thickness of muslin and strain the broth into a clean bowl (discard the chicken and vegetables). Season with salt, pepper and Tabasco to taste. Set aside.

4 To make the coriander pasta, sift the flour into a bowl and make a well in the centre. Whisk the egg and oil together and pour into the well. Mix together to make a soft pasta dough and knead on a lightly floured surface for 2 minutes, until smooth.

5 Divide the pasta dough into four even portions. Roll one portion out very thinly and cover with a layer of evenly spaced coriander leaves. Roll out another portion of pasta and lay this on top of the leaves, then gently roll the layers together. Repeat with the remaining pasta and coriander.

6 Cut out squares of pasta around the leaves. The pasta may then be left to sit and dry out if it is not needed immediately. When you are ready to serve, heat the chicken broth gently in a saucepan. As the broth simmers, add the pasta and cook for 1 minute. Serve immediately.

NUTRITION PER SERVE
Protein 25 g; Fat 4 g; Carbohydrate 18 g; Dietary Fibre 4 g; Cholesterol 90 mg; 915 kJ (220 cal)

HINT: Beg, borrow or steal a pasta machine for making this fine, delicate pasta. A rolling pin will suffice if necessary but you will need to roll the pasta as thinly as possible.

NOTE: The egg whites added to the vegetable and chicken stock pot make the broth very clear rather than leaving it with the normal cloudy appearance of chicken stock. This is called clarifying the stock. When you strain the broth through muslin or a tea towel, don't press the solids to extract the extra liquid or the broth will become cloudy. It is necessary to make a hole in the froth on top to prevent the stock boiling over.

Lay a second layer of thin pasta over the coriander leaves.

Put the chopped eggplant in a colander and sprinkle generously with salt.

Add the capsicum, garlic, zucchini and eggplant to the pan.

RATATOUILLE AND PASTA SOUP

Preparation time: 25 minutes
Total cooking time: 40 minutes
Serves 6

1 medium eggplant, chopped
salt
1 tablespoon olive oil
1 large onion, chopped
1 large red capsicum, chopped
1 large green capsicum, chopped
2 cloves garlic, crushed
3 zucchini, sliced
2 x 400 g (13 oz) cans crushed tomatoes
1 teaspoon dried oregano leaves
$1/2$ teaspoon dried thyme leaves
1 litre vegetable stock
$1/2$ cup (45 g/$1^1/2$ oz) pasta spirals

1 Spread the eggplant out in a colander and sprinkle generously with salt. Leave for 20 minutes; rinse and pat dry with paper towels.
2 Heat the oil in a large heavy-based pan and cook the onion for 10 minutes, or until soft and lightly golden. Add the capsicum, garlic, zucchini and eggplant and cook for 5 minutes.
3 Add the tomatoes, herbs and stock to the pan. Bring to the boil, then reduce the heat and simmer for 10 minutes, or until the vegetables are tender. Add the pasta and cook for 15 minutes, until al dente. Serve with Parmesan and bread.

NUTRITION PER SERVE
Protein 6 g; Fat 4 g; Carbohydrate 23 g; Dietary Fibre 5 g; Cholesterol 0 mg; 635 kJ (150 cal)

STORAGE: This soup will keep for up to 2 days in the refrigerator.

Dry-fry the pine nuts until golden brown, but take care not to let them burn.

Put the pine nuts, basil, rocket, garlic and Parmesan in a food processor.

PASTA AND WHITE BEAN SOUP

Preparation time: 30 minutes
Total cooking time: 20 minutes
Serves 6

1/3 cup (50 g/1¾ oz) pine nuts
1 cup (50 g/1¾ oz) basil leaves
50 g (1¾ oz) rocket leaves
2 cloves garlic, chopped
1/3 cup (35 g/1¼ oz) finely grated Parmesan
1/3 cup (80 ml/2¾ fl oz) olive oil
185 g (6 oz) spiral pasta
1.5 litres chicken stock
2 x 300 g (10 oz) cans cannellini beans, drained

1 Put the pine nuts in a frying pan and dry-fry them over moderate heat for 1–2 minutes, or until golden brown. Remove from the pan and allow to cool.

2 To make the pesto, mix the pine nuts, basil, rocket, garlic and Parmesan in a food processor and process until finely chopped. With the motor running, add the oil in a thin stream until well combined. Season to taste with salt and pepper. Set aside.

3 Cook the pasta until not quite tender. Heat the chicken stock in a large pan until it begins to boil. Reduce the heat to simmering point. Drain the pasta and add to the stock with the cannellini beans. Reheat and serve with a spoonful of pesto.

NUTRITION PER SERVE
Protein 15 g; Fat 20 g; Carbohydrate 40 g; Dietary Fibre 4 g; Cholesterol 5 mg; 1770 kJ (425 cal)

NOTE: Cannellini beans are small, white and slightly kidney-shaped and are much used in Italian cooking, particularly in Tuscany.

Remove wide strips of peel from the lemon and then remove the bitter white pith.

Cook for 10 minutes and then lift out the strips of lemon with a slotted spoon.

LEMON-SCENTED BROTH WITH TORTELLINI

Preparation time: 10 minutes
Total cooking time: 20 minutes
Serves 4–6

1 lemon
¹/₂ cup (125 ml/4 fl oz) white wine
440 g (14 oz) can chicken consommé
¹/₃ cup (20 g/³/₄ oz) chopped fresh parsley
375 g (12 oz) fresh or dried veal- or
    chicken-filled tortellini

1 Using a vegetable peeler, peel wide strips from the lemon. Remove the white pith with a small sharp knife and cut three of the wide pieces into fine strips. Set these aside for garnishing.
2 Place the wide lemon strips, white wine, consommé and 3 cups (750 ml/ 24 fl oz) water in a large deep pan. Cook for 10 minutes over low heat. Remove the lemon rind and bring to the boil.
3 Add half the parsley, the tortellini and a sprinkling of black pepper to the pan. Cook for 6–7 minutes or until the pasta is al dente. Garnish with the remaining parsley and the fine strips of lemon.

NUTRITION PER SERVE (6)
Protein 6 g; Fat 4 g; Carbohydrate 9 g; Dietary Fibre 2 g; Cholesterol 14 mg; 483 kJ (115 cal)

STORAGE: If you want, you can prepare the recipe up to the end of step 2 and then leave in the fridge for a day before adding the pasta.

Peel the pumpkin and potatoes and chop them into small cubes.

Add the pumpkin, potato and chicken stock, then cover the pan.

COUNTRY PUMPKIN AND PASTA SOUP

Preparation time: 25 minutes
Total cooking time: 20 minutes
Serves 4–6

750 g (1½ lb) pumpkin
2 potatoes
1 tablespoon olive oil
30 g (1 oz) butter
1 large onion, finely chopped
2 cloves garlic, crushed
3 litres chicken stock
125 g (4 oz) miniature pasta or risoni
1 tablespoon chopped fresh parsley, for
    serving

1 Peel the pumpkin and potatoes and chop into small cubes. Heat the oil and butter in a large pan. Add the onion and garlic and cook, stirring, for 5 minutes over low heat.
2 Add the pumpkin, potato and chicken stock. Increase the heat, cover and cook for 8 minutes or until the vegetables are tender.
3 Add the pasta and cook, stirring occasionally, for 5 minutes or until the pasta is al dente. Serve immediately, sprinkled with chopped parsley.

NUTRITION PER SERVE (6)
Protein 6 g; Fat 5 g; Carbohydrate 30 g; Dietary Fibre 3 g; Cholesterol 13 mg; 782 kJ (187 cal)

NOTES: Butternut or Japanese pumpkin will give this soup the sweetest flavor.
    Tiny star-shaped pasta look attractive in this soup.

Remove the rind and any excess fat from the bacon before you dice it.

Cook the bacon, butter, onion and celery in a large pan for 5 minutes.

BACON AND PEA SOUP

Preparation time: 20 minutes
Total cooking time: 15 minutes
Serves 4–6

4 rashers bacon, diced
50 g (1¹/₂ oz) butter
1 large onion, finely chopped
1 celery stalk, chopped into small pieces
2 litres chicken stock
1 cup (150 g/5 oz) frozen peas
250 g (8 oz) risoni
2 tablespoons chopped fresh parsley

1 Put the bacon, butter, onion and celery in a large heavy-based pan. Cook for 5 minutes over low heat, stirring occasionally.
2 Add the stock and peas and simmer, covered, for 5 minutes. Increase the heat and add the pasta. Cook uncovered, stirring occasionally, for 5 minutes. Add the parsley and serve.

NUTRITION PER SERVE (6)
Protein 10 g; Fat 9 g; Carbohydrate 35 g; Dietary Fibre 4 g; Cholesterol 28 mg; 1066 kJ (255 cal)

STORAGE: Store in an airtight container in the refrigerator for up to a day. Gently reheat before serving.

HINT: Double-smoked bacon will give the best flavor.

Stir the onion, carrot and celery over low heat until soft.

Add the sweet potato, drained corn kernels and the stock.

LOW-FAT VEGETABLE AND PASTA SOUP

Preparation time: 20 minutes
Total cooking time: 40 minutes
Serves 6

2 teaspoons olive oil
1 onion, chopped
1 carrot, chopped
2 celery stalks, chopped
350 g (11 oz) sweet potato, chopped
400 g (13 oz) can corn kernels, drained
1 litre vegetable stock
1 cup (90 g/3 oz) pasta spirals

1 Heat the oil in a large pan and add the onion, carrot and celery. Cook over low heat, stirring regularly, for 10 minutes, or until soft.
2 Add the sweet potato, corn kernels and stock. Bring to the boil, reduce the heat and simmer for 20 minutes, or until the vegetables are tender.
3 Add the pasta to the pan and return to the boil. Reduce the heat and simmer for 10 minutes, or until the pasta is al dente. Serve immediately.

NUTRITION PER SERVE
Protein 4 g; Fat 2 g; Carbohydrate 25 g; Dietary Fibre 5 g; Cholesterol 0 mg; 555 kJ (135 cal)

Pasta with Meat

PROSCIUTTO AND SWEET POTATO PENNE

Preparation time: 10 minutes
Total cooking time: 15 minutes
Serves 4

500 g (1 lb) penne
500 g (1 lb) orange sweet potato, diced
2 tablespoons extra virgin olive oil
5 spring onions, sliced
2 small cloves garlic, crushed
8 thin slices prosciutto, chopped
125 g (4 oz) sun-dried tomatoes in oil,
    drained and sliced
¼ cup (15 g/½ oz) shredded fresh basil
    leaves

1 Cook the penne in a large pan of rapidly boiling salted water until al dente. Drain well and return to the pan to keep warm.
2 Meanwhile, steam the sweet potato for 5 minutes, or until tender. Heat the oil in a saucepan, add the spring onion, garlic and sweet potato and stir over medium heat for 2–3 minutes, or until the spring onion is soft. Add the prosciutto and tomato and cook for a further 1 minute.
3 Add the sweet potato mixture to the penne and toss over low heat until heated through. Add the basil and season with black pepper. Serve immediately with crusty bread.

NUTRITION PER SERVE
Protein 20 g; Fat 20 g; Carbohydrate 115 g; Dietary Fibre 11 g; Cholesterol 5 mg; 3065 kJ (732 cal)

NOTE: Orange sweet potato is also known as kumera.

Cook the spring onion, garlic and sweet potato for 2–3 minutes.

Add the sweet potato mixture to the cooked pasta and heat through.

Cook the prosciutto and spring onion over medium heat until crisp.

Trim the stalks from the spinach, roughly chop the leaves and add to the pan.

FETTUCINE WITH SPINACH AND PROSCIUTTO

Preparation time: 10 minutes
Total cooking time: 15 minutes
Serves 4–6

500 g (1 lb) spinach or plain fettucine
2 tablespoons olive oil
8 thin slices prosciutto, chopped
3 spring onions, chopped
1 bunch English spinach
1 tablespoon balsamic vinegar
$^1/_2$ teaspoon caster sugar
grated Parmesan, for serving

1 Cook the pasta in a large pan of rapidly boiling salted water until al dente. Drain well and return to the pan to keep warm. Meanwhile, heat the oil in a large heavy-based deep pan. Add the prosciutto and spring onion and cook, stirring occasionally, over medium heat for 5 minutes or until the prosciutto is crisp.
2 Roughly chop the spinach and add to the pan. Stir in the vinegar and sugar, cover and cook for 1 minute or until the spinach has softened. Season with salt and pepper.
3 Add the sauce to the pasta and toss well. Sprinkle with Parmesan and serve immediately.

NUTRITION PER SERVE (6)
Protein 14 g; Fat 11 g; Carbohydrate 60 g; Dietary Fibre 5 g; Cholesterol 60 mg; 1670 kJ (400 cal)

STORAGE: This dish should be served as soon as it is cooked as the spinach turns a dull dark green if left standing.

VARIATION: Smoked bacon can be used instead of prosciutto.

Cook the onion until it is tender and then add the ham and cook for 1 minute.

Whisk together the eggs and milk, then stir in the pasta, Parmesan, herbs and onion mixture.

ITALIAN OMELETTE

Preparation time: 20 minutes
Total cooking time: 15 minutes
Serves 4

2 tablespoons olive oil
1 onion, finely chopped
125 g (4 oz) ham, sliced
6 eggs
3 tablespoons milk
2 cups (350 g/11 oz) cooked fusilli or spiral
    pasta (see NOTE)
$^1/_4$ cup (25 g/$^3/_4$ oz) grated Parmesan
2 tablespoons chopped fresh parsley
1 tablespoon chopped fresh basil
$^1/_2$ cup (60 g/2 o) grated Cheddar

1 Heat half the oil in pan. Add the onion and stir over low heat until tender. Add the ham and stir for 1 minute. Transfer to a plate.
2 Whisk together the eggs, milk, salt and pepper. Stir in the pasta, Parmesan, herbs and onion mixture.
3 Preheat the grill to hot. Heat the remaining oil in the same pan. Pour the egg mixture into the pan. Sprinkle with Cheddar. Cook over medium heat until the omelette begins to set around the edges then place under the grill until lightly browned on top. Cut into wedges for serving.

NUTRITION PER SERVE
Protein 30 g; Fat 32 g; Carbohydrate 30 g; Dietary Fibre 2 g; Cholesterol 327 mg; 2206 kJ (530 cal)

NOTE: To get 2 cups of cooked pasta you will need to start with about 150 g (5 oz) of uncooked dried pasta.

With clean hands, roll the mixture into balls and dust with flour.

Cook the meatballs in batches, turning frequently, until browned all over.

SPAGHETTI WITH MEATBALLS

Preparation time: 40 minutes
Total cooking time: 30 minutes
Serves 4

MEATBALLS
500 g (1 lb) beef mince
1/2 cup (40 g/1 1/4 oz) fresh breadcrumbs
1 onion, finely chopped
2 cloves garlic, crushed
2 teaspoons Worcestershire sauce
1 teaspoon dried oregano
1/4 cup (30 g/1 oz) plain flour
2 tablespoons olive oil

SAUCE
2 x 400 g (13 oz) cans chopped tomatoes
1 tablespoon olive oil
1 onion, finely chopped
2 cloves garlic, crushed
2 tablespoons tomato paste
1/2 cup (125 ml/4 fl oz) beef stock

2 teaspoons sugar
500 g (1 lb) spaghetti
grated Parmesan, to serve

1 Combine the mince, breadcrumbs, onion, garlic, Worcestershire sauce and oregano in a bowl and season to taste. Use your hands to mix the ingredients together well. Roll level tablespoons of the mixture into balls, dust lightly with the flour and shake off the excess. Heat the oil in a deep frying pan and cook the meatballs in batches, turning frequently, until browned all over. Drain well.
2 To make the sauce, purée the tomatoes in a food processor or blender. Heat the oil in the cleaned frying pan. Add the onion and cook over medium heat for a few minutes until soft and just lightly golden. Add the garlic and cook for 1 minute more. Add the puréed tomatoes, tomato paste, stock and sugar to the pan and stir to combine. Bring the mixture to the boil, and add the meatballs. Reduce the heat and simmer for 15 minutes, turning the meatballs once. Season with salt and pepper.

3 Meanwhile, cook the spaghetti in a large pan of rapidly boiling salted water until al dente. Drain, divide among serving plates and top with the meatballs and sauce. Serve with grated Parmesan.

NUTRITION PER SERVE
Protein 45 g; Fat 30 g; Carbohydrate 112 g; Dietary Fibre 11 g; Cholesterol 85 mg; 3875 kJ (925 cal)

Carefully remove the outer leaves and dark green section from the leeks.

Thoroughly clean the leeks, then use a large sharp knife to slice finely.

FUSILLI WITH BACON AND BROAD BEAN SAUCE

Preparation time: 30 minutes
Total cooking time: 25 minutes
Serves 4–6

500 g (1 lb) fusilli or penne
2 cups (300 g/10 oz) frozen broad beans
2 tablespoons olive oil
2 leeks, finely sliced
4 rashers bacon, diced
1¼ cups (315 ml/10 fl oz) cream
2 teaspoons grated lemon rind

1 Cook the pasta in a large pan of rapidly boiling salted water until al dente. Drain well and return to the pan to keep warm. While the pasta is cooking, plunge the broad beans into a pan of boiling water. Remove with a slotted spoon and place immediately in cold water. Drain and allow to cool, then peel (see NOTE).

2 Heat the oil in a heavy-based frying pan. Add the leek and bacon and cook over medium heat, stirring occasionally, for 8 minutes, or until the leek is golden. Add the cream and lemon rind and cook for 2 minutes. Add the broad beans and season well.

3 Add the sauce to the pasta and toss to combine. Serve at once.

NUTRITION PER SERVE (6)
Protein 20 g; Fat 30 g; Carbohydrate 62 g; Dietary Fibre 8 g; Cholesterol 83 mg; 2531 kJ (600 cal)

NOTE: Broad beans can be cooked and peeled in advance and refrigerated in an airtight container until needed. To peel them, break off the top and squeeze out the beans. Leaving the hard outside skin on the broad bean will change the delicate texture and flavor of this dish—it is worth the extra effort to peel them.

Very young fresh broad beans can be used without peeling.

Finely chop both the onions and then fry with the garlic, carrot and celery.

Stir the meat constantly and break up any lumps with the back of the spoon.

LOW-FAT SPAGHETTI BOLOGNESE

Preparation time: 30 minutes
Total cooking time: 1 hour 20 minutes
Serves 4–6

cooking oil spray
2 onions, finely chopped
2 cloves garlic, finely chopped
2 carrots, finely chopped
2 celery stalks, finely chopped
400 g (13 oz) lean beef mince
1 kg (2 lb) tomatoes, chopped
1/2 cup (125 ml/4 fl oz) red wine
350 g (11 oz) spaghetti

1 Lightly spray a large saucepan with oil. Heat over medium heat, add the onion, garlic, carrot and celery. Stir over medium heat for 5 minutes, or until the vegetables have softened. If you find the vegetables are sticking, add 1 tablespoon water.
2 Increase the heat to high, add the mince and cook for 5 minutes, or until browned. Stir constantly to prevent the meat sticking. Add the tomato, wine and 1 cup (250 ml/8 fl oz) water. Bring to the boil, reduce the heat and simmer, uncovered, for about 1 hour, until the sauce has thickened.
3 Cook the spaghetti in a large pan of rapidly boiling salted water until al dente. Drain and season well. Divide the spaghetti among pasta bowls and top with the Bolognese sauce. You can garnish with a little chopped fresh parsley or grated Parmesan cheese.

NUTRITION PER SERVE (6)
Protein 9 g; Fat 8 g; Carbohydrate 50 g; Dietary Fibre 7 g; Cholesterol 90 mg; 1695 kJ (405 cal)

Add the pasta to the pan with the lemon juice, thyme, tomato and pine nuts.

PENNE WITH SUN-DRIED TOMATOES AND LEMON

Preparation time: 10 minutes
Total cooking time: 15 minutes
Serves 4

250 g (8 oz) penne
3 tablespoons olive oil
3 rashers bacon, chopped
1 onion, chopped
1/3 cup (80 ml/2 3/4 fl oz) lemon juice
1 tablespoon fresh thyme leaves
1/3 cup (50 g/1 1/2 oz) chopped sun-dried tomatoes
1/2 cup (90 g/3 oz) pine nuts, toasted

1 Cook the pasta in a large pan of rapidly boiling salted water until al dente. Drain well and return to the pan to keep warm.
2 Heat the oil in a large pan. Add the bacon and onion and stir over medium heat for 4 minutes or until the bacon is brown and the onion has softened. Add the pasta, lemon juice, thyme, tomato and pine nuts. Stir over low heat for 2 minutes to heat through.

NUTRITION PER SERVE
Protein 13 g; Fat 25 g; Carbohydrate 47 g; Dietary Fibre 5 g; Cholesterol 10 mg; 1972 kJ (471 cal)

NOTE: Sun-dried tomatoes will become bitter if heated too much.

VARIATION: Use pancetta instead of bacon, if preferred.

Cut the broccoli into small florets and cook until tender, then drain.

Add the garlic, spring onion and mushrooms to the pan and stir well.

SPIRAL PASTA WITH HAM AND BROCCOLI

Preparation time: 10 minutes
Total cooking time: 15 minutes
Serves 4

400 g (13 oz) spiral pasta
250 g (8 oz) broccoli florets
30 g (1 oz) butter
250 g (8 oz) leg ham, cut into strips
2 cloves garlic, crushed
6 spring onions, chopped
200 g (6½ oz) mushrooms, sliced
1 cup (250 ml/8 fl oz) thick cream
½ cup (30 g/1 oz) chopped fresh parsley

1 Cook the pasta in a large pan of rapidly boiling salted water until al dente. Drain well and return to the pan to keep warm. Cook the broccoli in a small pan of rapidly boiling water for 2 minutes or until tender, then drain.
2 Heat the butter in a large pan. Add the ham and stir over medium heat for 2 minutes or until lightly browned.
3 Add the garlic, spring onion and mushrooms and stir for 2 minutes. Add the pasta, broccoli, cream and parsley and stir for 1 minute to heat through.

NUTRITION PER SERVE
Protein 29 g; Fat 30 g; Carbohydrate 74 g; Dietary Fibre 10 g; Cholesterol 74 mg; 2915 kJ (695 cal)

HINT: For the best flavor, use leg ham off the bone.

VARIATIONS: Add some cooked peas or diced, cooked carrots. Use coriander instead of parsley.

Cook the onion, garlic and sausage, stirring occasionally, for 5 minutes.

Add the crushed tomatoes, beans, basil, sage, parsley and seasoning.

RIGATONI WITH KIDNEY BEANS AND ITALIAN SAUSAGE

Preparation time: 25 minutes
Total cooking time: 30 minutes
Serves 4–6

1 tablespoon olive oil
1 large onion, chopped
2 cloves garlic, crushed
4 Italian sausages, chopped
825 g (1 lb 11 oz) can crushed tomatoes
425 g (14 oz) can kidney or borlotti beans,
   drained (see HINT)
2 tablespoons chopped fresh basil
1 tablespoon chopped fresh sage
1 tablespoon chopped fresh parsley
500 g (1 lb) rigatoni or large shells
3 tablespoons grated Parmesan, for serving

1 Heat the oil in a medium heavy-based pan. Add the onion, garlic and sausage and cook, stirring occasionally, over medium heat for 5 minutes.

2 Add the tomatoes, beans, basil, sage and parsley and season well. Reduce the heat and simmer for 20 minutes.

3 Meanwhile, cook the pasta in a large pan of rapidly boiling salted water until al dente. Drain well and return to the pan to keep warm. Divide among serving bowls and top with the sauce. Sprinkle with Parmesan and serve immediately.

NUTRITION PER SERVE (6)
Protein 27 g; Fat 10 g; Carbohydrate 65 g; Dietary Fibre 6 g; Cholesterol 232 mg; 1920 kJ (460 cal)

HINT: Dried beans can also be used. Soak overnight in water, then drain, place in a pan, cover well with water and boil for 20 minutes or until tender.

If you can't find a can of crushed tomatoes, use whole tomatoes and cut them in the tin.

Cook the prosciutto and onion until the prosciutto is golden and the onion softened.

PENNE WITH ROSEMARY AND PROSCIUTTO

Preparation time: 15 minutes
Total cooking time: 25 minutes
Serves 4–6

1 tablespoon olive oil
6 thin slices prosciutto, chopped
1 onion, finely chopped
825 g (1 lb 11 oz) can crushed tomatoes
1 tablespoon chopped fresh rosemary
500 g (1 lb) penne or macaroni
1/2 cup (50 g/1 1/2 oz) grated Parmesan, for
    serving

1 Heat the oil in a heavy-based frying pan. Add the prosciutto and onion and cook, stirring occasionally, over low heat for 5 minutes or until the prosciutto is golden and the onion has softened.
2 Add the tomatoes, rosemary and salt and pepper to the pan and simmer for 10 minutes.
3 Meanwhile, cook the pasta in a large pan of rapidly boiling salted water until al dente. Drain well and return to the pan to keep warm. Divide among warmed serving bowls and top with the sauce. sprinkle with Parmesan cheese and serve immediately.

NUTRITION PER SERVE (6)
Protein 40 g; Fat 8 g; Carbohydrate 65 g; Dietary Fibre 6 g; Cholesterol 13 mg; 1663 kJ (397 cal)

NOTE: Rosemary, commonly used in Mediterranean cookery, adds a distinctive flavor to this dish.

Cook the garlic and pancetta in the butter until the pancetta is crisp.

Add the risoni and stir until it is coated in the mixture, then add the stock.

RISONI RISOTTO WITH MUSHROOMS AND PANCETTA

Preparation time: 15 minutes
Total cooking time: 35 minutes
Serves 4–6

1 tablespoon butter
2 cloves garlic, finely chopped
150 g (5 oz) piece pancetta, diced
400 g (13 oz) button mushrooms, sliced
500 g (1 lb) risoni
1 litre chicken stock
$\frac{1}{2}$ cup (125 ml/4 fl oz) cream
$\frac{1}{2}$ cup (50 g/1$\frac{1}{2}$ oz) finely grated Parmesan
4 tablespoons finely chopped fresh flat-leaf
    parsley

1 Melt the butter in a saucepan, add the garlic and cook over medium heat for 30 seconds. Increase the heat to high, add the pancetta and cook for a further 3–5 minutes, or until crisp. Add the mushrooms and cook for 3–5 minutes, or until softened.
2 Add the risoni, stir until it is coated in the mixture, then add the stock and bring to the boil. Reduce the heat to medium and cook, covered, for 15–20 minutes, or until nearly all the liquid has evaporated and the risoni is tender.
3 Stir in the cream and cook, uncovered, for a further 3 minutes, stirring occasionally until the cream is absorbed. Stir in nearly all of the Parmesan and all the parsley and season to taste. Divide among four serving bowls and serve with the remaining Parmesan.

NUTRITION PER SERVE (6)
Protein 21.5 g; Fat 20 g; Carbohydrate 60 g; Dietary Fibre 4.5 g; Cholesterol 60 mg; 2110 kJ (505 cal)

Heat the oil in a large frying pan and brown the rabbit on all sides.

Stir in the flour and dried marjoram and cook for a minute.

PAPPARDELLE WITH RABBIT AND CAPSICUM

Preparation time: 20 minutes
Total cooking time: 2 hours
Serves 4

3 tablespoons olive oil
1 x 1 kg (2 lb) rabbit, jointed
2 rashers bacon, sliced
1 onion, sliced
2 celery stalks, chopped
1 clove garlic, crushed
2 tablespoons plain flour
1 teaspoon dried marjoram
425 g (14 oz) can crushed tomatoes
½ cup (125 ml/4 fl oz) red wine
3 tablespoons tomato paste
1 capsicum, seeded and sliced
1 eggplant, quartered and sliced
500 g (1 lb) pappardelle
2 tablespoons grated Parmesan, for serving

1 Heat the oil in a large frying pan. Add the rabbit and brown well on all sides. Transfer to a plate. Add the bacon, onion, celery and garlic to the same pan and stir over low heat until the onion is soft.

2 Stir in the flour and marjoram and cook for 1 minute. Add the crushed tomatoes, wine, tomato paste, ½ cup (125 ml/4 fl oz) water and salt and pepper. Stir well.

3 Bring to the boil, stirring constantly. Reduce the heat and return the rabbit to the pan. Simmer, covered, for 1½ hours or until the rabbit is very tender, adding more water as required. Remove the rabbit from the sauce and allow to cool slightly. Remove the meat from the bones.

4 Return the rabbit meat to the sauce with the capsicum and eggplant. Simmer for another 15–20 minutes. Meanwhile, cook the pasta in a large pan of rapidly boiling salted water until al dente. Drain well and return to the pan to keep warm. Serve the hot sauce over the pasta, sprinkled with a little Parmesan.

NUTRITION PER SERVE
Protein 80 g; Fat 13 g; Carbohydrate 102 g; Dietary Fibre 11 g; Cholesterol 166 mg; 3690 kJ (880 cal)

Brown the mince well in the oil, breaking up the lumps with the back of a fork.

Simmer the sauce for 20 minutes to reduce it by half before adding the parsley.

SPAGHETTI PIZZAIOLA

Preparation time: 15 minutes
Total cooking time: 30 minutes
Serves 4

2 tablespoons olive oil
2 cloves garlic, crushed
250 g (8 oz) beef or veal mince
2 x 425 g (14 oz) cans tomatoes
$^1/_2$ cup (125 ml/4 fl oz) red wine
1 tablespoon chopped capers
$^1/_2$ teaspoon dried marjoram
$^1/_2$ teaspoon dried basil
2 tablespoons chopped fresh parsley
500 g (1 lb) spaghetti

1 Heat the oil in a pan, add the garlic and stir over low heat for 1 minute. Add the mince and brown well, breaking up with a fork as it cooks.
2 Add the tomatoes, wine, capers, marjoram and basil and season with salt and pepper. Bring to the boil. Reduce the heat and simmer for 20 minutes or until the sauce is reduced by half. Add the parsley and stir well.
3 Meanwhile, cook the spaghetti in a large pan of rapidly boiling salted water until al dente. Drain well and return to the pan to keep warm. Add the sauce and toss together well. Serve immediately.

NUTRITION PER SERVE
Protein 28 g; Fat 18 g; Carbohydrate 95 g; Dietary Fibre 9 g; Cholesterol 40 mg; 2860 kJ (683 cal)

Slice the chorizo and cook in the oil for a couple of minutes.

Add the crushed tomatoes, wine and chilli and season with salt and pepper.

RIGATONI WITH CHORIZO AND TOMATO

Preparation time: 15 minutes
Total cooking time: 25 minutes
Serves 4

2 tablespoons olive oil
1 onion, sliced
250 g (8 oz) chorizo sausage, sliced
425 g (14 oz) can crushed tomatoes
$\frac{1}{2}$ cup (125 ml/4 fl oz) dry white wine
$\frac{1}{2}$–1 teaspoon chopped chilli, optional
375 g (12 oz) rigatoni
2 tablespoons chopped fresh parsley, for
    serving
2 tablespoons grated Parmesan, for serving

1 Heat the oil in a frying pan. Add the onion and stir over low heat until tender.
2 Add the sausage to the frying pan and cook, turning frequently, for 2–3 minutes. Add the tomatoes, wine and chilli and season with salt and pepper. Bring to the boil, reduce the heat and simmer for 15–20 minutes.
3 Meanwhile, cook the pasta in a large pan of rapidly boiling salted water until al dente. Drain well and return to the pan to keep warm. Add the sauce to the hot pasta with half the combined parsley and Parmesan cheese. Toss well. Serve sprinkled with the remaining combined parsley and Parmesan cheese.

NUTRITION PER SERVE
Protein 20 g; Fat 26 g; Carbohydrate 70 g; Dietary Fibre 6 g; Cholesterol 45 mg; 2578 kJ (616 cal)

VARIATION: Use different hot sausage in place of chorizo.

Grill the capsicums to remove the skins and then chop the flesh.

Brush the eggplant with a little oil and grill until golden on both sides.

ZITI WITH SAUSAGE

Preparation time: 10 minutes
Total cooking time: 35 minutes
Serves 4

1 red capsicum
1 green capsicum
1 small eggplant, sliced
3 tablespoons olive oil
1 onion, sliced
1 clove garlic, crushed
250 g (8 oz) chipolata sausages, sliced
425 g (14 oz) can crushed tomatoes
1/2 cup (125 ml/4 fl oz) red wine
3 tablespoons halved pitted black olives
1 tablespoon chopped fresh basil
1 tablespoon chopped fresh parsley
500 g (1 lb) ziti
2 tablespoons grated Parmesan, for serving

1 Cut both capsicums into large flat pieces, removing the seeds and membranes. Place under a hot grill until the skin blackens and blisters. Cover with a damp tea towel and then peel off the skin. Chop and set aside.
2 Brush the eggplant with a little oil. Grill until golden on each side, brushing with more oil as required. Set aside.
3 Heat the remaining oil in a frying pan. Add the onion and garlic and stir over low heat until the onion is tender. Add the chipolatas and cook until well browned.
4 Stir in the tomatoes, wine, olives, basil, parsley and salt and pepper. Bring to the boil. Reduce the heat and simmer for 15 minutes. Add the vegetables and heat through. Meanwhile, cook the ziti in a large pan of rapidly boiling salted water until al dente. Drain well and return to the pan to keep warm. Toss the vegetables and sauce through the hot pasta. Sprinkle with Parmesan cheese before serving.

NUTRITION PER SERVE
Protein 19 g; Fat 19 g; Carbohydrate 97 g; Dietary Fibre 11 g; Cholesterol 5 mg; 2756 kJ (650 cal)

NOTE: Ziti is a wide tubular pasta. You could use fettucine or spaghetti.

Rub the olive oil, oregano, garlic and salt mixture into the cut halves of the tomato.

Grill the prosciutto until crispy, then break into small pieces.

MEDITERRANEAN PASTA

Preparation time: 15 minutes
Total cooking time: 1 hour
Serves 4

2 tablespoons olive oil
1 teaspoon dried oregano
2 cloves garlic, finely chopped
6 Roma tomatoes, halved
500 g (1 lb) spaghetti
4 slices prosciutto
16 Kalamata olives
200 g (6½ oz) feta, cut into bite-size cubes
1 tablespoon balsamic vinegar
5 tablespoons olive oil, extra
3 cloves garlic, thinly sliced, extra
60 g (2 oz) rocket leaves, trimmed

1 Preheat the oven to slow 150°C (300°F/Gas 2). Combine the olive oil, oregano, garlic and 1 teaspoon salt in a bowl. Add the tomato and toss to combine, rubbing the mixture onto the cut halves of the tomato. Place the tomato cut-side-up on a lined baking tray and cook in the oven for 1 hour.

2 Meanwhile, cook the pasta in a large pan of rapidly boiling salted water until al dente. Drain well and return to the pan to keep warm. Place the prosciutto on a grill tray and cook under a hot grill, turning once, for 3–4 minutes, or until crispy. Break into pieces.

3 Toss the tomato, olives, feta, spaghetti and balsamic vinegar in a bowl and keep warm.

4 Heat the extra olive oil in a small saucepan and cook the extra garlic over low heat, without burning, for 1–2 minutes, or until the garlic has infused the oil.

5 Pour the garlic and oil over the spaghetti mixture, add the rocket leaves and toss well. Sprinkle with the prosciutto pieces and season well. Serve immediately.

NUTRITION PER SERVE
Protein 14 g; Fat 40 g; Carbohydrate 75 g; Dietary Fibre 9 g; Cholesterol 2.5 mg; 3020 kJ (720 cal)

Heat the oil in a large pan and brown the oxtail in batches.

Stir in the stock, crushed tomatoes, wine, cloves and bay leaves and season to taste.

PASTA WITH BRAISED OXTAIL AND CELERY

Preparation time: 20 minutes
Total cooking time: 3 hours 45 minutes
Serves 4

1.5 kg (3 lb) oxtail, jointed
3 tablespoons plain flour, seasoned
3 tablespoons olive oil
1 onion, finely chopped
2 cloves garlic, crushed
2 cups (500 ml/16 fl oz) beef stock
425 g (14 oz) can crushed tomatoes
1 cup (250 ml/8 fl oz) dry white wine
6 whole cloves
2 bay leaves
3 celery stalks, finely chopped
500 g (1 lb) penne
30 g (1 oz) butter or margarine
3 tablespoons grated Parmesan

1 Preheat the oven to warm 160°C (315°F/Gas 2–3). Dust the oxtail in the seasoned flour, shaking off the excess. Heat half the oil in a large pan and brown the oxtail over high heat in batches. Transfer the meat to a large casserole dish.
2 Wipe the pan clean with paper towels, add the remaining oil and the onion and garlic. Cook over low heat until the onion is tender. Stir in the stock, tomatoes, wine, cloves and bay leaves and season with salt and pepper. Bring to the boil and then pour over the oxtail.
3 Bake, covered, for 2¹/₂–3 hours. Add the celery and bake, uncovered, for another 30 minutes. Meanwhile, cook the pasta in a large pan of rapidly boiling salted water until al dente. Drain well and return to the pan to keep warm. Toss with butter and Parmesan. Serve the oxtail and sauce with the pasta.

NUTRITION PER SERVE
Protein 82 g; Fat 30 g; Carbohydrate 100 g; Dietary Fibre 8 g; Cholesterol 700 mg; 4388 kJ (1048 cal)

HINT: Seasoned flour is plain flour to which seasonings of your choice have been added, for example: herbs, salt, pepper or dried mustard.

Cut each cooked sausage into thick slices on the diagonal.

Add the pasta sauce and tomato to the pan and cook until the tomato is soft.

BEEF SAUSAGE PASTA

Preparation time: 10 minutes
Total cooking time: 15 minutes
Serves 4

150 g (5 oz) spiral pasta
4 thick beef sausages
2 tablespoons olive oil
1 large red onion, cut into wedges
1 cup (250 g/8 oz) tomato pasta sauce
4 small ripe tomatoes, peeled, seeded and
    chopped
2 tablespoons chopped fresh flat-leaf parsley

1 Cook the pasta in a large pan of rapidly boiling salted water until al dente. Drain well and return to the pan to keep warm, reserving ¼ cup (60 ml/2 fl oz) of the cooking water.
2 Meanwhile, prick the sausages all over with a fork. Heat a non-stick frying pan and cook the sausages over medium heat, turning often, for 5 minutes, or until cooked. Cut into thick diagonal slices and set aside.
3 Clean the frying pan and heat the oil. Cook the onion wedges over medium heat for 3 minutes, or until soft. Add the tomato pasta sauce and the tomato. Cook for 5 minutes, or until the tomato has softened. Add the sliced sausage and heat through for 1 minute.
4 Toss the pasta through the sauce, adding a little of the reserved pasta water, if necessary. Sprinkle with parsley and serve.

NUTRITION PER SERVE
Protein 12 g; Fat 18 g; Carbohydrate 44 g; Dietary Fibre 7.5 g; Cholesterol 17 mg; 1605 kJ (383 cal)

Discard the fat and rind from the bacon and chop the meat roughly into strips.

When the onion is softened, add the sliced mushrooms and stir while cooking.

LOW-FAT LINGUINE WITH BACON, MUSHROOMS AND PEAS

Preparation time: 20 minutes
Total cooking time: 25 minutes
Serves 4

3 bacon rashers
2 teaspoons olive oil
2–3 cloves garlic, crushed
1 red onion, chopped
185 g (6 oz) field mushrooms, sliced
$^1/_3$ cup (20 g/$^3/_4$ oz) chopped fresh parsley
1 cup (150 g/5 oz) peas
1$^1/_2$ cups (375 ml/12 fl oz) low-fat light
   evaporated milk
2 teaspoons cornflour
325 g (11 oz) linguine
25 g ($^3/_4$ oz) Parmesan shavings

1 Remove the fat and rind from the bacon and chop roughly. Heat the oil in a medium pan, add the garlic, onion and bacon and cook over low heat for 5 minutes, stirring frequently, until the onion and bacon are soft. Add the sliced mushrooms and cook, stirring, for another 5 minutes, or until soft.
2 Add the parsley, peas and milk to the pan. Mix the cornflour with 1 tablespoon of water until smooth, add to the mixture and stir over medium heat until slightly thickened.
3 Cook the pasta in a large pan of rapidly boiling salted water until al dente. Drain well and serve with the hot sauce and Parmesan shavings.

NUTRITION PER SERVE
Protein 30 g; Fat 7 g; Carbohydrate 80 g; Dietary Fibre 9 g; Cholesterol 25 mg; 2085 kJ (500 cal)

NOTE: Parmesan adds a nice flavor to this dish, but leave it out if you are wanting a meal with a very low fat content.

Remove the bacon, garlic, onion and spring onion from the heat. Stir in the ricotta and basil.

Bring a large pan of salted water to a rapid boil before adding the pasta.

PENNE WITH BACON, RICOTTA AND BASIL SAUCE

Preparation time: 20 minutes
Total cooking time: 15 minutes
Serves 4

2 teaspoons olive oil
2 rashers bacon, chopped
2–3 cloves garlic, crushed
1 onion, finely chopped
2 spring onions, finely chopped
250 g (8 oz) ricotta
1/2 cup (30 g/1 oz) finely chopped fresh basil
325 g (11 oz) penne
8 cherry tomatoes, halved

1 Heat the oil in a pan, add the bacon, garlic, onion and spring onion and stir over medium heat for 5 minutes, or until cooked. Remove from the heat, stir in the ricotta and chopped basil and beat until smooth.

2 Cook the pasta in a large pan of rapidly boiling salted water until al dente. Just prior to draining the pasta, add about a cup of the pasta cooking water to the ricotta mixture to thin the sauce. Add more water if you prefer an even thinner sauce. Season with salt and pepper.

3 Drain the pasta and stir the sauce and tomato halves through the pasta. Garnish with tiny fresh basil leaves.

NUTRITION PER SERVE
Protein 20 g; Fat 10 g; Carbohydrate 65 g; Dietary Fibre 5 g; Cholesterol 40 mg; 1885 kJ (450 cal)

Cook the sausage until well browned and then slice when cooled enough to hold.

Cook the onion and garlic until softened before adding the tomatoes, sugar and water.

PASTA SHELLS WITH SAUSAGE AND TOMATO

Preparation time: 15 minutes
Total cooking time: 20 minutes
Serves 4–6

500 g (1 lb) pasta shells or gnocchi
2 tablespoons olive oil
400 g (13 oz) thin Italian sausages
1 red onion, finely chopped
2 cloves garlic, finely chopped
2 x 415 g (13 oz) cans chopped tomatoes
1 teaspoon caster sugar
35 g (1 oz) fresh basil, torn
$^1/_2$ cup (45 g/$1^1/_2$ oz) grated pecorino cheese

1 Cook the pasta in a large pan of rapidly boiling salted water until al dente. Drain and return to the pan to keep warm. Meanwhile, heat 2 teaspoons of the oil in a large frying pan. Add the sausages and cook, turning, for 5 minutes, or until well browned and cooked through. Drain on paper towels, then slice when cooled enough to hold. Keep warm.

2 Wipe clean the frying pan and heat the remaining oil. Add the onion and garlic and cook over medium heat for 2 minutes, or until the onion has softened. Add the tomato, sugar and 1 cup (250 ml/8 fl oz) water and season well. Reduce the heat and simmer for 12 minutes, or until thickened and reduced a little.

3 Pour the sauce over the pasta and stir through the sausage, basil and half the cheese. Serve hot, sprinkled with the remaining cheese.

NUTRITION PER SERVE (6)
Protein 17 g; Fat 30 g; Carbohydrate 30 g; Dietary Fibre 4 g; Cholesterol 58 mg; 1905 kJ (455 cal)

Cook the onion, garlic and salami for 5 minutes, then add the capsicum and cover the pan.

Simmer the sauce uncovered for 15 minutes to reduce the liquid and thicken. Season well.

SPAGHETTI WITH SALAMI AND CAPSICUM

Preparation time: 15 minutes
Total cooking time: 55 minutes
Serves 4–6

2 tablespoons olive oil
1 large onion, finely chopped
2 cloves garlic, crushed
150 g (5 oz) spicy salami slices, cut into strips
2 large red capsicums, chopped
825 g (1 lb 11 oz) can crushed tomatoes
$\frac{1}{2}$ cup (125 ml/4 fl oz) dry white wine
1 teaspoon dried basil
500 g (1 lb) spaghetti

1 Heat the oil in a heavy-based frying pan. Add the onion, garlic and salami and cook, stirring, for 5 minutes over medium heat. Add the capsicum, cover the pan and cook for 5 minutes.
2 Add the crushed tomatoes, wine and basil. Bring to the boil, then reduce the heat and simmer, covered, for 15 minutes.
3 Uncover the pan and simmer for another 15 minutes, or until the sauce has thickened slightly. Season well.
4 Meanwhile, cook the pasta in a large pan of rapidly boiling salted water until al dente. Drain and toss with the sauce to serve.

NUTRITION PER SERVE (6)
Protein 15 g; Fat 13 g; Carbohydrate 66 g; Dietary Fibre 6 g; Cholesterol 16 mg; 1926 kJ (460 cal)

HINT: If you can't find canned crushed tomatoes, chop whole peeled tomatoes in the can with scissors.

Put the tomatoes at one end of the roasting tin and season well. Roast until soft.

Cook the bacon under a hot grill until crisp and golden, then roughly chop.

FETTUCINE WITH CHERRY TOMATOES, AVOCADO AND BACON

Preparation time: 15 minutes
Total cooking time: 30 minutes
Serves 4

4 cloves garlic, unpeeled
1/3 cup (80 ml/2¾ fl oz) olive oil
250 g (8 oz) cherry tomatoes
300 g (10 oz) short cut bacon (see Note)
350 g (11 oz) fresh fettucine
1 tablespoon white wine vinegar
2 tablespoons roughly chopped fresh basil
2 ripe avocados, diced

1 Preheat the oven to moderately hot 200°C (400°F/Gas 6). Place the garlic at one end of a roasting tin and drizzle with 2 tablespoons of the olive oil. Place the tomatoes at the other end and season well. Bake for 10 minutes, then remove the garlic. Return the tomatoes to the oven for a further 5–10 minutes, or until soft.
2 Cook the bacon under a hot grill for 4–5 minutes each side, or until crisp and golden. Roughly chop. Meanwhile, cook the pasta in a large pan of boiling salted water until al dente. Drain well and transfer to a large bowl. Drizzle 1 tablespoon of the olive oil over the pasta and toss well. Season with salt and pepper and keep warm.
3 Slit the skin of each garlic clove and squeeze the garlic out. Place in a screw-top jar with the vinegar, chopped basil and remaining oil and shake well to combine. Add the tomatoes and their juices, bacon and avocado to the fettucine, pour on the dressing and toss well. Garnish with a few whole fresh basil leaves and serve with crusty bread.

NUTRITION PER SERVE

Protein 28 g; Fat 44 g; Carbohydrate 51 g; Dietary Fibre 4 g; Cholesterol 106 mg; 2960 kJ (705 cal)

NOTE: Short cut bacon is the meaty end of the bacon rasher and is also sold as eye bacon.

Cook the pumpkin in boiling water until it is just tender, then drain.

Add the tomato, prosciutto, pumpkin and penne and toss gently.

PENNE WITH PUMPKIN, BAKED RICOTTA AND PROSCIUTTO

Preparation time: 15 minutes
Total cooking time: 15 minutes
Serves 4

500 g (1 lb) penne
460 g (15 oz) butternut pumpkin, cut into small cubes
¼ cup (60 ml/2 fl oz) extra virgin olive oil
2 cloves garlic, crushed
100 g (3½ oz) semi-dried tomatoes, chopped
4 slices prosciutto, chopped
250 g (8 oz) baked ricotta, cut into small cubes
3 tablespoons shredded fresh basil

1 Cook the pasta in a large pan of rapidly boiling salted water until al dente. Drain well. Meanwhile, cook the pumpkin in a saucepan of boiling water for 10–12 minutes, or until just tender, then drain.

2 Heat the oil in a large saucepan, add the garlic and cook over medium heat for 30 seconds. Add the tomato, prosciutto, pumpkin and penne and toss gently over low heat for 1–2 minutes, or until heated through.

3 Add the baked ricotta and the basil, season with salt and cracked black pepper and serve immediately.

NUTRITION PER SERVE
Protein 28.5 g; Fat 23 g; Carbohydrate 99 g; Dietary Fibre 8.5 g; Cholesterol 37 mg; 3020 kJ (720 cal)

Cook the bacon over medium heat for 3 minutes or until golden.

Add the bacon and spinach to the drained pasta and stir in the sweet chilli sauce.

FARFALLE WITH SPINACH AND BACON

Preparation time: 10 minutes
Total cooking time: 15 minutes
Serves 4

400 g (13 oz) farfalle
2 tablespoons extra virgin olive oil
250 g (8 oz) bacon, chopped
1 red onion, finely chopped
250 g (8 oz) baby spinach leaves
1–2 tablespoons sweet chilli sauce
¼ cup (30 g/1 oz) crumbled feta cheese

1 Cook the pasta in a large pan of rapidly boiling salted water until al dente. Drain and return to the pan to keep warm.

2 Meanwhile, heat the oil in a frying pan, add the bacon and cook over medium heat for 3 minutes, or until golden. Add the onion and cook for a further 4 minutes, or until softened. Toss the spinach leaves through the onion and bacon mixture for 30 seconds, or until just wilted.

3 Add the bacon and spinach mixture to the drained pasta, then stir in the sweet chilli sauce. Season to taste with salt and cracked black pepper and toss well. Spoon into warm pasta bowls and scatter with the crumbled feta. Serve immediately.

NUTRITION PER SERVE

Protein 28 g; Fat 19 g; Carbohydrate 73 g; Dietary Fibre 7 g; Cholesterol 42 mg; 2415 kJ (575 cal)

Cut the prosciutto into thin strips and cook in the oil for 2 minutes, or until crisp.

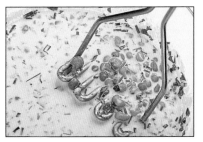

Add the cooked peas to the bowl of eggs, cream and Parmesan and then roughly mash.

CREAMY PASTA WITH PEAS AND PROSCIUTTO

Preparation time: 15 minutes
Total cooking time: 20 minutes
Serves 4

100 g (3¹/₂ oz) thinly sliced prosciutto
3 teaspoons oil
2 eggs
1 cup (250 ml/8 fl oz) cream
¹/₃ cup (35 g/1 oz) finely grated Parmesan
2 tablespoons chopped fresh flat-leaf parsley
1 tablespoon chopped fresh chives
250 g (8 oz) fresh or frozen peas
500 g pasta shells or gnocchi

1 Cut the prosciutto into thin strips. Heat the oil in a frying pan over medium heat, add the prosciutto and cook for 2 minutes, or until crisp. Drain on paper towels. Whisk together the eggs, cream, Parmesan and herbs in a large bowl.
2 Bring a large saucepan of salted water to the boil. Add the peas and cook for 5 minutes, or until just tender. Leaving the pan on the heat, use a slotted spoon and transfer the peas to the bowl of cream mixture, and then add 3 tablespoons of the cooking liquid to the same bowl. Using a potato masher or the back of a fork, roughly mash the peas.
3 Add the pasta to the boiling water and cook until al dente. Drain well, then return to the pan. Add the cream mixture, then warm through over low heat, gently stirring for about 30 seconds until the pasta is coated in the sauce. Season to taste with salt and cracked black pepper. Divide among warmed plates, top with the prosciutto and serve immediately.

NUTRITION PER SERVE
Protein 21 g; Fat 32.5 g; Carbohydrate 41 g; Dietary Fibre 6 g; Cholesterol 201 mg; 2260 kJ (540 cal)

NOTE: Be careful not to overheat or cook for too long or the egg will begin to set to scrambled egg.

Place the bay leaves and veal on top of the onion in the tin and roast until the veal is browned.

Cook the veal, covered and then uncovered, until it is falling away from the bone.

PENNE WITH VEAL RAGOUT

Preparation time: 15 minutes
Total cooking time: 2 hours 40 minutes
Serves 4

2 onions, sliced
2 bay leaves, crushed
1.5 kg (3 lb) veal shin, cut into osso buco
   pieces (see Note)
1 cup (250 ml/8 fl oz) red wine
2 x 400 g (13 oz) cans crushed tomatoes
1½ cups (375 ml/12 fl oz) beef stock
2 teaspoons chopped fresh rosemary
400 g (13 oz) penne
1 cup (150 g/5 oz) frozen peas

1 Preheat the oven to hot 220°C (425°F/Gas 7). Scatter the onion over the bottom of a large roasting tin, lightly spray with oil and place the bay leaves and veal pieces on top. Season with salt and pepper. Roast for 10–15 minutes, or until the veal is browned. Take care that the onion doesn't burn.

2 Pour the wine over the veal and return to the oven for a further 5 minutes. Reduce the heat to moderate 180°C (350°F/Gas 4), remove the tin from the oven and pour on the tomato, stock and 1 teaspoon of the rosemary. Cover with foil and return to the oven. Cook for 2 hours, or until the veal is starting to fall from the bone. Remove the foil and cook for a further 15 minutes, or until the meat loosens away from the bone and the liquid has evaporated slightly.

3 Cook the pasta in a large pan of rapidly boiling salted water until al dente. Drain and return to the pan to keep warm. Meanwhile, remove the veal from the oven and cool slightly. Add the peas and remaining rosemary and place over a hotplate. Cook over medium heat for 5 minutes, or until the peas are cooked. Serve the pasta topped with the ragout.

NUTRITION PER SERVE
Protein 52 g; Fat 5 g; Carbohydrate 81 g; Dietary Fibre 10 g; Cholesterol 125 mg; 2605 kJ (620 cal)

NOTE: Most butchers sell veal shin cut into osso buco pieces. If sold in a whole piece, ask the butcher to cut it for you (the pieces are about 3–4 cm thick). It is also available at some supermarkets. You can either remove the meat from the bone before serving, or leave it on.

Fry the pork in butter until it is golden brown and just cooked through, then cut into thin slices.

Toss together the onion, zucchini, basil, olives, pork and any juices.

PEPPERED PORK AND ZUCCHINI PASTA

Preparation time: 15 minutes
Total cooking time: 25 minutes
Serves 4

450 g (14 oz) pork fillet
3–4 teaspoons cracked black peppercorns
90 g (3 oz) butter
250 g (8 oz) pasta
1 onion, halved and thinly sliced
2 large zucchini, thinly sliced
²/₃ cup (20 g/³/₄ oz) fresh basil, torn
³/₄ cup (150 g/5 oz) baby black olives
¹/₂ cup (60 g/2 oz) grated Romano cheese

1 Cut the pork fillet in half widthways and roll in the cracked peppercorns and some salt. Heat half the butter in a large deep frying pan, add the pork and cook for 4 minutes each side, or until golden brown and just cooked through. Remove from the pan and cut into thin slices, then set aside and keep warm.
2 Cook the pasta in a large pan of rapidly boiling salted water until al dente. Drain and return to the pan to keep warm. Meanwhile, melt the remaining butter in the frying pan, add the onion and cook, stirring, over medium heat for about 3 minutes, or until soft. Add the zucchini and toss for 5 minutes, or until starting to soften. Add the basil, olives, sliced pork and any juices and toss well. Stir the pork mixture through the hot pasta, then season well. Serve immediately, topped with the cheese.

NUTRITION PER SERVE
Protein 39 g; Fat 22 g; Carbohydrate 53 g; Dietary Fibre 5 g; Cholesterol 114 mg; 2340 kJ (560 cal)

Heat a tablespoon of butter in a frying pan and cook the apple until golden.

Add the stock, cider, mustard and garlic and boil until the sauce has reduced and thickened.

PASTA WITH CREAMY PORK AND APPLE

Preparation time: 15 minutes
Total cooking time: 25 minutes
Serves 4

375 g (12 oz) pasta
60 g (2 oz) butter
2 Granny Smith apples, peeled, cored and
    cut into thin wedges
500 g (1 lb) pork fillets, thinly sliced
1½ cups (375 ml/12 fl oz) chicken stock
1 cup (250 ml/8 fl oz) dry alcoholic cider
3 teaspoons wholegrain mustard
2 cloves garlic, crushed
180 ml (6 fl oz) thick cream

1 Cook the pasta in a large pan of rapidly boiling salted water until al dente. Drain and return to the pan to keep warm.
2 Meanwhile, heat a tablespoon of the butter in a large frying pan, add the apple and cook over high heat, turning occasionally, for 4 minutes until golden. Remove from the pan, cover and keep warm. Add another tablespoon of butter to the same pan and stir-fry half the pork for 2–3 minutes, or until seared and just browned. Remove from the pan and keep warm. Repeat with the remaining butter and pork.
3 Add the stock, cider, mustard and garlic to the pan and boil for about 10 minutes, or until the sauce has reduced by half, scraping up any bits with a wooden spoon. Reduce the heat to medium and add the cream, pork and any cooking juices and cook for 2–3 minutes, or until the pork is just cooked through and tender.
4 Stir in two-thirds of the apple, being careful not to break it up, then mix in the pasta. Serve topped with a few pieces of the remaining apple.

NUTRITION PER SERVE
Protein 40 g; Fat 30 g; Carbohydrate 79 g; Dietary Fibre 7 g; Cholesterol 199 mg; 3195 kJ (765 cal)

NOTE: Don't use a non-stick frying pan to cook the apples or they will not caramelize properly.

Fry the sausages until they are well browned then slice them on the diagonal.

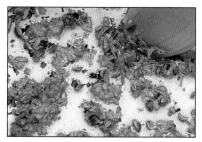

Cook the garlic, fennel seeds and chilli flakes in the oil.

BUCATINI WITH SAUSAGE AND FENNEL SEED

Preparation time: 10 minutes
Total cooking time: 40 minutes
Serves 4

500 g (1 lb) good-quality Italian sausages
2 tablespoons olive oil
3 cloves garlic, chopped
1 teaspoon fennel seeds
$^{1}/_{2}$ teaspoon chilli flakes
2 x 425 g (14 oz) cans crushed tomatoes
500 g (1 lb) bucatini
1 teaspoon balsamic vinegar
$^{1}/_{4}$ cup (7 g/$^{1}/_{4}$ oz) loosely packed fresh basil, chopped

1 Heat a frying pan over high heat, add the sausages and cook, turning, for 8–10 minutes, or until well browned and cooked through. Remove, cool slightly and slice thinly on the diagonal.

2 Heat the oil in a saucepan, add the garlic and cook over medium heat for 1 minute. Add the fennel seeds and chilli flakes and cook for a further minute. Stir in the tomato and bring to the boil, then reduce the heat and simmer, covered, for 20 minutes. Meanwhile, cook the pasta in a large pan of rapidly boiling salted water until al dente. Drain and return to the pan to keep warm.

3 Add the sausages to the sauce and cook, uncovered, for 5 minutes to heat through. Stir in the balsamic vinegar and basil. Divide the pasta among four bowls, top with the sauce and serve.

NUTRITION PER SERVE
Protein 34 g; Fat 51 g; Carbohydrate 96 g; Dietary Fibre 10 g; Cholesterol 95 mg; 4125 kJ (985 cal)

Add the artichokes and ham to the frying pan and cook for 2 minutes.

Add the cream and lemon rind, reduce the heat and simmer for 5 minutes.

LINGUINE WITH HAM, ARTICHOKE AND LEMON SAUCE

Preparation time: 15 minutes
Total cooking time: 10 minutes
Serves 4

500 g (1 lb) fresh linguine
1 tablespoon butter
2 large cloves garlic, chopped
150 g (5 oz) marinated artichokes, drained and quartered
150 g (5 oz) sliced leg ham, cut into strips
300 ml (10 fl oz) cream
2 teaspoons roughly grated lemon rind
1/2 cup (15 g/1/2 oz) fresh basil, torn
1/3 cup (35 g/1 oz) grated Parmesan

1 Cook the pasta in a large pan of rapidly boiling salted water until al dente. Drain and return to the pan to keep warm. Meanwhile, melt the butter in a large frying pan, add the garlic and cook over medium heat for 1 minute, or until fragrant. Add the artichokes and ham and cook for a further 2 minutes.

2 Add the cream and lemon rind, reduce the heat and simmer for 5 minutes, gently breaking up the artichokes with a wooden spoon. Pour the sauce over the pasta, then add the basil and Parmesan and toss well until the pasta is evenly coated. Serve immediately.

NUTRITION PER SERVE
Protein 26 g; Fat 42 g; Carbohydrate 91 g; Dietary Fibre 8 g; Cholesterol 143 mg; 3540 kJ (845 cal)

Cook the leek until it is soft but not browned and then add the wine.

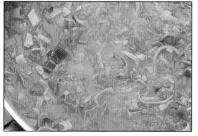

Add the tomato and salami to the sauce and simmer until it has reduced a little.

PAPPARDELLE WITH SALAMI, LEEK AND PROVOLONE CHEESE

Preparation time: 15 minutes
Total cooking time: 15 minutes
Serves 4

375 g (12 oz) pappardelle
2 tablespoons olive oil
2 leeks, thinly sliced (including some of the green section)
2 tablespoons white wine
2 x 400 g (13 oz) cans diced tomatoes
150 g (5 oz) sliced mild salami, cut into strips
¼ cup (7 g/¼ oz) fresh basil leaves, torn
125 g (4 oz) provolone cheese, sliced into strips
30 g (1 oz) grated Parmesan

1 Cook the pasta in a large pan of rapidly boiling salted water until al dente. Drain and return to the pan to keep warm. Meanwhile, heat the olive oil in a large deep frying pan, add the leek and cook over low heat for 4 minutes, or until soft but not browned. Increase the heat to medium, add the wine and stir until almost evaporated.

2 Add the tomato and salami, season with salt and cracked black pepper and simmer for 5 minutes, or until reduced slightly. Toss the tomato sauce mixture, basil and provolone lightly through the pasta. Sprinkle with Parmesan and serve.

NUTRITION PER SERVE
Protein 34 g; Fat 37 g; Carbohydrate 75 g; Dietary Fibre 6 g; Cholesterol 94 mg; 3250 kJ (775 cal)

Cook the veal in the butter in batches until it is golden brown.

Add the cream to the sauce and then simmer uncovered to allow it to thicken.

CREAMY VEAL AND MUSHROOM PASTA

Preparation time: 15 minutes
Total cooking time: 30 minutes
Serves 4

100 g (3½ oz) butter
500 g (1 lb) veal schnitzel, cut into bite-sized pieces
300 g (10 oz) Swiss brown mushrooms, sliced
3 cloves garlic, crushed
¾ cup (185 ml/6 fl oz) dry white wine
½ cup (125 ml/4 fl oz) chicken stock
200 ml (6½ fl oz) thick cream
1–2 tablespoons lemon juice
400 g (13 oz) pappardelle

1 Melt half the butter in a large frying pan over medium heat. Add the veal in batches and cook for 2–3 minutes, or until golden brown. Remove the veal from the pan and keep warm.

2 Add the remaining butter to the same pan and heat until foaming. Add the mushrooms and garlic and cook, stirring, over low heat for 5 minutes. Pour in the wine and stock, scraping the bottom of the pan with a wooden spoon, and simmer, covered, for 10 minutes.

3 Remove the lid, add the cream and simmer for 5 minutes, or until the sauce thickens. Stir in the lemon juice, veal and any juices until warmed through. Season to taste. Meanwhile, cook the pasta in a large pan of rapidly boiling salted water until al dente. Drain well, toss the sauce through the pasta and serve immediately.

NUTRITION PER SERVE
Protein 45 g; Fat 41 g; Carbohydrate 74 g; Dietary Fibre 5 g; Cholesterol 236 mg; 3660 kJ (875 cal)

Pasta with Chicken

SPAGHETTI WITH CHICKEN MEATBALLS

Preparation time: 30 minutes + chilling
Total cooking time: 1 hour 30 minutes
Serves 4–6

500 g (1 lb) chicken mince
60 g (2 oz) freshly grated Parmesan
2 cups (160 g/5½ oz) fresh white
  breadcrumbs
2 cloves garlic, crushed
1 egg
1 tablespoon chopped fresh flat-leaf parsley
1 tablespoon chopped fresh sage
3 tablespoons vegetable oil
500 g (1 lb) spaghetti
2 tablespoons chopped fresh oregano, to
  serve

TOMATO SAUCE
1 tablespoon olive oil
1 onion, finely chopped
2 kg (4 lb) ripe tomatoes, roughly chopped
2 bay leaves
1 cup (30 g/1 oz) fresh basil leaves, loosely
  packed
1 teaspoon coarse ground black pepper

1 In a large bowl, mix together the mince, Parmesan, breadcrumbs, garlic, egg, pepper and herbs. Shape tablespoons of the mixture into small balls and chill for 30 minutes to firm. Heat the oil in a shallow pan and fry the balls in batches until golden brown; turn often by shaking the pan. Drain on paper towels.
2 To make the tomato sauce, heat the oil in a large pan, add the onion and fry for 1–2 minutes. Add the tomato and bay leaves, cover and bring to the boil, stirring occasionally. Reduce the heat to low, partially cover and cook for 50–60 minutes.
3 Add the meatballs, basil leaves and pepper and simmer for 10–15 minutes, uncovered. Meanwhile, cook the spaghetti in a large pan of rapidly boiling salted water until al dente. Drain well and return to the pan. Add some sauce to the pasta and toss. Serve the pasta in individual bowls with sauce and meatballs, sprinkled with fresh oregano and a litte extra Parmesan cheese.

NUTRITION PER SERVE (6)
Protein 30 g; Fat 23 g; Carbohydrate 86 g;
Dietary Fibre 10 g; Cholesterol 60 mg; 2876 kJ
(690 cal)

Shape tablespoons of the mixture into small balls
and then chill for 30 minutes to firm up.

Add the meatballs, basil and pepper to the tomato
mixture.

Fry the eggplant in a large frying pan until golden and cooked through.

Chargrill the chicken breast fillets until browned and cooked through on both sides.

CHICKEN AND EGGPLANT PASTA

Preparation time: 15 minutes
Total cooking time: 15 minutes
Serves 4

375 g (12 oz) penne
100 ml (3¹/₂ fl oz) olive oil
4 slender eggplants, thinly sliced on the diagonal
2 chicken breast fillets
2 teaspoons lemon juice
¹/₂ cup (15 g/¹/₂ oz) chopped fresh flat-leaf parsley
270 g (9 oz) chargrilled red capsicum, drained and sliced (see Note)
150 g (5 oz) fresh asparagus, trimmed, blanched and cut into short lengths
90 g (3 oz) semi-dried tomatoes, finely sliced

1 Cook the pasta in a large pan of rapidly boiling salted water until al dente. Drain and return to the pan to keep warm. Meanwhile, heat 2 tablespoons of the oil in a large frying pan over high heat and cook the eggplant for 4–5 minutes, or until golden and cooked through.
2 Heat a lightly oiled chargrill pan over high heat and cook the chicken for 5 minutes each side, or until browned and cooked through. Cut into thick slices. Combine the lemon juice, parsley and the remaining oil in a small jar and shake well. Return the pasta to the heat, toss through the dressing, chicken, eggplant, capsicum, asparagus and tomato until well mixed and warmed through. Season with black pepper. Serve warm with a little grated Parmesan.

NUTRITION PER SERVE
Protein 50 g; Fat 28 g; Carbohydrate 72 g; Dietary Fibre 7.5 g; Cholesterol 114 mg; 3120 kJ (745 cal)

NOTE: Jars of chargrilled capsicum can be bought at the supermarket; otherwise, visit your local deli.

If you are using fresh fettucine it will have a shorter cooking time than dried.

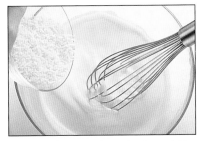

Lightly beat the eggs and cream together and stir in the grated Parmesan.

CHICKEN CARBONARA

Preparation time: 10 minutes
Total cooking time: 20 minutes
Serves 4

500 g (1 lb) fresh tomato fettucine
600 g (1¹/₄ lb) chicken tenderloins
40 g (1¹/₄ oz) butter
3 eggs
300 ml (10 fl oz) cream
¹/₂ cup (50 g/1¹/₂ oz) grated Parmesan
shaved Parmesan and fresh basil leaves, to
   garnish

1 Cook the pasta in a large pan of rapidly boiling salted water until al dente. Drain and return to the pan to keep warm.
2 Trim and slice the tenderloins in half on the diagonal. Melt the butter in a frying pan and cook the chicken for 4–5 minutes, or until browned. Lightly beat the eggs and cream together and stir in the grated Parmesan. Season with salt to taste and stir through the chicken.
3 Combine the chicken and cream mixture with the fettucine in the frying pan. Reduce the heat and cook, stirring constantly, for 10–15 seconds, or until the sauce is slightly thickened. Do not keep on the heat too long or the eggs will set and scramble. Season with black pepper and serve, garnished with the extra Parmesan and basil leaves.

NUTRITION PER SERVE
Protein 54 g; Fat 52 g; Carbohydrate 64 g; Dietary Fibre 4.5 g; Cholesterol 348 mg; 3927 kJ (938 cal)

VARIATION: Saffron fettucine can be purchased from delicatessens or pasta shops, and is a good substitute for tomato fettucine.

Place the chicken between two sheets of plastic wrap and flatten slightly with your hand.

Brown the chicken until cooked through and then cut into slices.

WARM MINTED CHICKEN PASTA

Preparation time: 15 minutes
Total cooking time: 20 minutes
Serves 4

250 g (8 oz) pasta
1/2 cup (125 ml/4 fl oz) olive oil
1 large red capsicum
3 chicken breast fillets
6 spring onions, cut into short lengths
4 cloves garlic, thinly sliced
3/4 cup (35 g/1 1/4 oz) chopped fresh mint
1/3 cup (80 ml/2 3/4 fl oz) cider vinegar
100 g (3 1/2 oz) baby English spinach

1 Cook the pasta in a large pan of rapidly boiling salted water until al dente. Drain, return to the pan to keep warm and toss with a tablespoon of the oil.

2 Meanwhile, cut the capsicum into quarters, removing the seeds and membrane. Place, skin-side-up, under a hot grill for 8–10 minutes, or until the skin blackens and blisters. Cool in a plastic bag, then peel away the skin. Cut into thin strips. Place the chicken between two sheets of plastic wrap and press with the palm of your hand until slightly flattened.

3 Heat 1 tablespoon of the oil in a large frying pan, add the chicken and cook over medium heat for 2–3 minutes each side, or until light brown and cooked through. Remove from the pan and cut into thin slices.

4 Add another tablespoon of the oil to the pan and add the spring onion, garlic and capsicum. Cook, stirring, for 2–3 minutes, or until starting to soften. Add most of the mint, the vinegar and the remaining oil and stir until warmed through. Toss together the pasta, chicken, spinach, onion mixture and remaining mint. Serve warm.

NUTRITION PER SERVE
Protein 47 g; Fat 30 g; Carbohydrate 47g; Dietary Fibre 6 g; Cholesterol 84 mg; 2705 kJ (645 cal)

Cook the leek in the oil for 3–4 minutes, or until it is soft.

Add the cream and chicken and simmer until the sauce has slightly thickened.

SMOKED CHICKEN LINGUINE

Preparation time: 15 minutes
Total cooking time: 20 minutes
Serves 4

1 tablespoon olive oil
1 leek, thinly sliced
3 large cloves garlic, finely chopped
1/2 cup (125 ml/4 fl oz) dry white wine
300 g (10 oz) Swiss brown mushrooms, sliced
2 teaspoons chopped fresh thyme
300 ml (10 fl oz) thick cream
2 smoked chicken breast fillets, thinly sliced (see Note)
350 g (11 oz) fresh linguine

1 Heat the oil in a saucepan. Add the leek and cook, stirring, over low heat for 3–4 minutes, or until soft. Add the garlic and cook for another minute. Pour in the wine and simmer for 2–3 minutes, or until the liquid has reduced by half.
2 Increase the heat to medium, add the mushrooms and thyme and cook for 5 minutes, or until any excess liquid has been absorbed, then add the cream and sliced chicken. Reduce the heat and simmer for 4–5 minutes, or until the sauce has slightly thickened.
3 Meanwhile, cook the pasta in a large pan of rapidly boiling salted water until al dente. Drain and divide among serving plates. Spoon on the sauce and serve.

NUTRITION PER SERVE
Protein 33 g; Fat 40 g; Carbohydrate 53 g; Dietary Fibre 4 g; Cholesterol 207 mg; 2990 kJ (715 cal)

NOTE: Buy smoked chicken at the deli section of good supermarkets.

Drain the cooked rigatoni and then return to the pan to keep warm.

Cook the chicken over high heat until browned and cooked through.

CREAMY RIGATONI WITH CHICKEN AND SUN-DRIED TOMATO SAUCE

Preparation time: 5 minutes
Total cooking time: 20 minutes
Serves 4–6

500 g (1 lb) rigatoni
1 tablespoon olive oil
4 chicken breast fillets, thinly sliced
4 ripe tomatoes, diced
150 g (5 oz) sun-dried tomatoes in oil, thinly sliced
2 tablespoons sun-dried tomato paste (see NOTE)
handful of small fresh basil leaves
300 ml (10 fl oz) cream
200 ml (6¹/₂ fl oz) chicken stock

1 Cook the pasta in a large pan of rapidly boiling salted water until al dente. Drain and return to the pan to keep warm.
2 Meanwhile, heat the oil in a deep frying pan and cook the chicken over high heat for 4 minutes each side, or until browned and cooked through. Remove from the pan and keep warm.
3 Return the pan to the heat and add the tomato, sun-dried tomato, sun-dried tomato paste and half the basil leaves. Cook over medium heat for 5 minutes, or until the tomato starts to soften. Stir in the cream and hicken stock and bring to the boil, stirring constantly.
4 Reduce the heat and return the chicken to the pan. Add the rigatoni and season with pepper. Heat gently until the chicken and pasta are warmed through. Top with the remaining basil leaves and serve immediately with crusty bread.

NUTRITION PER SERVE (6)
Protein 45 g; Fat 50 g; Carbohydrate 90 g; Dietary Fibre 8 g; Cholesterol 195 mg; 4227 kJ (1010 cal)

NOTE: Sun-dried tomato paste is available in good supermarkets. Or, you can make your own by processing whole sun-dried tomatoes in oil with a little of their oil until a smooth paste is formed.

Cut the chicken in half to make four flat fillets that will cook through quickly.

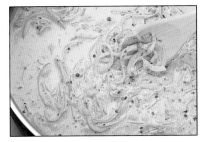

Stir in the cream and cook for 4–5 minutes, or until the sauce thickens slightly.

CREAMY CHICKEN AND PEPPERCORN PAPPARDELLE

Preparation time: 15 minutes
Total cooking time: 15 minutes
Serves 4

2 chicken breast fillets
30 g (1 oz) butter
1 onion, halved and thinly sliced
2 tablespoons drained green peppercorns,
  slightly crushed
1/2 cup (125 ml/4 fl oz) white wine
300 ml (10 fl oz) cream
400 g (13 oz) pappardelle
90 g (3 oz) sour cream (optional)
2 tablespoons chopped fresh chives

1 Cut the chicken in half so that you have four flat fillets and season with salt and pepper. Melt the butter in a frying pan, add the chicken and cook for 3 minutes each side, or until lightly browned and cooked through. Remove from the pan, cut into slices and keep warm.

2 Add the onion and peppercorns to the same pan and cook over medium heat for 3 minutes, or until the onion has softened slightly. Add the wine and cook for 1 minute, or until reduced by half. Stir in the cream and cook for 4–5 minutes, or until thickened slightly, then season with salt and pepper.

3 Meanwhile, cook the pasta in a large pan of rapidly boiling salted water until al dente. Drain and return to the pan to keep warm. Mix together the pasta, chicken with any juices and cream sauce. Divide the pasta among serving bowls, top with a dollop of sour cream and sprinkle with chives.

NUTRITION PER SERVE
Protein 38 g; Fat 50 g; Carbohydrate 60 g; Dietary Fibre 1.5 g; Cholesterol 250 mg; 3580 kJ (855 cal)

Roll heaped tablespoons of the mixture into balls and place on the lined tray.

Simmer the meatballs in the sauce, turning once, until they are cooked through.

LASAGNETTE WITH SPICY CHICKEN MEATBALLS

Preparation time: 10 minutes
Total cooking time: 15 minutes
Serves 4

750 g (1½ lb) chicken mince
2 tablespoons chopped fresh coriander
   leaves
1½ tablespoons red curry paste
2 tablespoons oil
1 red onion, finely chopped
3 cloves garlic, crushed
3½ cups (875 g/1 lb 13 oz) tomato pasta
   sauce
2 teaspoons soft brown sugar
350 g (11 oz) lasagnette

1 Line a tray with baking paper. Combine the mince, coriander and 1 tablespoon of the curry paste in a bowl. Roll heaped tablespoons of the mixture into balls and put on the tray—you should get about 20 balls. Refrigerate until ready to use.

2 Heat the oil in a large deep frying pan and cook the onion and garlic over medium heat for 2–3 minutes, or until softened. Add the remaining curry paste and cook, stirring, for 1 minute, or until fragrant. Add the pasta sauce and sugar and stir well. Reduce the heat, add the meatballs and cook, turning halfway through, for 10 minutes, or until the meatballs are cooked through.

3 Meanwhile, cook the pasta in a large pan of rapidly boiling salted water until al dente. Drain and divide among four serving bowls. Top with the sauce and meatballs and sprinkle with fresh coriander to serve.

NUTRITION PER SERVE
Protein 52 g; Fat 29 g; Carbohydrate 79 g; Dietary Fibre 8.5 g; Cholesterol 185 mg; 3300 kJ (790 cal)

Separate the leaves of the bok choy then blanch in boiling water until tender.

Remove the duck meat from the bones and then finely shred.

CHINESE ROAST DUCK WITH PAPPARDELLE

Preparation time: 15 minutes
Total cooking time: 15 minutes
Serves 4–6

250 g (8 oz) baby bok choy, leaves
    separated
600 g (1¼ lb) fresh pappardelle
1 Chinese roast duck, skin removed (see
    NOTE)
⅓ cup (80 ml/3¾ fl oz) peanut oil
3 cloves garlic, crushed
3 teaspoons grated fresh ginger
¾ cup (35 g/1 oz) chopped fresh coriander
    leaves
2 tablespoons hoisin sauce
2 tablespoons oyster sauce

1 Bring a large pan of water to the boil and blanch the bok choy for 1–2 minutes, or until tender but still crisp. Remove with a slotted spoon and keep warm. Cook the pasta in the water until al dente. Drain well and return to the pan to keep warm.
2 Remove and shred the duck meat. Heat the peanut oil in a small pan over high heat until smoking. Remove from the heat and cool for 1 minute, then swirl in the garlic and ginger to infuse the oil. Be careful not to allow the garlic to burn or it will turn bitter.
3 Pour the hot oil over the pasta and add the bok choy, duck, coriander, hoisin and oyster sauces. Toss well, season and serve immediately.

NUTRITION PER SERVE (6)
Protein 29 g; Fat 20 g; Carbohydrate 76 g; Dietary Fibre 4.5 g; Cholesterol 105 mg; 2490 kJ (595 cal)

NOTE: Chinese roast duck can be bought from Asian barbecue food shops or restaurants.

You can either fry or chargrill the chicken breast fillets, then thinly slice.

Cook the prosciutto under a hot grill until crisp. Allow to cool, then break into pieces.

PASTA WITH ARTICHOKES AND CHARGRILLED CHICKEN

Preparation time: 10 minutes
Total cooking time: 30 minutes
Serves 6

1 tablespoon olive oil
3 chicken breast fillets
500 g (1 lb) pasta
8 slices prosciutto
280 g (9 oz) jar artichokes in oil, drained and quartered, oil reserved
150 g (5 oz) semi-dried tomatoes, thinly sliced
90 g (3 oz) baby rocket leaves
2–3 tablespoons balsamic vinegar

1 Lightly brush a chargrill or frying pan with the oil and heat over high heat. Cook the chicken for 6–8 minutes each side, or until cooked through. Thinly slice and set aside.

2 Cook the pasta in a large pan of rapidly boiling salted water until al dente. Drain and return to the pan to keep warm. Meanwhile, place the prosciutto on a grill tray and cook under a hot grill for 2 minutes each side, or until crisp. Cool slightly and break into pieces. Combine the pasta with the chicken, prosciutto, artichokes, tomato and rocket in a bowl and toss. Whisk together ¼ cup (60 ml/2 fl oz) of the reserved artichoke oil and the balsamic vinegar and toss through the pasta mixture. Season and serve.

NUTRITION PER SERVE
Protein 30 g; Fat 9 g; Carbohydrate 51 g; Dietary Fibre 4 g; Cholesterol 103 mg; 1705 kJ (410 cal)

Fry the onion and garlic in the butter and oil until the onion is tender.

Add the tomato and tomato paste and stir in, then add the wine.

PENNE WITH CHICKEN AND MUSHROOMS

Preparation time: 15 minutes
Total cooking time: 25 minutes
Serves 4

30 g (1 oz) butter
1 tablespoon olive oil
1 onion, sliced
1 clove garlic, crushed
60 g (2 oz) prosciutto, chopped
250 g (8 oz) chicken thigh fillets, trimmed and sliced
125 g (4 oz) mushrooms, sliced
1 tomato, peeled, halved and sliced
1 tablespoon tomato paste
1/2 cup (125 ml/4 fl oz) white wine
1 cup (250 ml/8 fl oz) cream
500 g (1 lb) penne
2 tablespoons grated Parmesan, for serving

1 Heat the butter and oil in a large frying pan. Add the onion and garlic and stir over low heat until the onion is tender. Add the prosciutto and fry until crisp.

2 Add the chicken and cook over medium heat for 3 minutes. Add the mushrooms and cook for another 2 minutes. Stir in the tomato and tomato paste and then the wine. Bring to the boil. Reduce the heat and simmer until reduced by half.

3 Stir in the cream, salt and pepper. Bring to the boil. Reduce the heat and simmer until the sauce begins to thicken. Meanwhile, cook the pasta in a large pan of rapidly boiling salted water until al dente. Drain and return to the pan. Add the sauce and toss to combine. Serve immediately, sprinkled with Parmesan.

NUTRITION PER SERVE
Protein 23 g; Fat 60 g; Carbohydrate 14 g; Dietary Fibre 3 g; Cholesterol 255 mg; 2888 kJ (700 cal)

HINT: If you prefer, you can use chicken mince in this recipe instead of sliced chicken fillets.

Trim any fat or gristle from the chicken liver before cutting them into small pieces.

Cook the onion and garlic until the onion is tender and then add the livers.

TAGLIATELLE WITH CHICKEN LIVERS AND CREAM

Preparation time: 20 minutes
Total cooking time: 15 minutes
Serves 4

2 tablespoons olive oil
1 onion, finely chopped
1 clove garlic, crushed
300 g (10 oz) chicken livers, chopped into
   small pieces
1 cup (250 ml/8 fl oz) cream
1 tablespoon snipped chives
1 teaspoon wholegrain mustard
2 eggs, beaten
375 g (12 oz) tagliatelle
2 tablespoons grated Parmesan, for serving

1 Heat the oil in a large frying pan. Add the onion and garlic and stir over low heat until the onion is tender. Add the chicken livers to the pan and cook gently for 2–3 minutes. Remove from the heat.

2 Stir in the cream, chives and mustard and season with salt and pepper. Return to the heat and bring the sauce to the boil. Add the eggs, stirring gently. Remove from the heat.

3 Meanwhile, cook the pasta in a large pan of rapidly boiling salted water until al dente. Drain and return to the pan to keep warm. Add the sauce and toss well to combine. Serve in warmed pasta bowls with grated Parmesan.

NUTRITION PER SERVE

Protein 25 g; Fat 35 g; Carbohydrate 70 g; Dietary Fibre 5 g; Cholesterol 70 mg; 2914 kJ (700 cal)

Cook the pasta, drain well and then return to the pan to keep warm.

The woody ends of the asparagus will snap off easily when you gently bend the stalk.

PENNE WITH SAUTEED CHICKEN, ASPARAGUS AND GOATS CHEESE

Preparation time: 15 minutes
Total cooking time: 35 minutes
Serves 4

500 g (1 lb) penne
350 g (11 oz) fresh asparagus spears
1 tablespoon olive oil
2 chicken breast fillets, cut into small cubes
1 tablespoon finely chopped fresh thyme
1 cup (250 ml/8 fl oz) chicken stock
1/3 cup (80 ml/2¾ fl oz) balsamic vinegar
150 g (5 oz) goats cheese, crumbled

1 Cook the pasta in a large pan of rapidly boiling salted water until al dente. Drain and return to the pan to keep warm.
2 Remove the woody ends from the asparagus, cut into short lengths and cook in a pan of boiling water for 3 minutes, or until just tender.
3 Heat the oil in a pan over high heat. Add the chicken and cook in batches, stirring occasionally, for 5 minutes, or until browned. Return all the chicken to the pan. Add the thyme and cook for 1 minute. Add the stock and vinegar and bring to the boil. Reduce the heat and simmer, stirring, for 3–4 minutes, or until the sauce has reduced slightly, then add the asparagus. Toss the pasta with the chicken in a serving bowl and sprinkle with the cheese. Season and serve.

NUTRITION PER SERVE
Protein 45 g; Fat 17 g; Carbohydrate 90 g; Dietary Fibre 7.5 g; Cholesterol 75 mg; 2957 kJ (705 cal)

VARIATION: You can use feta instead of goats cheese.

Pasta with Seafood

TAGLIATELLE WITH OCTOPUS

Preparation time: 15 minutes
Total cooking time: 20 minutes
Serves 4

500 g (1 lb) tagliatelle
2 tablespoons olive oil
1 onion, sliced
1 clove garlic, crushed
425 g (14 oz) can crushed tomatoes
$^{1}/_{2}$ cup (125 ml/4 fl oz) dry white wine
1 tablespoon chilli sauce
1 tablespoon chopped fresh basil
1 kg (2 lb) baby octopus, cleaned and halved
    (see NOTE)

1 Cook the pasta in a large pan of rapidly boiling salted water until al dente. Drain and return to the pan to keep warm.

2 Meanwhile, heat the oil in a large frying pan. Add the onion and garlic and stir over low heat until the onion is tender. Add the crushed tomatoes, wine, chilli sauce, basil and season with salt and pepper. Bring to the boil. Reduce the heat and simmer for 10 minutes.

3 Add the octopus to the sauce. Simmer for 5–10 minutes or until the octopus is tender. Pour over the pasta and serve immediately.

NUTRITION PER SERVE
Protein 58 g; Fat 14 g; Carbohydrate 96 g; Dietary Fibre 9 g; Cholesterol 50 mg; 3230 kJ (772 cal)

NOTE: To clean octopus, use a small sharp knife and remove the gut by either cutting off the head entirely or by slicing open the head and removing the gut. Pick up the body and use your index finger to push the beak up. Remove the beak. Wash the octopus thoroughly. Cut the sac into two or three pieces.

Use your index finger to push up from underneath the octopus so you can remove the beak.

Once the tomato sauce is cooked, add the octopus and simmer for 5–10 minutes.

Cook the spring onion and mushrooms over medium heat until soft.

Add the wine and cream to the saucepan and bring to the boil.

SMOKED SALMON PASTA

Preparation time: 10 minutes
Total cooking time: 15 minutes
Serves 4

500 g (1 lb) pasta
1 tablespoon olive oil
4 spring onions, finely chopped
180 g (6 oz) button mushrooms, sliced
1 cup (250 ml/8 fl oz) dry white wine
300 ml (10 fl oz) cream
1 tablespoon finely chopped fresh dill
1 tablespoon lemon juice
90 g (3 oz) Parmesan, grated
200 g (6½ oz) smoked salmon, cut into
    strips
shaved Parmesan and lemon wedges, to
    serve

1 Cook the pasta in a large pan of rapidly boiling salted water until al dente. Drain and return to the pan to keep warm.
2 Meanwhile, heat the oil in a small saucepan, add the spring onion and mushrooms and cook over medium heat for 1–2 minutes, or until soft. Add the wine and cream and bring to the boil, then reduce the heat and simmer for 1 minute.
3 Pour the mushroom sauce over the pasta and stir through the dill and lemon juice. Add the Parmesan and stir until warmed through. Remove from the heat and stir in the smoked salmon. Season with pepper and serve with Parmesan shavings and lemon wedges.

NUTRITION PER SERVE
Protein 40 g; Fat 60 g; Carbohydrate 90 g; Dietary Fibre 8 g; Cholesterol 184 mg; 4608 kJ (1101 cal)

Transfer the pasta to a bowl to cool and toss with a little oil.

Cook the garlic for a few seconds before adding the wine and lemon juice.

ANGEL HAIR PASTA WITH GARLIC, SCALLOPS AND ROCKET

Preparation time: 10 minutes
Total cooking time: 15 minutes
Serves 4

20 large scallops with roe
250 g (8 oz) angel hair pasta
150 ml (5 fl oz) extra virgin olive oil
2 cloves garlic, finely chopped
1/4 cup (60 ml/2 fl oz) white wine
1 tablespoon lemon juice
100 g (3 1/2 oz) baby rocket leaves
1/2 cup (30 g/1 oz) chopped fresh coriander
   leaves

1 Pull or trim any veins, membrane or hard white muscle from the scallops. Pat the scallops dry with paper towels. Cook the pasta in a large pan of rapidly boiling salted water until al dente. Drain and transfer to a bowl. Toss with 1 tablespoon of the oil.
2 Meanwhile, heat 1 tablespoon oil in a frying pan, add the garlic and cook for a few seconds, or until fragrant. Do not brown. Add the wine and lemon juice, and remove from the heat.
3 Heat a chargrill pan or barbecue grill plate over high heat and brush with a little oil. Season the scallops with salt and pepper and cook for 1 minute each side, or until just cooked. Gently reheat the garlic mixture, add the rocket and stir over medium heat for 1–2 minutes, or until wilted. Toss through the pasta and mix together well. Add the remaining oil and half the coriander and mix well. Divide the pasta among four bowls, arrange the scallops over the top and garnish with the remaining coriander.

NUTRITION PER SERVE
Protein 15 g; Fat 37 g; Carbohydrate 45 g; Dietary Fibre 4 g; Cholesterol 20 mg; 2425 kJ (580 cal)

VARIATION: Add 1/2 teaspoon dried chilli flakes just before the wine and lemon juice for an added kick.

Using a sharp knife, roughly chop the vine-ripened tomatoes.

Cook the garlic and tuna over medium heat for 1 minute.

SPAGHETTI WITH TUNA, BASIL AND CAPERS

Preparation time: 10 minutes
Total cooking time: 15 minutes
Serves 4

500 g (1 lb) spaghetti
1 tablespoon extra virgin olive oil
2 cloves garlic, crushed
250 g (8 oz) can tuna in brine, drained and broken into chunks
2 cups (60 g/2 oz) fresh basil leaves, torn
4 vine-ripened tomatoes, roughly chopped
2 tablespoons capers, roughly chopped
90 g (3 oz) Parmesan, grated

1 Cook the pasta in a large pan of rapidly boiling salted water until al dente. Drain and return to the pan to keep warm.
2 Meanwhile, heat the oil in a small saucepan, add the garlic and tuna and cook over medium heat for 1 minute, or until the garlic is fragrant and the tuna is warmed through.
3 Add the tuna mixture, basil, tomato, capers and Parmesan to the spaghetti and mix together well. Season and serve with crusty bread.

NUTRITION PER SERVE
Protein 48 g; Fat 20 g; Carbohydrate 93 g; Dietary Fibre 9.5 g; Cholesterol 60 mg; 3147 kJ (752 cal)

Combine the milk, cream and lemon juice and stir slowly into the sauce.

Once the sauce is cooked, add the drained pasta to the pan and toss well.

SALMON AND PASTA MORNAY

Preparation time: 10 minutes
Total cooking time: 15 minutes
Serves 4

400 g (13 oz) small shell pasta
30 g (1 oz) butter
6 spring onions, chopped
2 cloves garlic, crushed
1 tablespoon plain flour
1 cup (250 ml/8 fl oz) milk
1 cup (250 g/8 oz) sour cream
1 tablespoon lemon juice
425 g (14 oz) can salmon, drained and
  flaked
1/2 cup (15 g/1/2 oz) chopped fresh parsley

1 Cook the pasta in a large pan of rapidly boiling salted water until al dente. Drain and return to the pan to keep warm.
2 Meanwhile, melt the butter in a pan and cook the onion and garlic over low heat for 3 minutes or until soft. Add the flour and stir for 1 minute. Mix together the milk, cream and lemon juice and slowly add to the pan, stirring constantly. Stir over medium heat for 3 minutes or until the sauce boils and thickens.
3 Add the salmon and parsley to the sauce and stir for 1 minute to heat through. Toss with the pasta and season before serving.

NUTRITION PER SERVE
Protein 39 g; Fat 42 g; Carbohydrate 78 g; Dietary Fibre 6 g; Cholesterol 192 mg; 3530 kJ (852 cal)

STORAGE: The sauce can be kept for up to a day, covered in the fridge. Cook the pasta and reheat the sauce just before serving.

VARIATION: Use canned tuna instead of salmon. Add 1 teaspoon of mustard to the sauce.

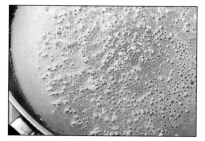

Cook the mushrooms, garlic, prawns and salmon until the fish just starts to flake.

Add the wine, stock and saffron to the pan. Scrape the bits from the bottom of the pan.

SALMON WITH PASTA AND SAFFRON CREAM SAUCE

Preparation time: 15 minutes
Total cooking time: 20 minutes
Serves 4

500 g (1 lb) pappardelle pasta
50 g (1¾ oz) butter
4 cloves garlic, crushed
150 g (5 oz) oyster mushrooms
800 g (1 lb 10 oz) raw prawns, peeled and
    deveined
2 x 400 g (13 oz) salmon fillets, skin
    removed, cut into small cubes
1 cup (250 ml/8 fl oz) white wine
1 cup (250 ml/8 fl oz) fish stock
¼ teaspoon saffron threads
400 ml (13 fl oz) crème fraîche
125 g (4 oz) sugar snap peas or snow peas

1 Cook the pasta in a large pan of rapidly boiling salted water until al dente. Drain and return to the pan to keep warm.

2 Meanwhile, melt the butter in a large deep frying pan, add the garlic and oyster mushrooms and cook for 1 minute. Add the prawns and salmon and cook for 2–3 minutes, or until the prawns are cooked and the salmon starts to flake but is still rare in the centre. Be careful not to burn the garlic. Transfer to a bowl.

3 Pour the wine and stock into the pan and add the saffron. Scrape the bottom of the pan with a wooden spoon. Bring to the boil, then reduce the heat and simmer rapidly for 5 minutes, or until reduced by half. Add the crème fraîche and sugar snap peas and stir through. Bring to the boil, then reduce the heat and simmer, stirring occasionally, for 3–4 minutes, until the liquid has slightly thickened.

4 Return the seafood and any juices to the pan and gently stir over medium heat until warmed through. Serve immediately over the pasta.

NUTRITION PER SERVE
Protein 98 g; Fat 48 g; Carbohydrate 96 g; Dietary Fibre 9.5 g; Cholesterol 456 mg; 5240 kJ (1250 cal)

The easiest way to mince the anchovies is with a mortar and pestle.

Cook the spaghetti in a pan of lightly salted boiling water until al dente.

SPAGHETTI WITH OLIVE, CAPER AND ANCHOVY SAUCE

Preparation time: 15 minutes
Total cooking time: 20 minutes
Serves 6

375 g (12 oz) spaghetti
1/3 cup (80 ml/2³/₄ fl oz) olive oil
2 onions, finely chopped
3 cloves garlic, finely chopped
1/2 teaspoon chilli flakes
6 large ripe tomatoes, diced
4 tablespoons capers in brine, rinsed, drained
7–8 anchovies in oil, drained, minced
150 g (5 oz) Kalamata olives
3 tablespoons chopped fresh flat-leaf parsley

1 Cook the pasta in a large pan of rapidly boiling salted water until al dente. Drain and return to the pan to keep warm.
2 Meanwhile, heat the oil in a saucepan, add the onion and cook over medium heat for 5 minutes. Add the garlic and chilli flakes, and cook for 30 seconds, then add the tomato, capers and anchovies. Simmer over low heat for 5–10 minutes, or until thick and pulpy, then stir in the olives and parsley.
3 Stir the pasta through the sauce. Season and serve immediately with crusty bread.

NUTRITION PER SERVE
Protein 10 g; Fat 15 g; Carbohydrate 49 g; Dietary Fibre 6.5 g; Cholesterol 2 mg; 1563 kJ (373 cal)

Cook the pasta in a large pan of rapidly boiling water until al dente.

Add the tomatoes, wine, parsley and sugar and stir well.

PASTA WITH CLAMS

Preparation time: 25 minutes + overnight soaking
Total cooking time: 20 minutes
Serves 4

2 tablespoons salt
2 tablespoons plain flour
1 kg (2 lb) clams or pipis
500 g (1 lb) shell pasta
1 tablespoon olive oil
2 cloves garlic, crushed
2 x 425 g (14 oz) cans crushed tomatoes
¼ cup (60 ml/2 fl oz) red wine
2 tablespoons chopped fresh parsley
1 teaspoon sugar

1 Blend the salt and plain flour with enough water to make a paste. Add to a large pan of cold water and soak the shellfish overnight. This will draw out sand from inside the shells. Scrub the shells well. Rinse and drain.

2 Cook the pasta in a large pan of rapidly boiling salted water until al dente. Drain and return to the pan to keep warm. Meanwhile, heat the oil in a large pan. Add the garlic and cook over low heat for 30 seconds. Add the tomatoes, wine, parsley and sugar and season. Stir and bring to the boil. Reduce the heat and simmer, stirring occasionally, for 5 minutes.

3 Add the clams to the sauce and cook for 3–5 minutes, stirring occasionally, until opened. Discard any clams that do not open in the cooking time. Serve over the pasta.

NUTRITION PER SERVE
Protein 35 g; Fat 25 g; Carbohydrate 55 g; Dietary Fibre 7 g; Cholesterol 355 mg; 2420 kJ (580 cal)

Pull the tentacles from the squid body, then pull the quill from the pouch.

Cook the leek and garlic to soften before adding the chilli and cayenne pepper.

SPAGHETTI WITH CHILLI CALAMARI

Preparation time: 10 minutes
Total cooking time: 20 minutes
Serves 4

500 g (1 lb) calamari, cleaned
500 g (1 lb) spaghetti
2 tablespoons olive oil
1 leek, chopped
2 cloves garlic, crushed
1–2 teaspoons chopped chilli
$^{1}/_{2}$ teaspoon cayenne pepper
425 g (14 oz) can crushed tomatoes
$^{1}/_{2}$ cup (125 ml/4 fl oz) fish stock (see NOTE)
1 tablespoon chopped fresh basil
2 teaspoons chopped fresh sage
1 teaspoon chopped fresh marjoram

1 Pull the tentacles from the calamari bodies. Use your fingers to pull the quills away from the pouches. Pull the skin away from the flesh and discard. Using a sharp knife, slit the tubes up one side, lay out flat and score one side in a diamond pattern. Cut each piece into four.
2 Cook the pasta in a large pan of rapidly boiling salted water until al dente. Drain and return to the pan to keep warm. While the pasta is cooking, heat the oil in a large frying pan. Add the leek and cook for 2 minutes. Add the garlic and stir over low heat for 1 minute. Stir in the chilli and cayenne pepper. Add the tomatoes, stock and herbs. Bring to the boil. Reduce the heat and simmer for 5 minutes.
3 Add the calamari to the sauce and simmer for another 5–10 minutes or until tender. Serve over the spaghetti.

NUTRITION PER SERVE
Protein 36 g; Fat 13 g; Carbohydrate 92 g; Dietary Fibre 9 g; Cholesterol 250 mg; 2671 kJ (638 cal)

NOTE: Make your own fish stock by putting fish bones and trimmings, 1 roughly chopped onion, 1 celery stalk and 1 carrot in a large saucepan or stockpot and covering with cold water. Bring to the boil, then reduce the heat and simmer for 30 minutes. Drain well, discarding the solids, and use the stock immediately.

Cook the pasta in a large saucepan until al dente, then drain well.

Cook the prawns in batches until they are pink and tender.

SAFFRON PASTA WITH GARLIC PRAWNS AND PRESERVED LEMON

Preparation time: 20 minutes
Total cooking time: 20 minutes
Serves 4

1/2 cup (125 ml/4 fl oz) dry white wine
pinch of saffron threads
500 g (1 lb) fresh saffron or plain angel-hair pasta
1 tablespoon virgin olive oil
30 g (1 oz) butter
750 g (1 1/2 lb) raw prawns, peeled and deveined
3 cloves garlic, crushed
100 g (3 1/2 oz) butter, for pan-frying, extra
1/2 preserved lemon, rinsed, pith and flesh removed, cut into thin strips
1 tablespoon lemon juice
4 spring onions, thinly sliced
4 kaffir lime leaves, thinly shredded
1/2 cup (125 ml/4 fl oz) chicken stock
2 tablespoons snipped chives

1 Place the wine and saffron in a small saucepan and boil for 3 minutes, or until reduced by half. Remove from the heat.
2 Cook the pasta in a large pan of rapidly boiling salted water until al dente. Drain and return to the pan to keep warm.
3 Heat the oil and butter in a large frying pan and cook the prawns in batches over high heat for 3 minutes, or until pink and tender. Cut into thirds, then transfer to a plate and keep warm.
4 Add the garlic and extra butter to the same pan and cook over medium heat for 3 minutes, or until golden. Add the wine and stir to remove any sediment from the bottom of the pan. Add the preserved lemon, lemon juice, spring onion, lime leaves and stock and bring to the boil, then reduce the heat and simmer for 2 minutes.
5 Return the prawns to the frying pan and heat through. Serve the pasta topped with some of the prawns and sauce and sprinkle with chives.

NUTRITION PER SERVE
Protein 15 g; Fat 27 g; Carbohydrate 90 g; Dietary Fibre 7.5 g; Cholesterol 64 mg; 2888 kJ (690 cal)

Cook the scallops over high heat, making sure they are well spaced in the pan.

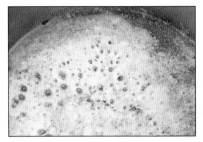

Cook the butter for 4 minutes, or until it is foaming and golden brown.

CAJUN SCALLOPS WITH PASTA AND BUTTERY CORN SAUCE

Preparation time: 15 minutes
Total cooking time: 15 minutes
Serves 4

350 g (11 oz) small pasta shells
20 large scallops, without roe
2 tablespoons Cajun spice mix
2 tablespoons corn oil
250 g (8 oz) butter
3 cloves garlic, crushed
400 g (13 oz) can corn kernels, drained
1/4 cup (60 ml/2 fl oz) lime juice
4 tablespoons finely chopped fresh
   coriander leaves

1 Cook the pasta in a large pan of rapidly boiling salted water until al dente. Drain and return to the pan to keep warm. Meanwhile, pat the scallops dry with paper towel and lightly coat in the spice mix. Heat the oil in a large frying pan and cook the scallops for 1 minute each side over high heat (ensuring they are well spaced), then remove from the pan, cover and keep warm.

2 Reduce the heat to medium, add the butter and cook for 4 minutes, or until foaming and golden brown. Remove from the heat, add the garlic, corn and lime juice. Gently toss the corn mixture through the pasta with 2 tablespoons of the coriander and season well. Divide among four serving plates, top with the scallops, drizzle with any juices and sprinkle with the remaining coriander.

NUTRITION PER SERVE
Protein 20 g; Fat 61 g; Carbohydrate 75 g; Dietary Fibre 7 g; Cholesterol 174.5 mg; 3850 kJ (920 cal)

NOTES: Scallops should not be crowded when they are cooked or they will release all their juices, causing them to stew and toughen.
   Don't use a non-stick frying pan.
To really achieve the most delicious flavors, don't use a non-stick frying pan—they can prevent the butter from properly browning and the juices from caramelising.

Blanch the broccoli in boiling salted water, then plunge into chilled water and drain well.

Add the cream and half the basil and cook until the sauce has reduced.

PASTA WITH ANCHOVIES, BROCCOLI AND BASIL

Preparation time: 15 minutes
Total cooking time: 25 minutes
Serves 4–6

600 g (1¼ lb) broccoli, cut into florets
500 g (1 lb) orecchiette
1 tablespoon olive oil
4 cloves garlic, finely chopped
8 anchovy fillets, roughly chopped
1 cup (250 ml/8 fl oz) cream
1 cup (30 g/1 oz) fresh basil, torn
2 teaspoons finely grated lemon rind
100 g (3½ oz) Parmesan, grated

1 Blanch the broccoli in a large saucepan of boiling salted water for 3–4 minutes. Remove and plunge into chilled water. Drain well with a slotted spoon. Cook the pasta in a large pan of rapidly boiling salted water until al dente. Drain and return to the pan to keep warm, reserving 2 tablespoons of the cooking water.

2 Meanwhile, heat the oil in a frying pan over medium heat. Add the garlic and anchovies and cook for 1–2 minutes, or until the garlic begins to turn golden. Add the broccoli and cook for a further 5 minutes. Add the cream and half the basil and cook for 10 minutes, or until the cream has reduced and slightly thickened and the broccoli is very tender.

3 Purée half the mixture in a food processor until nearly smooth, then return to the pan with the lemon rind, half the Parmesan and 2 tablespoons of the reserved water. Stir together well, then season. Add the warm pasta and remaining basil, and toss until well combined. Sprinkle with the remaining Parmesan and serve immediately.

NUTRITION PER SERVE (6)
Protein 23 g; Fat 28 g; Carbohydrate 61 g; Dietary Fibre 9 g; Cholesterol 77 mg; 2455 kJ (585 cal)

Add the cooked pasta to the mixture and then the eggs.

Cook the frittata over low heat for 25 minutes and then place under the grill to brown.

CRAB, CAMEMBERT AND FUSILLI FRITTATA

Preparation time: 15 minutes
Total cooking time: 50 minutes
Serves 4–6

1 cup (90 g/3 oz) fusilli
1 tablespoon olive oil
1 very small red onion, finely chopped
1 large Roma tomato, roughly chopped
1/3 cup (60 g/2 oz) semi-dried tomatoes, roughly chopped
2 tablespoons finely chopped fresh coriander leaves
2/3 cup (150 g/5 oz) cooked fresh or canned crab meat
150 g (5 oz) Camembert, rind removed, cut into small pieces
6 eggs plus 2 egg yolks

1 Cook the pasta in a large pan of rapidly boiling salted water until al dente. Drain and set aside to cool a little.

2 Meanwhile, heat half the oil in a small frying pan over low heat, add the onion and cook for 4–5 minutes, or until softened but not browned. Transfer to a bowl and add the Roma tomato, semi-dried tomatoes and coriander. Squeeze out any excess moisture from the crab meat and add to the bowl. Add half the cheese and the cooled pasta. Mix well. Beat together the six eggs and the two extra yolks, then stir into the frittata mixture. Season with salt and pepper.

3 Heat the remaining oil in the frying pan, pour in the frittata mixture and cook over low heat for 25 minutes. Preheat the grill to low. Scatter the remaining Camembert over the frittata before placing it under the grill for 10–15 minutes, or until cooked and golden brown on top. Remove from the grill and leave for 5 minutes. Cut into slices and serve immediately.

NUTRITION PER SERVE (6)
Protein 19 g; Fat 17 g; Carbohydrate 13 g; Dietary Fibre 2 g; Cholesterol 293 mg; 1155 kJ (275 cal)

Sear the tuna over medium heat and then cut it into bite-sized cubes.

Cook the garlic, onion, lemon rind, capers and parsley, then add the lemon juice.

FETTUCINE WITH BALSAMIC-SEARED TUNA

Preparation time: 15 minutes + 10 minutes marinating
Total cooking time: 15 minutes
Serves 4–6

4 x 200 g (6½ oz) tuna steaks
⅔ cup (170 ml/5½ oz) balsamic vinegar
½ cup (125 ml/4 fl oz) good-quality olive oil
1 lemon
1 clove garlic, finely chopped
1 red onion, finely chopped
2 tablespoons capers, rinsed and dried
½ cup (15 g/½ oz) fresh flat-leaf parsley, finely chopped
500 g (1 lb) fresh fettucine

1 Place the tuna steaks in a non-metallic dish and cover with the balsamic vinegar. Turn to coat evenly and marinate for 10 minutes. Heat 2 tablespoons of the oil in a large frying pan over medium heat and cook the tuna for 2–3 minutes each side. Remove from the pan, cut into small cubes and transfer to a bowl.

2 Finely grate the rind from the lemon to give ½ teaspoon rind, then squeeze the lemon to give ¼ cup (60 ml/2 fl oz) juice. Wipe the frying pan clean, and heat 2 tablespoons of the olive oil over medium heat, then add the garlic and cook for 30 seconds. Stir in the chopped onion and cook for 2 minutes. Add the lemon rind and capers and cook for 1 minute, then stir in the parsley and cook for 1 minute. Add the lemon juice and remaining oil and gently toss together. Season to taste.

3 Cook the pasta in a large pan of rapidly boiling salted water until al dente. Drain, return to the pan and toss with the caper mixture. Divide the pasta among serving bowls and arrange the tuna pieces over the top.

NUTRITION PER SERVE (6)

Fat 26 g; Protein 43 g; Carbohydrate 60 g; Dietary Fibre 4.5 g; Cholesterol 48 mg; 2740 kJ (655 Cal)

Process the mascarpone, egg yolks and garlic until smooth.

Flavor the oil with garlic and then use to cook the breadcrumbs until brown and crunchy.

TAGLIATELLE WITH SALMON ROE AND HERB BREADCRUMBS

Preparation time: 15 minutes
Total cooking time: 20 minutes
Serves 6

8 slices white bread
250 g (8 oz) mascarpone
2 egg yolks
4 cloves garlic, peeled
200 ml (6¹/₂ fl oz) olive oil
500 g (1 lb) fresh tagliatelle
3 tablespoons chopped fresh dill
100 g (3¹/₂ oz) Parmesan, grated
60 g (2 oz) salmon roe

1 Place the slices of bread in a food processor or blender and process until fine breadcrumbs form. Remove from the food processor. Place the mascarpone, egg yolks and 1 clove garlic in the food processor or blender and process until smooth. With the motor running, gradually add half the oil in a thin stream.
2 Cook the pasta in a large pan of rapidly boiling salted water until al dente. Drain and return to the pan to keep warm. Meanwhile, heat the remaining oil in a heavy-based frying pan and cook the remaining garlic cloves over medium heat for 2–3 minutes, or until golden brown. Remove the cloves from the oil and discard. Add the fresh breadcrumbs to the warm oil and cook over low heat for 15 minutes, or until golden and crunchy. Remove from the pan and drain on paper towels. When cool, stir in the dill and season lightly with salt and cracked black pepper.

3 Add the mascarpone mixture and the Parmesan to the pasta and toss together well. Divide among six serving plates, sprinkle with the breadcrumbs, top with the salmon roe and serve immediately.

NUTRITION PER SERVE
Protein 26 g; Fat 54 g; Carbohydrate 78 g; Dietary Fibre 6 g; Cholesterol 152 mg; 3745 kJ (895 cal)

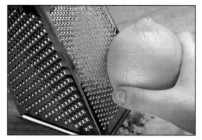

Grate the lemon rind on the finest side of the grater, avoiding the white pith beneath the rind.

Toss together the pasta and tuna mixture, then garnish with the egg and parsley.

SPAGHETTI NICOISE

Preparation time: 10 minutes
Total cooking time: 15 minutes
Serves 4–6

350 g (11 oz) spaghetti
8 quail eggs (or 4 hen eggs)
1 lemon
3 x 185 g (6 oz) cans tuna in oil
1/3 cup (60 g/2 oz) pitted and halved
    Kalamata olives
100 g (3½ oz) semi-dried tomatoes, halved
    lengthways
4 anchovy fillets, chopped into small pieces
3 tablespoons baby capers, drained
3 tablespoons chopped fresh flat-leaf parsley

1 Cook the pasta in a large pan of rapidly boiling salted water until al dente. Drain and return to the pan to keep warm. Meanwhile, place the eggs in a saucepan of cold water, bring to the boil and cook for 4 minutes (10 minutes for hen eggs). Drain, cool under cold water, then peel. Cut the quail eggs in half or the hen eggs into quarters. Finely grate the rind of the lemon to give 1 teaspoon of grated rind. Then, squeeze the lemon to give |2 tablespoons juice.

2 Empty the tuna and its oil into a large bowl. Add the olives, tomato halves, anchovies, lemon rind and juice, capers and 2 tablespoons of the parsley. Drain the pasta and rinse in a little cold water, then toss gently through the tuna mixture. Garnish with egg and the extra chopped fresh parsley to serve.

NUTRITION PER SERVE (6)
Protein 32 g; Fat 26 g; Carbohydrate 47 g;
Dietary Fibre 5 g; Cholesterol 153 mg; 2300 kJ
(550 cal)

Cook the salmon for 2 minutes on each side to sear it, then cut into cubes.

Add the cream, dill and mustard powder and simmer until the sauce thickens.

TAGLIATELLE WITH SALMON AND CREAMY DILL DRESSING

Preparation time: 10 minutes
Total cooking time: 15 minutes
Serves 4

350 g (11 oz) fresh tagliatelle
¼ cup (60 ml/2 fl oz) olive oil
3 x 200 g (6½ oz) salmon fillets, skinned and boned (ask your fishmonger to do this for you)
3 cloves garlic, crushed
1½ cups (375 ml/12 fl oz) cream
1½ tablespoons chopped fresh dill
1 teaspoon mustard powder
1 tablespoon lemon juice
30 g (1 oz) Parmesan, shaved

1 Cook the pasta in a large pan of rapidly boiling salted water until al dente. Drain, toss with 1 tablespoon of the oil and return to the pan to keep warm. Meanwhile, heat the remaining oil in a large deep frying pan and cook the salmon for 2 minutes each side, or until crisp on the outside but still pink inside. Remove from the pan, cut into small cubes and keep warm.
2 In the same pan, cook the garlic for 30 seconds, or until fragrant. Add the cream, dill and mustard powder, bring to the boil, then reduce the heat and simmer, stirring, for 4–5 minutes, or until thickened. Season.
3 Add the salmon and any juices plus the lemon juice to the creamy dill sauce and stir until warmed through. Gently toss the sauce and salmon through the pasta and divide among four serving bowls. Sprinkle with the Parmesan and serve.

NUTRITION PER SERVE
Protein 45 g; Fat 66 g; Carbohydrate 51 g; Dietary Fibre 1.5 g; Cholesterol 215 mg; 4100 kJ (980 cal)

Scrub the mussels and then pull away the hairy beards that grow between the shells.

Cook the mussels and clams in the sauce for 3 minutes, discarding any that don't open.

SPAGHETTI WITH SHELLFISH AND WHITE WINE SAUCE

Preparation time: 15 minutes
Total cooking time: 15 minutes
Serves 4

500 g (1 lb) mussels
1 kg (2 lb) clams
400 g (13 oz) spaghetti
2 tablespoons olive oil
4 French shallots, finely chopped
2 cloves garlic, crushed
1 cup (250 ml/8 fl oz) dry white wine
3 tablespoons chopped fresh flat-leaf parsley

1 Scrub the mussels with a stiff brush and remove any barnacles with a knife. Pull away the beards. Discard any mussels or clams that are broken or open ones that do not close when tapped on the work surface. Wash them both thoroughly under cold running water. Cook the pasta in a large pan of rapidly boiling salted water until al dente. Drain and return to the pan to keep warm.

2 Meanwhile, heat the oil in a large saucepan over medium heat and cook the shallots for 4 minutes, or until softened. Add the garlic and cook for a further 1 minute. Pour in the wine, bring to the boil and cook for 2 minutes, or until reduced slightly. Add the clams and mussels, tossing to coat them in the liquid, then cover the pan. Cook, shaking the pan regularly, for about 3 minutes, or until the shells have opened. Discard any clams or mussels that do not open in the cooking time. Toss the clam mixture through the spaghetti, scatter with parsley and transfer to a warmed serving dish. Season and serve with salad and bread.

NUTRITION PER SERVE
Protein 37 g; Fat 12 g; Carbohydrate 76 g; Dietary Fibre 6 g; Cholesterol 68 mg; 2520 kJ (600 cal)

Add the Champagne to the sauce, then add the cream and simmer to thicken.

Toss the sauce and other ingredients with the warm pasta just before serving.

SMOKED SALMON PASTA IN CHAMPAGNE SAUCE

Preparation time: 15 minutes
Total cooking time: 15 minutes
Serves 4

375 g (12 oz) pappardelle
1 tablespoon olive oil
2 large cloves garlic, crushed
1/2 cup (125 ml/4 fl oz) Champagne
1 cup (250 ml/8 fl oz) thick cream
200 g (6 1/2 oz) smoked salmon, cut into thin strips
2 tablespoons small capers in brine, rinsed and dried
2 tablespoons chopped fresh chives
2 tablespoons chopped fresh dill

1 Cook the pasta in a large pan of rapidly boiling salted water until al dente. Drain and keep warm. Heat the oil in a frying pan; cook the garlic over medium heat for 30 seconds. Pour in the Champagne and cook for 2–3 minutes, or until reduced slightly. Add the cream and cook for 3–4 minutes, or until thickened.
2 Toss the sauce and remaining ingredients with the pasta and serve.

NUTRITION PER SERVE
Protein 24 g; Fat 33 g; Carbohydrate 55 g; Dietary Fibre 1.5 g; Cholesterol 165 mg; 2600 kJ (620 cal)

Cook the garlic and mushrooms until soft before adding the lobster meat.

Add the cream to the sauce, then reduce the heat and simmer to thicken.

PAPPARDELLE WITH LOBSTER AND SAFFRON CREAM SAUCE

Preparation time: 10 minutes
Total cooking time: 20 minutes
Serves 4–6

400 g (13 oz) pappardelle
60 g (2 oz) butter
4 large cloves garlic, crushed
250 g (8 oz) Swiss brown mushrooms, sliced
500 g (1 lb) fresh or frozen lobster tail meat or raw bug tails
1/2 cup (125 ml/4 fl oz) white wine
1/2 teaspoon saffron threads
700 ml (23 fl oz) thick cream
2 egg yolks

1 Cook the pasta in a large pan of rapidly boiling salted water until al dente. Drain and return to the pan to keep warm. Meanwhile, melt the butter in a large deep frying pan, add the garlic and mushrooms and cook over medium heat for 2–3 minutes, or until soft. Add the lobster and cook for 4–5 minutes, or until just cooked through. Remove from the pan.
2 Add the wine and saffron to the pan, scraping the bottom to collect any bits. Bring to the boil and cook for 2–3 minutes, or until reduced. Add the cream, reduce the heat and simmer for 5 minutes. Whisk through the egg yolks until thickened. Return the lobster mixture to the pan and stir until warmed through. Drain the pasta and divide among serving dishes. Spoon on the lobster sauce and season to taste. Serve immediately.

NUTRITION PER SERVE (6)
Protein 29 g; Fat 55 g; Carbohydrate 52 g; Dietary Fibre 3 g; Cholesterol 309 mg; 3430 kJ (820 cal)

Make the gremolata by mixing together the parsley, lemon rind and garlic.

Remove the skin and any bones from the salmon—lift out small bones with tweezers.

PAPPARDELLE WITH FRESH SALMON AND GREMOLATA

Preparation time: 15 minutes
Total cooking time: 15 minutes
Serves 4

¹/₂ cup (30 g/1 oz) chopped fresh flat-leaf
   parsley
3 teaspoons grated lemon rind
2 cloves garlic, finely chopped
400 g (13 oz) pappardelle
¹/₄ cup (60 ml/2 fl oz) virgin olive oil
500 g (1 lb) salmon fillet
2 teaspoons olive oil, extra

1 To make the gremolata, put the parsley, lemon rind and garlic in a bowl and mix together well. Cook the pasta in a large pan of rapidly boiling salted water until al dente. Drain, transfer to a bowl, then add the virgin olive oil and toss gently. Add the gremolata and toss again.
2 Remove the skin and any bones from the salmon. Heat the extra olive oil in a frying pan and cook the salmon over medium heat for 3–4 minutes, turning once during cooking. Take care not to overcook the fish. Flake the salmon into large pieces and toss through the pasta. Season to taste with salt and cracked black pepper, divide among four warm serving plates and serve.

NUTRITION PER SERVE

Protein 38 g; Fat 25 g; Carbohydrate 71 g; Dietary Fibre 4 g; Cholesterol 83 mg; 2755 kJ (660 cal)

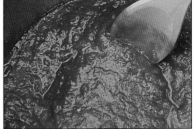

Simmer the garlic, saffron and pasta sauce until thickened slightly.

You can use the same water in which you cooked the pasta for blanching the spinach.

SEAFOOD LASAGNE

Preparation time: 15 minutes
Total cooking time: 15 minutes
Serves 4

1 tablespoon olive oil
2 cloves garlic, crushed
¹/₄ teaspoon saffron threads
600 g (1¹/₄ lb) bottled tomato pasta sauce
750 g (1¹/₂ lb) mixed raw seafood, cut into
    bite-sized pieces (use scallops and peeled
    prawns or prepared marinara mix)
4 fresh lasagne sheets, cut into twelve 10 x
    16 cm (4 x 7 inch) rectangles
120 g (4 oz) English spinach
³/₄ cup (185 g/6 oz) mascarpone
³/₄ cup (90 g/3 oz) grated Parmesan

1 Heat the oil in a large saucepan, add the garlic, saffron and pasta sauce, reduce the heat and simmer for 8 minutes, or until thickened slightly. Add the seafood and cook for 2 minutes, or until cooked, then season. Remove from the heat.

2 Cook the pasta in a large pan of boiling water for 1–2 minutes, or until al dente. Remove and arrange the sheets on a tray to prevent them sticking. Blanch the spinach in the same pan of boiling water for 30 seconds. Remove with tongs, transfer to a colander and drain well.

3 To assemble, lay a pasta rectangle on each of four ovenproof serving plates. Spread half the mascarpone over the pasta sheets. Top with half the spinach and half the seafood sauce. Sprinkle with one third of the Parmesan. Repeat to give two layers, finishing with a third pasta sheet. Sprinkle with the remaining cheese. Place under a medium grill for 2 minutes, or until the cheese is slightly melted. Serve immediately.

NUTRITION PER SERVE
Protein 53 g; Fat 29 g; Carbohydrate 47 g; Dietary Fibre 5 g; Cholesterol 364 mg; 2750 kJ (655 cal)

Toss the sweet potato in 2 tablespoons of oil and roast until tender.

Process the coriander, parsley, garlic, cumin and black pepper, then add the lemon juice and oil.

TUNA AND CHERMOULA ON PAPPARDELLE

Preparation time: 15 minutes + 20 minutes marinating
Total cooking time: 30 minutes
Serves 4

500 g (1 lb) sweet potato, cut into small cubes
100 ml (3¹/₂ fl oz) olive oil
2 cups (60 g/2 oz) fresh coriander leaves, finely chopped
2 cups (60 g/2 oz) fresh flat-leaf parsley, chopped
3 cloves garlic, crushed
3 teaspoons ground cumin
¹/₄ cup (60 ml/2 fl oz) lemon juice
4 x 180 g (6 oz) tuna steaks
400 g (13 oz) pappardelle

1 Preheat the oven to moderately hot 200°C (400°F/Gas 6). Toss the sweet potato in 2 tablespoons of the oil, place on a baking tray and roast for 25–30 minutes, or until tender.
2 To make the chermoula, place the coriander, parsley, garlic, cumin and ³/₄ teaspoon cracked black pepper in a small food processor and process to a rough paste. Transfer to a bowl and stir in the lemon juice and 1 table-spoon of the oil. Place the tuna in a non-metallic bowl, cover with 2 tablespoons of the chermoula and toss until it is evenly coated. Marinate in the refrigerator for 20 minutes. Meanwhile, cook the pasta in a large pan of rapidly boiling salted water until al dente. Drain and return to the pan to keep warm. Toss with the remaining chermoula and oil.
3 Heat a lightly oiled chargrill pan over high heat. Cook the tuna for 2 minutes each side, or until done to your liking. Cut into small cubes, toss through the pasta with the sweet potato and serve.

NUTRITION PER SERVE
Protein 62 g; Fat 34 g; Carbohydrate 90 g; Dietary Fibre 7 g; Cholesterol 83 mg; 3830 kJ (915 cal)

Peel the tomatoes and then cook to a sauce with the garlic and sugar. Add the oil and parsley.

Top the pasta with tomato sauce, then smoked salmon and rocket leaves.

WARM PASTA AND SMOKED SALMON STACK

Preparation time: 15 minutes
Total cooking time: 15 minutes
Serves 4

1.5 kg (3 lb) vine-ripened tomatoes
2 cloves garlic, crushed
1 teaspoon sugar
$\frac{1}{3}$ cup (80 ml/2$\frac{3}{4}$ fl oz) olive oil
3 tablespoons chopped fresh flat-leaf parsley
6 fresh lasagne sheets
400 g (13 oz) smoked salmon
100 g (3$\frac{1}{2}$ oz) baby rocket leaves
extra virgin olive oil, for drizzling

1 Score a cross in the base of each tomato and place in a bowl of boiling water for 1 minute. Plunge into cold water and peel the skin away from the cross. Remove the core, then transfer to a food processor or blender and, using the pulse button, process until roughly chopped. Transfer to a saucepan with the garlic and sugar, bring to the boil, then reduce the heat and simmer for 5 minutes, or until reduced slightly. Remove from the heat and gradually whisk in the oil. Stir in the parsley and season. Keep warm.

2 Cut the lasagne sheets in half widthways to give 12 pieces, each about 12 cm (5 inches) squares. Cook the pasta in a large saucepan of boiling water in two batches until al dente. Remove from the water and lay out flat to prevent sticking.

3 Place a pasta sheet on each of four plates. Set aside $\frac{1}{3}$ cup of the tomato mix. Spoon half the remaining tomato mixture over the pasta sheets, then half the smoked salmon and rocket leaves. Repeat to give two layers. Finish with a third sheet of pasta.

4 Top each pasta stack with a tablespoon of the tomato sauce, drizzle with a little extra virgin olive oil and serve immediately.

NUTRITION PER SERVE
Protein 32 g; Fat 25 g; Carbohydrate 35 g; Dietary Fibre 6.5 g; Cholesterol 48 mg; 2065 kJ (495 cal)

Top each salmon fillet with dill, shredded lemon rind and a cube of butter.

Fold each parcel over twice at the top and tuck the ends under.

SEAFOOD SPAGHETTI PAPER PARCELS

Preparation time: 20 minutes
Total cooking time: 35 minutes
Makes 6

185 g (6 oz) thin spaghetti
4 ripe Roma tomatoes
1 tablespoon olive oil
4 spring onions, finely chopped
1 celery stalk, finely chopped
$1/3$ cup (80 ml/$2^3/4$ fl oz) white wine
$1/2$ cup (125 ml/4 fl oz) tomato pasta sauce
4 gherkins, finely diced
2 tablespoons drained bottled capers, chopped
6 x 175 g (6 oz) pieces of skinless salmon fillet or ocean trout, boned
6 large dill sprigs
shredded rind of 2 lemons
30 g (1 oz) butter, cut into small cubes

1 Preheat the oven to moderate 180°C (350°F/Gas 4). Cook the pasta in a large pan of rapidly boiling salted water until al dente. Drain and run under cold water. Transfer to a bowl.
2 Score a cross in the base of each tomato. Place in a heatproof bowl and cover with boiling water. Leave for 1 minute, transfer to cold water, drain and peel the skin away from the cross. Halve each tomato, scoop out the seeds and chop the flesh.
3 Heat the oil in a frying pan, add the spring onion and celery and stir for 2 minutes. Add the tomato and wine and bring to the boil. Boil for 3 minutes to reduce. Reduce the heat and stir in the pasta sauce, gherkins and capers. Season well. Mix thoroughly through the pasta.
4 To assemble, cut six 30 cm (12 inch) square sheets (depending on the shape of your fish) of baking paper and brush the outside edges with oil. Divide the pasta among the sheets, using a fork to curl the pasta. Place a piece of salmon on top of each, then top with dill and lemon rind. Divide the butter among the parcels.

5 Fold into parcels, turning over twice at the top to seal. Tuck the ends under and bake on a baking tray for 20 minutes. To serve, cut or pull open the parcel and serve in the paper, or if you prefer, slide off the paper onto serving plates.

NUTRITION PER PARCEL
Protein 40 g; Fat 13 g; Carbohydrate 28 g; Dietary Fibre 3 g; Cholesterol 135 mg; 1674 kJ (400 cal)

NOTE: The parcels can be assembled a few hours ahead and refrigerated until required. If you do this, allow a couple of extra minutes cooking.

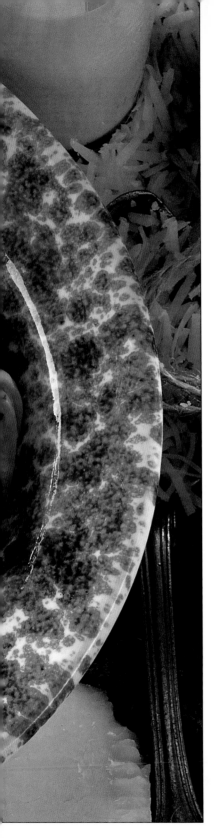

Pasta with Vegetables

TAGLIATELLE WITH ASPARAGUS AND HERBS

Preparation time: 15 minutes
Total cooking time: 15 minutes
Serves 4–6

500 g (1 lb) tagliatelle
1 bunch asparagus
2 tablespoons butter
1 tablespoon chopped fresh parsley
1 tablespoon chopped fresh basil
1¼ cups (310 ml/10 fl oz) cream
½ cup (60 g/2 oz) grated Parmesan

1 Cook the pasta in a large pan of rapidly boiling salted water until al dente. Drain and return to the pan to keep warm.
2 Meanwhile, snap the woody ends from the asparagus and cut the stems into short lengths. Heat the butter in a medium pan and stir the asparagus over medium heat for 2 minutes or until just tender.
3 Add the chopped parsley and basil, cream, salt and pepper and cook for 2 minutes.
4 Add the Parmesan cheese and stir well. Toss through the pasta and serve in warmed bowls.

NUTRITION PER SERVE (6)
Protein 14 g; Fat 30 g; Carbohydrate 60 g; Dietary Fibre 4 g; Cholesterol 95mg; 2418 kJ (580 cal)

NOTE: Will serve eight people as a first course.

Snap the woody ends from the asparagus and then cut the spears into short pieces.

Heat the butter and then stir the asparagus over medium heat until just tender.

Cook the spaghetti until al dente, then drain and return to the pan to keep warm.

Cook the breadcrumbs and half the garlic until lightly golden.

SPAGHETTI WITH HERBS, BABY SPINACH AND GARLIC CRUMBS

Preparation time: 15 minutes
Total cooking time: 15 minutes
Serves 4

375 g (12 oz) spaghetti
125 g (4 oz) day-old crusty Italian bread, crusts removed
100 ml (3¹/₂ fl oz) extra virgin olive oil, plus extra for serving
4 cloves garlic, finely chopped
400 g (13 oz) baby English spinach leaves
4 tablespoons chopped fresh basil
¹/₂ cup (30 g/1 oz) chopped fresh flat-leaf parsley
1 tablespoon fresh thyme leaves
30 g (1 oz) shaved Parmesan

1 Cook the pasta in a large pan of rapidly boiling salted water until al dente. Drain and return to the pan to keep warm, reserving ¹/₂ cup (125 ml/4 fl oz) of the cooking water.
2 To make the garlic breadcrumbs, mix the bread in a food processor or blender until coarse crumbs form. Heat 1 tablespoon oil in a saucepan. Add the breadcrumbs and half the garlic and toss for 2–3 minutes, or until lightly golden. Remove and clean the pan with paper towels.
3 Heat 2 tablespoons of the oil in the same pan. Add the spinach and remaining garlic, toss together for 1 minute, then add the herbs. Cook, tossing frequently, for a further 1 minute to wilt the herbs a little and to heat through. Toss through the pasta with the remaining oil and reserved pasta water. Divide among serving bowls and scatter with the garlic crumbs. Serve hot sprinkled with Parmesan and drizzled with extra virgin olive oil.

NUTRITION PER SERVE
Protein 19 g; Fat 23.5 g; Carbohydrate 82 g; Dietary Fibre 9 g; Cholesterol 7 mg; 2590 kJ (620 cal)

Add the flour with one hand while kneading it into the potato with the other.

Gently knead the mixture until all the flour is mixed in and the dough is smooth.

BLUE CHEESE GNOCCHI

Preparation time: 20 minutes
Total cooking time: 20 minutes
Serves 4

500 g (1 lb) potatoes, quartered
1¼ cups (150 g/5 oz) plain flour

SAUCE
300 ml (10 fl oz) cream
125 g (4 oz) Gorgonzola cheese, roughly
    chopped
2 tablespoons chopped fresh chives

1 Cook the potatoes in boiling salted water for 15–20 minutes or in the microwave until tender. Stir through a generous amount of salt. Drain the potatoes then mash until completely smooth. Transfer to a bowl.

2 Sprinkle the flour into the bowl with one hand while kneading it into the potato mixture with the other hand. Continue kneading until all the flour is worked in and the dough is smooth. This should take a few minutes and will be sticky at first.

3 Divide the dough into three and roll each portion into a sausage that is 2 cm (¾ inch) thick. Cut into 2.5 cm (1 inch) lengths and, using floured hands, press each gnocchi against a fork to flatten it and indent one side (the indentation helps the sauce to stick to the cooked gnocchi).

4 Bring a large pan of water to the boil. When rapidly boiling, drop in the gnocchi, then reduce the heat and simmer until the gnocchi rise to the surface. This will take 2–3 minutes. Lift the gnocchi out of the water with a slotted spoon and drain well. Keep warm on a serving dish.

5 Put the cream in a small pan and bring to the boil. Boil rapidly, stirring constantly, for about 5 minutes, or until the sauce has reduced by a third. Remove from the heat and stir through the cheese. Season and pour over the gnocchi. Scatter the chives over the top and serve immediately.

NUTRITION PER SERVE
Protein 20 g; Fat 45 g; Carbohydrate 45 g; Dietary Fibre 3.5 g; Cholesterol 130 mg; 2736 kJ (655 cal)

CARAMELIZED PUMPKIN AND RICOTTA LASAGNE WITH LIME BUTTER

Preparation time: 30 minutes
Total cooking time: 30 minutes
Serves 4 as an entrée

½ butternut pumpkin (600 g/1¼ lb), peeled and seeded
2 tablespoons olive oil
3 teaspoons finely chopped fresh rosemary
1 teaspoon sea salt flakes
¼ cup (60 ml/2 fl oz) lime juice
¼ cup (60 ml/2 fl oz) white wine
¼ cup (60 ml/2 fl oz) vegetable stock
3 French shallots, finely chopped
1 clove garlic, crushed
¼ teaspoon white pepper
1 tablespoon cream
150 g (5 oz) butter, chilled and cut into small cubes
2 teaspoons finely diced mustard fruit (see NOTE)
100 g (3½ oz) fresh lasagne sheets, cut into eight 8 cm (3 inch) squares
100 g (3½ oz) ricotta
1 amaretti cookie, crushed (optional) (see NOTE)
small sprigs fresh rosemary, to garnish

1 Preheat the oven to moderately hot 200°C (400°F/Gas 6). Cut the piece of pumpkin in half, then each half into eight slices. Place half the oil, 2 teaspoons of the rosemary and the salt in a bowl and toss the pumpkin slices through the mixture.

2 Put the pumpkin in a single layer on a baking tray and bake for 25–30 minutes, or until cooked and slightly caramelized. Remove from the oven, cover and keep warm.

3 Meanwhile, combine the lime juice, wine, stock, shallots, garlic, white pepper and the remaining rosemary in a small saucepan and simmer for about 15–20 minutes, or until the liquid has reduced to about 2 tablespoons. Strain into a small clean saucepan, then add the cream and simmer for 2–3 minutes, or until thickened slightly. Whisk in the butter a few cubes at a time until all the butter is incorporated and the sauce is thickened, smooth and glossy. Remove from the heat and stir in the mustard fruit. Season with salt and pepper and leave covered.

4 Fill a large saucepan with water, add the remaining oil and bring to the boil, then reduce to a simmer. Add the lasagne squares in batches and cook, stirring, for 1–2 minutes, or until al dente. Drain well.

5 Gently reheat the pumpkin and the lime butter if necessary. To assemble, place one lasagne square on each plate. Place two slices of pumpkin onto each square, top with one quarter of the ricotta, then top with another two slices of pumpkin and finish with a final layer of lasagne. Give the lime butter a quick whisk, then spoon a little over the top and around the lasagne on the plate. Season with salt and pepper. Sprinkle the top of each lasagne with a little of the crushed amaretti and some fresh rosemary.

NUTRITION PER SERVE
Protein 11 g; Fat 16 g; Carbohydrate 34 g; Dietary Fibre 4.5 g; Cholesterol 20 mg; 1413 kJ (340 cal)

NOTE: Mustard fruit is a piquant fruit relish made from crystallised fruits preserved in white wine, honey and mustard. Buy it and amaretti from delicatessens and gourmet food stores.

Cut the piece of pumpkin in half, then cut each half into eight slices.

Add the tomatoes, sugar and seasoning to the frying vegetables.

Use a wooden spoon to beat the eggs into the mashed potato.

POTATO GNOCCHI WITH TOMATO AND BASIL SAUCE

Preparation time: 1 hour
Total cooking time: 50 minutes
Serves 4–6

TOMATO SAUCE
1 tablespoon oil
1 onion, chopped
1 celery stalk, chopped
2 carrots, chopped
2 x 425 g (14 oz) cans crushed tomatoes
1 teaspoon sugar
$1/2$ cup (30 g/1 oz) fresh basil, chopped

1 kg (2 lb) potatoes, roughly chopped
30 g (1 oz) butter
2 cups (250 g/8 oz) plain flour
2 eggs, beaten
grated Parmesan, for serving

1 To make the tomato sauce, heat the oil in a large frying pan and cook the onion, celery and carrots for 5 minutes, stirring regularly. Add the tomatoes and sugar and season. Bring to the boil, reduce the heat to very low and simmer for 20 minutes. Mix until smooth in a food processor. Add the basil leaves and set aside.

2 To make gnocchi, cook the potatoes in boiling water for 15 minutes or until very tender. Drain well and mash until smooth. Using a wooden spoon, stir in the butter and the flour, then beat in the eggs. Leave to cool.

3 Turn the potato mixture out onto a floured surface and divide in two. Roll each half into a long sausage shape. Cut into 3–4 cm ($1^1/4$–$1^1/2$ inch) pieces and press each piece with the back of a fork to give the gnocchi ridges.

4 Bring a large pan of water to the boil, add the gnocchi and cook for 3 minutes, or until they rise to the surface. Drain with a slotted spoon and serve with the tomato sauce and grated Parmesan cheese.

NUTRITION PER SERVE (6)
Protein 15 g; Fat 10 g; Carbohydrate 60 g; Dietary Fibre 5 g; Cholesterol 75 mg; 1680 kJ (400 cal)

Coarsely grate the zucchini and then fry with the garlic until softened.

Toss the zucchini into the pasta and then add the grated Parmesan.

FETTUCINE WITH ZUCCHINI

Preparation time: 15 minutes
Total cooking time: 15 minutes
Serves 4–6

500 g (1 lb) tagliatelle or fettucine
60 g (2 oz) butter
2 cloves garlic, crushed
500 g (1 lb) zucchini, grated
³/₄ cup (75 g/2¹/₂ oz) grated Parmesan
1 cup (250 ml/8 fl oz) olive oil
16 basil leaves (see HINT)

1 Cook the pasta in a large pan of rapidly boiling water until al dente. Drain and return to the pan.
2 Meanwhile, heat the butter in a deep heavy-based pan over low heat until it is foaming. Add the garlic and cook for 1 minute. Add the zucchini and cook, stirring occasionally, for 1–2 minutes or until the zucchini has softened.
3 Add the sauce to the pasta. Add the Parmesan cheese and toss well.
4 To make basil leaves crisp, heat the oil in a small pan, add two leaves at a time and cook for 1 minute or until crisp. Drain on paper towels. Serve with the pasta.

NUTRITION PER SERVE (6)
Protein 15 g; Fat 53 g; Carbohydrate 60 g; Dietary Fibre 5.5 g; Cholesterol 37 mg; 3245 kJ (775 cal)

HINT: Basil leaves can be fried up to 2 hours in advance. Store in an airtight container after cooling.

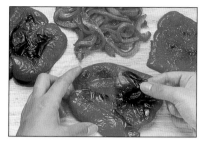

Grill the capsicum until the skin is blackened and will peel away easily.

Add the capsicum, garlic, chilli and cream and cook for 2 minutes.

LINGUINE WITH RED PEPPER SAUCE

Preparation time: 20 minutes
Total cooking time: 30 minutes
Serves 4–6

3 red capsicums
3 tablespoons olive oil
1 large onion, sliced
2 cloves garlic, crushed
$1/4$–$1/2$ teaspoon chilli flakes or powder
$1/2$ cup (125 ml/4 fl oz) cream
2 tablespoons chopped fresh oregano
500 g (1 lb) linguine or spaghetti

1 Halve each capsicum, removing the membrane and seeds and cut into large pieces. Place skin-side-up under a hot grill and cook for 8 minutes or until black and blistered. Cover with a damp tea towel and allow to cool. Peel off the skin and cut the capsicum into thin strips.
2 Heat the oil in a large heavy-based pan. Add the onion and cook, stirring, over low heat for 8 minutes or until soft. Add the capsicum, garlic, chilli and cream and cook for 2 minutes, stirring occasionally. Add salt and pepper and the oregano.
3 Meanwhile, cook the pasta in a large pan of rapidly boiling salted water until al dente. Drain and return to the pan to keep warm. Add the sauce to the pasta and toss well before serving.

NUTRITION PER SERVE (6)
Protein 11 g; Fat 20 g; Carbohydrate 62 g; Dietary Fibre 5 g; Cholesterol 62 mg; 1970 kJ (470 cal)

HINT: If you use dried oregano use about one-third of the quantity as dried herbs are stronger in flavor.

VARIATION: For a stronger capsicum flavor, omit the cream.

Wipe the mushrooms clean and slice them. Cut the eggplant into small cubes.

Heat the oil in a pan and cook the mushrooms, eggplant and garlic.

BUCATINI WITH EGGPLANT AND MUSHROOMS

Preparation time: 20 minutes
Total cooking time: 25 minutes
Serves 4–6

2 tablespoons olive oil
250 g (8 oz) mushrooms, sliced
1 eggplant, diced
2 cloves garlic, crushed
825 g (1 lb 11 oz) can tomatoes
500 g (1 lb) bucatini or spaghetti
1/4 cup (15 g/1/2 oz) chopped fresh parsley

1 Heat the oil in a pan and cook the mushrooms, eggplant and garlic, stirring, for 4 minutes. Add the tomatoes, cover and simmer for 15 minutes.
2 Meanwhile, cook the pasta in a large pan of rapidly boiling salted water until al dente. Drain and return to the pan to keep warm. Season the sauce and stir in the parsley. Toss with the pasta and serve immediately.

NUTRITION PER SERVE (6)
Protein 12 g; Fat 8 g; Carbohydrate 65 g; Dietary Fibre 8 g; Cholesterol 0 mg; 1600 kJ (383 cal)

HINT: If the pasta is cooked before you are ready to serve you can prevent it sticking together by tossing it with a little olive oil after draining.

Toss the sweet potato with the flavored oil and then roast in the oven until soft.

Cook the onion in the butter over low heat until soft and caramelized.

FETTUCINE WITH SWEET POTATO, FETA AND OLIVES

Preparation time: 15 minutes
Total cooking time: 35 minutes
Serves 6

1.5 kg (3 lb) orange sweet potato, cut into small cubes
$^1/_3$ cup (80 ml/2$^3/_4$ fl oz) olive oil
4 cloves garlic, crushed
2 tablespoons butter
4 red onions, sliced into thin wedges
500 g (1 lb) fresh basil fettucine
400 g (13 oz) soft feta cheese, diced
200 g (6$^1/_2$ oz) small black olives
$^1/_2$ cup (30 g/1 oz) firmly packed fresh basil, torn

1 Preheat the oven to moderately hot 200°C (400°F/Gas 6). Place the sweet potato, oil and garlic in a bowl and toss to coat the sweet potato. Lay out the sweet potato in a roasting tin and roast for 15 minutes. Turn and roast for another 15 minutes, until tender and golden—make sure the sweet potato is not too soft or it will not hold its shape. Keep warm.
2 Meanwhile, melt the butter in a deep frying pan and cook the onion over low heat, stirring occasionally, for 25–30 minutes, or until soft and slightly caramelized.
3 Cook the pasta in a large pan of rapidly boiling salted water until al dente. Drain and return to the pan. Add the onion to the pasta and toss together. Add the sweet potato, feta, olives and basil and gently toss. Serve drizzled with extra virgin olive oil.

NUTRITION PER SERVE
Protein 28 g; Fat 33 g; Carbohydrate 91 g; Dietary Fibre 7 g; Cholesterol 124 mg; 3195 kJ (765 cal)

Toss the pumpkin through the herbs and oil, then season with salt and roast until soft.

Put the cooked pumpkin and cream in a food processor and mix until smooth.

ROAST PUMPKIN SAUCE ON PAPPARDELLE

Preparation time: 15 minutes
Total cooking time: 35 minutes
Serves 4

1.5 kg (3 lb) butternut pumpkin, cut into
    small cubes
4 cloves garlic, crushed
3 teaspoons fresh thyme leaves
100 ml (3½ fl oz) olive oil
500 g (1 lb) pappardelle
2 tablespoons cream
¾ cup (185 ml/6 fl oz) hot chicken stock
30 g (1 oz) shaved Parmesan

1 Preheat the oven to moderately hot 200°C (400°F/Gas 6). Place the pumpkin, garlic, thyme and ¼ cup (60 ml/2 fl oz) of the olive oil in a bowl and toss together. Season with salt, transfer to a baking tray and cook for 30 minutes, or until tender and golden. Meanwhile, cook the pasta in a large pan of rapidly boiling salted water until al dente. Drain and return to the pan. Toss through the remaining oil and keep warm.
2 Place the pumpkin and cream in a food processor or blender and process until smooth. Add the hot stock and process until smooth. Season with salt and cracked black pepper and gently toss through the pasta. Serve with Parmesan and extra thyme leaves.

NUTRITION PER SERVE
Protein 26 g; Fat 30 g; Carbohydrate 110 g; Dietary Fibre 8 g; Cholesterol 43 mg; 3400 kJ (810 cal)

NOTE: The sauce becomes thick on standing, so serve immediately.

Add the garlic and marjoram to the softened mushrooms and cook for another 2 minutes.

Cook the pasta in a large saucepan of boiling water until al dente.

PENNE WITH MUSHROOM AND HERB SAUCE

Preparation time: 15 minutes
Total cooking time: 25 minutes
Serves 4

2 tablespoons olive oil
500 g (1 lb) button mushrooms, sliced
2 cloves garlic, crushed
2 teaspoons chopped fresh marjoram
1/2 cup (125 ml/4 fl oz) dry white white
1/3 cup (80 ml/2³/₄ fl oz) light cream
375 g (12 oz) penne
1 tablespoon lemon juice
1 teaspoon finely grated lemon rind
2 tablespoons chopped fresh parsley
1/2 cup (60 g/2 oz) grated Parmesan

1 Heat the oil in a large heavy-based frying pan over high heat. Add the mushrooms and cook for 3 minutes, stirring constantly. Add the garlic and marjoram and cook for 2 minutes.
2 Add the dry white wine, reduce the heat and simmer for 5 minutes, or until nearly all the liquid has evaporated. Stir in the cream and continue to cook over low heat for 5 minutes, or until the sauce has thickened.
3 Meanwhile, cook the pasta in a large pan of rapidly boiling salted water until al dente. Drain and return to the pan to keep warm.
4 Add the lemon juice, rind, parsley and half the Parmesan to the sauce. Season to taste. Toss the penne through the sauce and sprinkle with the remaining Parmesan.

NUTRITION PER SERVE
Protein 20 g; Fat 18 g; Carbohydrate 67 g; Dietary Fibre 6.5 g; Cholesterol 25 mg; 2275 kJ (545 cal)

Peel the carrot if it needs it, before grating. Peel the tomatoes and roughly chop.

Cook the onion and celery before adding the tomatoes, carrot, parsley, vinegar and wine.

TAGLIATELLE WITH SWEET TOMATO AND WALNUT SAUCE

Preparation time: 20 minutes
Total cooking time: 45 minutes
Serves 4–6

4 ripe Roma tomatoes
1 tablespoon oil
1 onion, finely chopped
1 celery stalk, finely chopped
1 carrot, grated
2 tablespoons chopped fresh parsley
1 teaspoon red wine vinegar
1/4 cup (60 ml/2 fl oz) white wine
500 g (1 lb) tagliatelle or fettucine
1 tablespoon olive oil, extra
3/4 cup (90 g/3 oz) walnuts, roughly chopped
grated Parmesan, for serving

1 Score a cross on the bottom of each tomato, place in boiling water for 1 minute, then plunge into cold water. Peel the skin away from the cross and roughly chop the tomatoes.
2 Heat oil in a large heavy-based pan and cook the onion and celery for 5 minutes over low heat, stirring regularly. Add the tomatoes, carrot, parsley and combined vinegar and wine. Reduce the heat and simmer for 25 minutes. Season to taste.
3 Meanwhile, cook the pasta in a large pan of rapidly boiling salted water until al dente. Drain and return to the pan to keep warm.
4 Heat the extra oil in a frying pan and stir the walnuts over low heat for 5 minutes. Toss the pasta and sauce together and serve topped with walnuts and Parmesan cheese.

NUTRITION PER SERVE (6)
Protein 13 g; Fat 10 g; Carbohydrate 61 g; Dietary Fibre 6 g; Cholesterol 7 mg; 1654 kJ (395 Cal)

Roast the sweet potatoes in their skins for an hour and then pierce to check they are soft.

Peel the sweet potatoes and then mash with a potato masher or fork.

ROASTED SWEET POTATO AND DITALINI PATTIES

Preparation time: 15 minutes
Total cooking time: 1 hour 10 minutes
Serves 4

800 g (1 lb 10 oz) orange sweet potatoes
$\frac{1}{2}$ cup (90 g/3 oz) ditalini
30 g (1 oz) toasted pine nuts
2 cloves garlic, crushed
4 tablespoons finely chopped fresh basil
$\frac{1}{2}$ cup (60 g/2 oz) grated Parmesan
$\frac{1}{3}$ cup (35 g/1 oz) dry breadcrumbs
plain flour, for dusting
olive oil, for shallow-frying

1 Preheat the oven to very hot 250°C (500°F/Gas 10). Pierce the whole sweet potatoes several times with a fork, then place in a roasting tin and roast for about 1 hour, or until soft. Remove from the oven and cool. Meanwhile, cook the pasta in a large pan of rapidly boiling salted water until al dente. Drain and rinse under cold water.

2 Peel the sweet potato and mash with a potato masher or fork. Add the pine nuts, garlic, basil, Parmesan, breadcrumbs and the pasta and mix together. Season.

3 Shape the mixture into eight even patties with floured hands, then lightly dust the patties with flour. Heat the oil in a large frying pan and cook the patties in batches over medium heat for 2 minutes each side, or until golden and heated through. Drain on crumpled paper towels, sprinkle with salt and serve immediately.

NUTRITION PER SERVE
Protein 14 g; Fat 15 g; Carbohydrate 51 g; Dietary Fibre 6 g; Cholesterol 12 mg; 1650 kJ (395 cal)

NOTE: To save time, drop spoonfuls of the mixture into the pan and flatten with an oiled spatula.

SERVING SUGGESTION: The patties are great with aïoli—mix 1 clove of crushed garlic into $\frac{1}{3}$ cup (90 g/3 oz) mayonnaise with a squeeze of lemon juice and season well.

Blanch the broccoli in boiling water for a couple of minutes then cool in iced water.

Simmer the tomato sauce for 5 minutes or until it has thickened.

FARMHOUSE PASTA

Preparation time: 10 minutes
Total cooking time: 15 minutes
Serves 4

375 g (12 oz) pasta
1 large potato, cut into small cubes
400 g (13 oz) broccoli
1/3 cup (80 ml/2¾ fl oz) olive oil
3 cloves garlic, crushed
1 small fresh red chilli, finely chopped
2 x 400 g (13 oz) cans diced tomatoes
1/4 cup (30 g/1 oz) grated Pecorino cheese

1 Bring a large saucepan of salted water to the boil and cook the pasta and potato together for 8–10 minutes, or until the pasta is al dente. Drain and return to the saucepan. Meanwhile, trim the broccoli into florets and discard the stems. Place in a saucepan of boiling water and cook for 1–2 minutes, then drain and plunge into iced water. Drain and add to the cooked pasta and potato.
2 Heat the oil in a saucepan, add the garlic and chilli and cook for 30 seconds. Add the tomato and simmer for 5 minutes, or until slightly reduced and thickened. Season to taste with salt and cracked black pepper.
3 Pour the tomato mixture over the pasta, potato and broccoli. Toss well and stir over low heat until warmed through. Serve sprinkled with grated Pecorino cheese.

NUTRITION PER SERVE
Protein 20 g; Fat 22 g; Carbohydrate 77 g;
Dietary Fibre 11 g; Cholesterol 6 mg; 2445 kJ
(585 cal)

Bake the bread and the walnuts on the same tray to dry out the bread and toast the nuts.

Cook the pasta in a large pan of rapidly boiling water until it is tender.

PASTA SHELLS WITH WALNUT PESTO

Preparation time: 15 minutes
Total cooking time: 15 minutes
Serves 4–6

125 g (4 oz) day-old crusty bread, crusts removed
1½ cups (185 g/6 oz) walnut pieces
500 g (1 lb) pasta shells
½ cup (30 g/1 oz) firmly packed fresh basil, roughly chopped
2–3 cloves garlic, peeled
1 small fresh red chilli, seeded and roughly chopped
½ teaspoon finely grated lemon rind
¼ cup (60 ml/2 fl oz) lemon juice
½ cup (125 ml/4 fl oz) olive oil

1 Preheat the oven to warm 160°C (315°F/Gas 2–3). Cut the bread into 2 cm (¾ inch) thick slices and place on a baking tray with the walnuts. Bake for 8–10 minutes, or until the bread is dried out a little and the walnuts are lightly toasted. Don't overcook the walnuts or they will become bitter.
2 Meanwhile, cook the pasta in a large pan of rapidly boiling salted water until al dente. Drain and return to the pan to keep warm.
3 Break the bread into chunks and mix in a food processor with the walnuts, basil, garlic, chilli, lemon rind and juice. Use the pulse button to chop the mixture without forming a paste. Transfer to a bowl and stir in the oil. Toss through the pasta, then season to taste with salt and pepper.

NUTRITION PER SERVE (6)
Protein 15 g; Fat 39 g; Carbohydrate 70 g; Dietary Fibre 7 g; Cholesterol 0 mg; 2870 kJ (685 cal)

HINT: Don't add the oil to the food processor or the pesto will lose its crunchy texture.

Add the chives, basil, sage and thyme to the sauce and cook for another minute.

Add the herb sauce and the stock to the pasta and return to the heat.

CAVATELLI WITH HERB SAUCE AND PECORINO

Preparation time: 10 minutes
Total cooking time: 15 minutes
Serves 4

400 g (13 oz) cavatelli
90 g (3 oz) butter
2 cloves garlic, crushed
3 tablespoons chopped fresh chives
3 tablespoons shredded fresh basil
1 tablespoon shredded fresh sage
1 teaspoon fresh thyme
1/4 cup (60 ml/2 fl oz) warm vegetable stock
60 g (2 oz) Pecorino cheese, grated

1 Cook the pasta in a large pan of rapidly boiling salted water until al dente. Drain and return to the pan to keep warm. Meanwhile, heat the butter in a small saucepan over medium heat, add the garlic and cook for 1 minute, or until fragrant. Add the chives, basil, sage and thyme and cook for a further minute.
2 Add the herb mixture and stock to the pasta in the pan. Return to the heat for 2–3 minutes, or until warmed through. Season to taste, add the Pecorino and stir well. Divide among bowls and garnish with sage leaves.

NUTRITION PER SERVE (6)
Protein 16 g; Fat 22 g; Carbohydrate 71 g; Dietary Fibre 6 g; Cholesterol 65 mg; 2280 kJ (545 cal)

NOTE: Pecorino is Italian sheep's milk cheese with a sharp flavor. If you can't find it, use Parmesan instead.

Toss the pumpkin cubes with oil and then roast for 30 minutes until crisp.

Cook the pasta until tender, then drain and return to the pan to keep warm.

PASTA EARS WITH SPICED PUMPKIN AND YOGHURT

Preparation time: 15 minutes
Total cooking time: 35 minutes
Serves 6

1 kg (2 lb) pumpkin, cut into small cubes
1/3 cup (80 ml/2¾ fl oz) olive oil
500 g (1 lb) orecchiette
2 cloves garlic, crushed
1 teaspoon dried chilli flakes
1 teaspoon coriander seeds, crushed
1 tablespoon cumin seeds, crushed
200 g (6½ oz) Greek-style natural yoghurt
3 tablespoons chopped fresh coriander
   leaves

1 Preheat the oven to moderately hot 200°C (400°F/Gas 6). Toss the pumpkin in 2 tablespoons of the oil, place in a roasting tin and cook for 30 minutes, turning once, until crisp.
2 Meanwhile, cook the pasta in a large pan of rapidly boiling salted water until al dente. Drain and return to the pan to keep warm.
3 Heat the remaining oil in a saucepan. Add the garlic, chilli, coriander and cumin and cook for 30 seconds, or until fragrant. Toss the spice mix and pumpkin through the pasta, then stir in the yoghurt and fresh coriander and season to taste. Serve immediately.

NUTRITION PER SERVE
Protein 15 g; Fat 15 g; Carbohydrate 75 g; Dietary Fibre 7 g; Cholesterol 6 mg; 2035 kJ (485 cal)

Discard the stalks of the tomatoes, then cut in half lengthways.

Add the stock, wine and vinegar to the baking dish and bring to the boil.

PASTA WITH ROASTED TOMATO SAUCE

Preparation time: 25 minutes
Total cooking time: 50 minutes
Serves 4

1 kg (2 lb) ripe Roma tomatoes
8 cloves garlic, unpeeled
2 tablespoons olive oil
2 teaspoons dried basil
1 cup (250 ml/8 fl oz) vegetable stock
$^{1}/_{2}$ cup (125 ml/4 fl oz) dry white wine
2 tablespoons balsamic vinegar
500 g (1 lb) tagliatelle
2 tablespoons grated Parmesan

1 Preheat the oven to moderate 180°C (350°F/Gas 4). Cut the tomatoes in half lengthways and arrange, cut-side-up, in a baking dish. Sprinkle with 1 tablespoon water to prevent the tomatoes sticking. Add the garlic to the pan and drizzle or brush the oil over the tomatoes and garlic. Sprinkle with basil, salt and freshly ground black pepper. Bake for 25 minutes, or until soft, and gently remove from the pan.
2 Heat the baking dish over low heat and add the stock, white wine and vinegar. Bring to the boil, reduce the heat and simmer for 20 minutes. Roughly chop the tomatoes, retaining all the juices. Squeeze the garlic out of the skin and add the tomato and garlic to the simmering sauce. Taste and adjust the seasonings.
3 Cook the pasta in a large pan of rapidly boiling salted water until al dente. Drain and return to the pan to keep warm. Serve the sauce over the pasta and sprinkle with Parmesan.

NUTRITION PER SERVE

Protein 20 g; Fat 3.5 g; Carbohydrate 95 g; Dietary Fibre 10 g; Cholesterol 5 mg; 2060 kJ (515 cal)

Cook the pasta in boiling water until it is tender, then drain well.

Add the garlic, chickpeas, tomato and parsley and stir to warm through.

ROTELLE WITH CHICKPEAS, TOMATO AND PARSLEY

Preparation time: 10 minutes
Total cooking time: 15 minutes
Serves 4

375 g (12 oz) rotelle
1 tablespoon ground cumin
$^1/_2$ cup (125 ml/4 fl oz) olive oil
1 red onion, halved and thinly sliced
3 cloves garlic, crushed
400 g (13 oz) can chickpeas, drained
3 large tomatoes, diced
$^1/_2$ cup (15 g/$^1/_2$ oz) chopped fresh flat-leaf
  parsley
$^1/_4$ cup (60 ml/2 fl oz) lemon juice

1 Cook the pasta in a large pan of rapidly boiling salted water until al dente. Drain and return to the pan to keep warm.
2 Meanwhile, heat a large frying pan over medium heat, add the cumin and cook, tossing, for 1 minute, or until fragrant. Remove from the pan. Heat half the oil in the same pan and cook the onion over medium heat for 2–3 minutes, or until soft. Stir in the garlic, chickpeas, tomato and parsley and stir until warmed through. Gently toss through the pasta.
3 Place the lemon juice, cumin and remaining oil in a jar with a lid and shake together well. Add the dressing to the saucepan with the pasta and chickpea mixture, return to the stove-top over low heat and stir until warmed through. Season well with salt and cracked black pepper. Serve hot with grated Parmesan, or serve cold. If serving cold, rinse the pasta under cold water before adding the chickpea mixture and do not return to the heat.

NUTRITION PER SERVE
Protein 17 g; Fat 27 g; Carbohydrate 80 g; Dietary Fibre 10 g; Cholesterol 0 mg; 2655 kJ (635 cal)

Drain the pasta well and toss with a little olive oil to prevent it sticking.

Cook the onion, carrot and celery for 10 minutes or until browned.

PENNE WITH RUSTIC LENTIL SAUCE

Preparation time: 10 minutes
Total cooking time: 30 minutes
Serves 4

1 litre vegetable or chicken stock
350 g (11 oz) penne
$^1/_3$ cup (80 ml/2$^3/_4$ fl oz) virgin olive oil, plus
   extra for serving
1 onion, chopped
2 carrots, diced
3 celery stalks, diced
3 cloves garlic, crushed
1 tablespoon plus 1 teaspoon chopped fresh
   thyme
400 g (13 oz) can lentils, drained

1 Boil the chicken stock in a large saucepan for 10 minutes, or until reduced by half. Meanwhile, cook the pasta in a large pan of rapidly boiling salted water until al dente. Drain well and toss with 2 tablespoons of the olive oil.

2 Heat the remaining oil in a large, deep frying pan, add the onion, carrot and celery and cook over medium heat for 10 minutes, or until browned. Add two-thirds of the crushed garlic and 1 tablespoon of the thyme and cook for a further 1 minute. Add the stock, bring to the boil and cook for 8 minutes, or until tender. Stir in the lentils and heat through.

3 Stir in the remaining garlic and thyme and season well—the stock should be slightly syrupy at this point. Combine the pasta with the lentil sauce in a large bowl and drizzle with virgin olive oil to serve.

NUTRITION PER SERVE
Protein 17 g; Fat 18 g; Carbohydrate 72 g; Dietary Fibre 9 g; Cholesterol 0 mg; 2165 kJ (515 cal)

Blanch the broad beans in boiling water then iced water and then slip out of their skins.

Add the asparagus to the pan and cook until bright green and just tender.

COTELLI WITH SPRING VEGETABLES

Preparation time: 15 minutes
Total cooking time: 20 minutes
Serves 4

500 g (1 lb) cotelli
2 cups (300 g/10 oz) frozen peas
2 cups (300 g/10 oz) frozen broad beans
$^1/_3$ cup (80 ml/2$^3/_4$ fl oz) olive oil
6 spring onions, cut into short pieces
2 cloves garlic, finely chopped
1 cup (250 ml/8 fl oz) chicken stock
12 asparagus spears, chopped
1 lemon

1 Cook the pasta in a large pan of rapidly boiling salted water until al dente. Drain and return to the pan to keep warm.
2 Meanwhile, cook the peas in a saucepan of boiling water for 1–2 minutes, or until tender. Remove with a slotted spoon and plunge into cold water. Add the broad beans to the same saucepan of boiling water and cook for 1–2 minutes, then drain and plunge into cold water. Remove and slip out of their skins.
3 Heat 2 tablespoons of the oil in a frying pan. Add the spring onion and garlic and cook over medium heat for 2 minutes, or until softened. Pour in the stock and cook for 5 minutes, or until slightly reduced. Add the asparagus and cook for 3–4 minutes, or until bright green and just tender. Stir in the peas and broad beans and cook for 2–3 minutes to heat through.
4 Toss the remaining oil through the pasta, then add the vegetable mixture, $^1/_2$ teaspoon finely grated lemon rind and $^1/_4$ cup (60 ml/2 fl oz) lemon juice. Season and toss together well. Serve with Parmesan shavings.

NUTRITION PER SERVE
Protein 25 g; Fat 21 g; Carbohydrate 103 g; Dietary Fibre 19 g; Cholesterol 0 mg; 2935 kJ (700 cal)

Soak the porcini mushrooms in boiling water to soften them.

Cook the garlic and button mushrooms for 4 minutes before adding the porcini.

PASTA WITH ROCKET AND MUSHROOMS

Preparation time: 15 minutes + 10 minutes soaking
Total cooking time: 15 minutes
Serves 4

15 g (1/2 oz) dried porcini mushrooms
375 g (12 oz) pasta
1 tablespoon butter
1/4 cup (60 ml/2 fl oz) extra virgin olive oil
2 cloves garlic, crushed
250 g (8 oz) button mushrooms, sliced
1/4 cup (60 ml/2 fl oz) lemon juice
1/3 cup (30 g/1 oz) grated Parmesan
90 g (3 oz) baby rocket leaves

1 Soak the porcini mushrooms in 1/3 cup (80 ml/2 3/4 fl oz) boiling water for 10 minutes to soften. Cook the pasta in a large pan of rapidly boiling salted water until al dente. Drain and return to the pan to keep warm.
2 Meanwhile, heat the butter and oil over medium heat in a frying pan. Add the garlic and button mushrooms and cook for 4 minutes, tossing occasionally. Drain the porcini mushrooms, reserving the soaking liquid. Chop all of the mushrooms, then add them to the frying pan with the soaking liquid. Bring to a simmer.
3 Add the mushroom mixture, lemon juice and Parmesan to the saucepan with the pasta and toss together. Season to taste with salt and cracked black pepper. Toss through the rocket just before serving.

NUTRITION PER SERVE
Protein 16 g; Fat 23 g; Carbohydrate 68 g; Dietary Fibre 7 g; Cholesterol 22 mg; 2265 kJ (540 cal)

Drizzle the cubes of pumpkin with olive oil, using Parmesan-infused oil if available.

Roast the pumpkin, garlic and tomatoes until they are tender.

PASTA WITH BABY SPINACH, ROASTED PUMPKIN & TOMATO

Preparation time: 15 minutes
Total cooking time: 1 hour
Serves 4

750 g (1½ lb) pumpkin
2 tablespoons olive oil (see Notes)
16 unpeeled cloves garlic
250 g (8 oz) cherry tomatoes, halved
500 g (1 lb) pasta
200 g (6½ oz) baby English spinach leaves
200 g (6½ oz) marinated Persian feta (see Notes)
¼ cup (60 ml/2 fl oz) sherry vinegar
2 tablespoons walnut oil

1 Preheat the oven to moderately hot 200°C (400°F/Gas 6). Cut the pumpkin into large cubes, place in a roasting tin and drizzle with oil. Roast for 30 minutes, then add the garlic. Arrange the tomatoes on a baking tray. Put all the vegetables in the oven and roast for 10–15 minutes, or until tender. Don't overcook the tomatoes or they will break up.
2 Cook the pasta in a large pan of rapidly boiling salted water until al dente. Drain and return to the pan to keep warm.
3 Toss together the pasta, tomatoes, pumpkin, garlic and spinach.
4 Drain the feta, reserving ¼ cup (60 ml/2 fl oz) marinade. Whisk this with the vinegar and walnut oil. Pour over the pasta and sprinkle with feta.

NUTRITION PER SERVE
Protein 29 g; Fat 34 g; Carbohydrate 105 g; Dietary Fibre 13 g; Cholesterol 34 mg; 3524 kJ (842 cal)

NOTES: If you can find it, use Parmesan-infused olive oil. It is available at gourmet food stores and adds depth of flavor.
Persian feta is softer and creamier than other feta and is marinated in oil, herbs and garlic.

VARIATION: Toss in 200 g marinated Kalamata olives for added flavor.

Add the tomato sauce, stock, olives and anchovies to the sauce and heat through.

POTATO GNOCCHI WITH TOMATO-OLIVE SAUCE

Preparation time: 10 minutes
Total cooking time: 15 minutes
Serves 4

500 g (1 lb) fresh potato gnocchi
2 tablespoons oil
1 leek, sliced
1 cup (250 g/8 oz) bottled tomato pasta
    sauce
²/₃ cup (170 ml/5¹/₂ fl oz) vegetable stock
¹/₃ cup (60 g/2 oz) chopped black olives
6 anchovies, chopped

1 Cook the gnocchi in a large pan of rapidly boiling salted water until it floats to the surface. Lift out with a slotted spoon. Meanwhile, heat the oil in a large pan and add the leek. Stir over medium heat for 2 minutes or until tender. Add the tomato sauce, stock, olives and anchovies and stir for 5 minutes to heat through. Serve over the gnocchi.

NUTRITION PER SERVE
Protein 6 g; Fat 11 g; Carbohydrate 25 g; Dietary Fibre 5 g; Cholesterol 2 mg; 930 kJ (222 cal)

STORAGE: The sauce will keep for a day, covered, in the fridge.

NOTE: Fresh potato gnocchi is available from supermarkets and delicatessens. Use any other dried or fresh pasta if you prefer.

Stir the garlic, peas and mint into the stock and leek mixture.

Stir in the cream, nutmeg and grated Parmesan and check the seasoning.

TAGLIATELLE WITH ASPARAGUS, PEAS AND HERB SAUCE

Preparation time: 20 minutes
Total cooking time: 25 minutes
Serves 4

375 g (12 oz) tagliatelle
2 leeks, thinly sliced
1 cup (250 ml/8 fl oz) chicken or vegetable
    stock
3 cloves garlic, crushed
1 1/2 cups (250 g/8 oz) shelled fresh peas
1 tablespoon finely chopped fresh mint
400 g (13 oz) asparagus spears, cut into 5
    cm (2 inch) lengths
1/4 cup (15 g/1/2 oz) finely chopped fresh
    parsley
1/2 cup (30 g/1 oz) shredded fresh basil
1/3 cup (80 m/2 3/4 fl oz) light cream

pinch of grated nutmeg
1 tablespoon grated Parmesan
2 tablespoons extra virgin olive oil, to serve

1 Cook the pasta in a large pan of rapidly boiling salted water until al dente. Drain and return to the pan to keep warm.
2 Put the leeks and 1/2 cup (125 ml/ 4 fl oz) of the stock in a large, deep, frying pan. Cook over low heat, stirring often, for 4–5 minutes. Stir in the garlic, peas and mint and cook for 1 minute. Add the remaining stock and 1/2 cup (125 ml/4 fl oz) water and bring to the boil. Simmer for 5 minutes. Add the asparagus, parsley and basil and season well. Simmer for 3–4 minutes, or until the asparagus is just tender. Gradually increase the heat to thicken the sauce until it will just coat a spoon. Stir in the cream, nutmeg and Parmesan and season.
3 Add the tagliatelle to the sauce and toss lightly to coat. Serve drizzled with the extra virgin olive oil and some more grated Parmesan.

NUTRITION PER SERVE
Protein 21 g; Fat 11 g; Carbohydrate 76 g; Dietary Fibre 9 g; Cholesterol 32 mg; 2080 kJ (495 cal)

Simmer the balsamic vinegar and brown sugar until the liquid becomes syrupy.

Toss the peas, asparagus, zucchini, rocket, basil and olive oil together.

FRESH VEGETABLE LASAGNE WITH ROCKET

Preparation time: 20 minutes
Total cooking time: 20 minutes
Serves 4

BALSAMIC SYRUP
1/3 cup (80 ml/2¾ fl oz) balsamic vinegar
1½ tablespoons brown sugar

1 cup (150 g/5 oz) fresh or frozen peas
16 asparagus spears, trimmed and cut into
    short lengths
2 large zucchini, cut into thin ribbons
2 fresh lasagne sheets (each sheet 24 x 35
    cm/10 x 14 inches)
100 g (3½ oz) rocket leaves
1 cup (30 g/1 oz) fresh basil, torn
2 tablespoons extra virgin olive oil
250 g (8 oz) low-fat ricotta
150 g (5 oz) semi-dried tomatoes
Parmesan shavings, to garnish

1 To make the syrup, place the vinegar and brown sugar in a small saucepan and stir over medium heat until the sugar dissolves. Reduce the heat and simmer for 3–4 minutes, or until the sauce becomes syrupy. Remove from the heat.

2 Bring a large saucepan of salted water to the boil. Blanch the peas, asparagus and zucchini in separate batches until just tender, removing each batch with a slotted spoon and refreshing in cold water. Reserve the cooking liquid and return to the boil.

3 Cook the lasagne sheets in the boiling water for 1–2 minutes, or until al dente. Refresh in cold water and drain well. Cut each sheet in half lengthways.

4 Toss the vegetables and the rocket with the basil and olive oil. Season.

5 To assemble, place one strip of pasta on a serving plate—one third on the centre of the plate and two thirds overhanging one side. Place a small amount of the salad on the centre one third, topped with some ricotta and tomato. Season lightly and fold over one third of the lasagne sheet. Top with another layer of salad, ricotta and tomato. Fold back the final layer of pasta and garnish with a little salad and tomato. Repeat with the remaining pasta strips, salad, ricotta and tomato to make four individual servings. Just before serving, drizzle with the balsamic syrup and garnish with Parmesan shavings.

NUTRITION PER SERVE
Fat 16 g; Protein 18 g; Fat 16 g; Carbohydrate 36 g; Dietary Fibre 6 g; Cholesterol 63 mg; 1515 kJ (360 cal)

Cook the capers over high heat until they are crisp and golden.

Mix the lemon juice, basil and olive oil in a food processor until smooth.

COTELLI WITH CAPERS, BOCCONCINI AND BASIL OIL

Preparation time: 10 minutes
Total cooking time: 20 minutes
Serves 4–6

1/2 cup (125 ml/4 fl oz) olive oil
125 g (4 oz) jar capers in brine, drained
500 g (1 lb) cotelli
2 tablespoons lemon juice
2 cups (100 g/3 1/2 oz) firmly packed fresh
  basil
1/3 cup (35 g/1 oz) grated Parmesan
250 g (8 oz) cherry tomatoes, quartered
8 bocconcini, quartered
extra virgin olive oil, for serving

1 Heat half the olive oil in a pan, add the capers and cook over high heat for 3–4 minutes, or until crisp and golden. Drain on paper towels and set aside.

2 Cook the pasta in a large pan of rapidly boiling salted water until al dente. Drain and return to the pan to keep warm. Meanwhile, mix the lemon juice, 1 1/2 cups (75 g/2 1/2 oz) of the basil and the remaining olive oil in a food processor until smooth. Season.

3 Roughly tear the remaining basil leaves, then toss through the warm pasta with the basil mixture, 2 tablespoons of the Parmesan and the cherry tomatoes. Spoon into warmed bowls and top with the bocconcini and capers. Drizzle with extra virgin olive oil and garnish with the remaining grated Parmesan. Serve immediately.

NUTRITION PER SERVE (6)

Protein 21 g; Fat 26 g; Carbohydrate 61 g; Dietary Fibre 5.5 g; Cholesterol 23.5 mg; 2375 kJ (565 cal)

Cook the pasta in a large pan of rapidly boiling water until it is tender.

Add the broccoli, chopped nuts, lemon juice and chilli and warm through.

LINGUINE WITH BROCCOLI, PINE NUTS AND LEMON

Preparation time: 15 minutes
Total cooking time: 15 minutes
Serves 4–6

500 g (1 lb) linguine
600 g (1¼ lb) broccoli, cut into small florets
½ cup (90 g/3 oz) pine nuts
½ cup (125 ml/4 fl oz) extra virgin olive oil
2 teaspoons finely grated lemon rind
¼ cup (60 ml/2 fl oz) lemon juice
1 teaspoon dried chilli flakes
½ cup (60 g/2 oz) finely grated Parmesan

1 Cook the pasta in a large pan of rapidly boiling salted water until al dente. Drain and return to the pan to keep warm. Meanwhile, bring a saucepan of water to the boil and cook the broccoli for 2 minutes, or until just tender but still bright green. Drain and set aside.

2 Heat a large non-stick frying pan and dry-fry the pine nuts for 2–3 minutes, or until just golden, shaking the pan to prevent them burning. Remove from the pan and roughly chop. Reduce the heat to low, add the oil and lemon rind to the frying pan and gently heat until fragrant. Add the broccoli, chopped nuts, lemon juice and chilli and stir until warmed through. Season with salt and pepper. Add to the pasta with the Parmesan and toss to combine. Divide among serving bowls.

NUTRITION PER SERVE (6)
Protein 19 g; Fat 27 g; Carbohydrate 60 g; Dietary Fibre 9 g; Cholesterol 8 mg; 2355 kJ (560 cal)

Add the spinach, stock and cream to the sauce and simmer rapidly.

Transfer the spinach sauce to a food processor and mix until smooth.

FETTUCINE WITH CREAMY SPINACH AND ROAST TOMATO

Preparation time: 10 minutes
Total cooking time: 35 minutes
Serves 4–6

6 Roma tomatoes
2 tablespoons butter
2 cloves garlic, crushed
1 onion, chopped
500 g (1 lb) English spinach
1 cup (250 ml/8 fl oz) vegetable stock
$\frac{1}{2}$ cup (125 ml/4 fl oz) thick cream
500 g (1 lb) fresh spinach fettucine
60 g (2 oz) shaved Parmesan

1 Preheat the oven to hot 220°C (425°F/Gas 7). Cut the tomatoes in half lengthways, then cut each half into three wedges. Place the wedges on a lightly greased baking tray and bake for 30–35 minutes, or until softened and slightly golden. Meanwhile, heat the butter in a large frying pan. Add the garlic and onion and cook over medium heat for 5 minutes, or until the onion is soft. Add the spinach, stock and cream, increase the heat to high and bring to the boil. Simmer rapidly for 5 minutes then season well and process in a food processor until smooth.
2 Meanwhile, cook the pasta in a large pan of rapidly boiling salted water until al dente. Drain and return to the pan to keep warm. Toss with the spinach sauce. Divide among serving bowls and top with the roasted tomatoes and Parmesan shavings.

NUTRITION PER SERVE (6)
Protein 17 g; Fat 18 g; Carbohydrate 65 g; Dietary Fibre 8 g; Cholesterol 49 mg; 2035 kJ (485 cal)

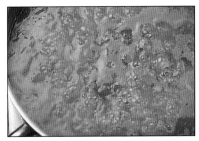

Add the tomato, sugar, wine, herbs and water and bring to the boil.

Add the pasta to the sauce, breaking the strands if they're too long.

PASTA PRONTO

Preparation time: 10 minutes
Total cooking time: 15 minutes
Serves 4

2 tablespoons extra virgin olive oil
4 cloves garlic, finely chopped
1 small fresh red chilli, finely chopped
3 x 400 g (13 oz) cans crushed tomatoes
1 teaspoon sugar
1/3 cup (80 ml/2¾ fl oz) dry white wine
3 tablespoons chopped fresh herbs (e.g. basil or parsley)
400 g (13 oz) vermicelli
30 g (1 oz) shaved Parmesan

1 Heat the oil in a large deep frying pan and cook the garlic and chilli for 1 minute. Add the tomato, sugar, wine, herbs and 1¾ cups (440 ml/14 fl oz) water. Bring to the boil and season.
2 Reduce the heat to medium and add the pasta, breaking the strands if they are too long. Cook for 10 minutes, or until the pasta is cooked, stirring often to prevent sticking. The pasta will thicken the sauce as it cooks. Season and serve with shaved Parmesan.

NUTRITION PER SERVE
Protein 17 g; Fat 14 g; Carbohydrate 82 g; Dietary Fibre 10 g; Cholesterol 7 mg; 2225 kJ (530 cal)

Add the thyme and all the mushrooms to the pan, then add the porcini soaking liquid.

Toss the lasagne sheets gently through the egg, cream and Parmesan mixture.

FREE-FORM WILD MUSHROOM LASAGNE

Preparation time: 10 minutes + 15 minutes soaking
Total cooking time: 15 minutes
Serves 4

10 g (¼ oz) dried porcini mushrooms
350 g (11 oz) wild mushrooms (e.g. shiitake, oyster, Swiss brown)
30 g (1 oz) butter
1 small onion, halved and thinly sliced
1 tablespoon chopped fresh thyme
3 egg yolks
½ cup (125 ml/4 fl oz) thick cream
1 cup (100 g/3½ oz) grated Parmesan
8 fresh lasagne sheets (10 x 25 cm/ 4 x 10 inches)

1 Soak the porcini in ¼ cup (60 ml/ 2 fl oz) boiling water for 15 minutes. Strain through a sieve, reserving the liquid. Cut the larger of all the mushrooms in half. Heat the butter in a frying pan and cook the onion over medium heat for 1–2 minutes, or until just soft. Add the thyme and mushrooms (including the porcini) and cook for 1–2 minutes, or until softened. Pour in the reserved mushroom liquid and cook for 1–2 minutes, or until the liquid has evaporated. Set aside.

2 Beat the egg yolks, cream and half the Parmesan in a large bowl. Cook the lasagne sheets in a large saucepan of boiling water for 2–3 minutes, stirring gently. Drain well and toss the sheets gently through the egg mixture while hot. Reheat the mushrooms quickly. To serve, place a sheet of folded lasagne on a plate, top with some mushrooms, then another sheet of folded lasagne. Drizzle with any remaining egg mixture and sprinkle with the remaining Parmesan.

NUTRITION PER SERVE
Protein 20 g; Fat 30 g; Carbohydrate 30 g; Dietary Fibre 4.5 g; Cholesterol 213 mg; 1950 kJ (465 cal)

Roast the walnuts in the oven until they are golden, then roughly chop.

Cook the sauce until the cheese has melted and the sauce has thickened.

BLUE CHEESE AND WALNUT LASAGNETTE

Preparation time: 10 minutes
Total cooking time: 15 minutes
Serves 4

375 g (12 oz) lasagnette
1 cup (100 g/3½ oz) walnuts
2 tablespoons butter
3 French shallots, finely chopped
1 tablespoon brandy
1 cup (250 ml/8 fl oz) crème fraîche
200 g (6½ oz) Gorgonzola cheese, crumbled
   (see NOTE)
75 g (2½ oz) baby English spinach

1 Preheat the oven to moderately hot 200°C (400°F/Gas 6). Cook the pasta in a large pan of rapidly boiling salted water until al dente. Drain and return to the pan to keep warm. Meanwhile, place the walnuts on a baking tray and roast for 5 minutes, or until golden and toasted. Cool, then roughly chop.
2 Heat the butter in a large saucepan, add the shallots and cook over medium heat for 1–2 minutes, or until soft but not brown. Add the brandy and simmer for 1 minute. Stir in the crème fraîche and Gorgonzola. Cook for 3–4 minutes, or until the cheese has melted and the sauce has thickened. Stir in the spinach and walnuts, reserving 1 tablespoon to garnish. Heat gently until the spinach has just wilted. Season and gently mix the sauce through the pasta. Sprinkle with the reserved walnuts to serve.

NUTRITION PER SERVE
Protein 32 g; Fat 64 g; Carbohydrate 69 g; Dietary Fibre 4.5 g; Cholesterol 152 mg; 4095 kJ (980 cal)

NOTE: Use young Gorgonzola that has a sweeter, milder flavor than mature.

Heat the oil in a frying pan and cook the garlic and chilli for 1 minute over low heat.

Pour the contents of the frying pan over the pasta and add the herbs and salt and pepper.

PASTA WITH RICOTTA, CHILLI AND HERBS

Preparation time: 15 minutes
Total cooking time: 20 minutes
Serves 4

500 g (1 lb) spiral pasta or penne
3 tablespoons olive oil
3 cloves garlic, crushed
2 teaspoons very finely chopped fresh chilli
1 cup (30 g/1 oz) fresh flat-leaf parsley
 leaves, roughly chopped
$1/2$ cup (15 g/$1/2$ oz) fresh basil leaves,
 shredded
$1/2$ cup (15 g/$1/2$ oz) fresh oregano leaves,
 roughly chopped
200 g ($6^1/2$ oz) ricotta cheese, cut into small
 cubes

1 Cook the pasta in a large pan of rapidly boiling salted water until al dente. Drain and return to the pan. Meanwhile, heat the oil in a non-stick heavy-based frying pan. Add the garlic and chilli to the frying pan and stir for 1 minute over low heat.

2 Pour the contents of the frying pan over the pasta and add the herbs. Season to taste and toss well.

3 Add the cubes of ricotta to the pasta and serve immediately.

NUTRITION PER SERVE
Protein 20 g; Fat 20 g; Carbohydrate 90 g; Dietary Fibre 7 g; Cholesterol 24 mg; 2635 kJ (630 cal)

While the pasta is cooking, dice the eggplant and chop the olives.

Cook the garlic for 30 seconds, then add the eggplant and cook until tender.

GREEN OLIVE AND EGGPLANT TOSS

Preparation time: 20 minutes
Total cooking time: 20 minutes
Serves 4

500 g (1 lb) fettucine or tagliatelle
1 cup (185 g/6 oz) green olives
1 large eggplant
2 tablespoons olive oil
2 cloves garlic, crushed
1/2 cup (125 ml/4 fl oz) lemon juice
2 tablespoons chopped fresh parsley
1/2 cup (50 g/1 3/4 oz) freshly grated
   Parmesan

1 Cook the pasta in a large pan of rapidly boiling salted water until it is al dente. Drain and return to the pan. While the pasta is cooking, chop the olives (removing the stones) and cut the eggplant into small cubes.
2 Heat the oil in a heavy-based frying pan. Add the garlic and stir for 30 seconds. Add the eggplant and cook over medium heat, stirring frequently, for 6 minutes or until the eggplant is tender.
3 Add the olives, lemon juice and salt and pepper to the pan. Tip the sauce into the pasta and toss well. Serve sprinkled with parsley and Parmesan.

NUTRITION PER SERVE
Protein 20 g; Fat 17 g; Carbohydrate 92 g;
Dietary Fibre 10 g; Cholesterol 12 mg; 2572 kJ
(615 cal)

Filled Pasta

SPINACH AND RICOTTA SHELLS

Preparation time: 15 minutes
Total cooking time: 15 minutes
Serves 4

20 giant pasta shells (conchiglie)
1 tablespoon oil
2 rashers bacon, finely chopped
1 onion, finely chopped
500 g (1 lb) English spinach, chopped
750 g (1½ lb) ricotta
⅓ cup (30 g/1 oz) grated Parmesan
1 cup (250 g/8 oz) bottled tomato pasta
    sauce
toasted pine nuts, for serving

1 Cook the pasta in a large pan of rapidly boiling salted water until al dente. Drain well. Meanwhile, heat the oil in a pan and cook the bacon and onion over medium heat for 3 minutes or until lightly browned. Add the spinach and stir over low heat until wilted. Add the ricotta and stir until combined.
2 Spoon the filling into the pasta shells and sprinkle with Parmesan. Place on a cold, lightly oiled grill tray and grill under medium-high heat for 3 minutes or until lightly browned and heated through.
3 Heat the tomato pasta sauce in a small pan for 1 minute or until heated through. Spoon the sauce onto serving plates and top with the filled shells. Sprinkle with pine nuts to serve.

NUTRITION PER SERVE
Protein 33 g; Fat 31 g; Carbohydrate 37 g; Dietary Fibre 4 g; Cholesterol 109 mg; 2344 kJ (560 cal)

STORAGE: The shells can be filled several hours before required. Store, covered, in the fridge and grill just before serving.

Cook the bacon and onion until lightly browned, then add the spinach and stir until wilted.

Spoon the filling into the cooked pasta shells and then sprinkle with Parmesan.

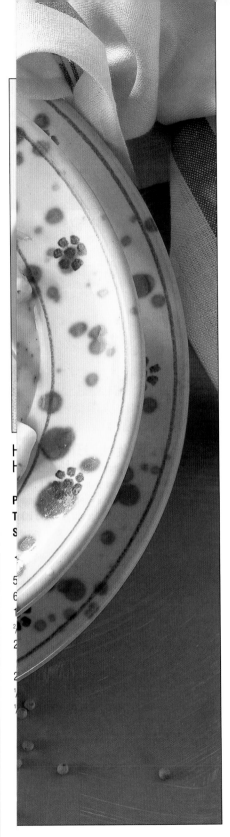

CREAMY SEAFOOD RAVIOLI

Preparation time: 45 minutes + 30 minutes standing
Total cooking time: 15 minutes
Serves 4

PASTA
2 cups (250 g/8 oz) plain flour
pinch of salt
3 eggs
1 tablespoon olive oil
1 egg yolk, extra

FILLING
50 g (1¾ oz) butter, softened
3 cloves garlic, finely chopped
2 tablespoons finely chopped fresh flat-leaf parsley
100 g (3½ oz) scallops, cleaned and finely chopped
100 g (3½ oz) raw prawn meat, finely chopped

SAUCE
3 tablespoons butter
3 tablespoons plain flour
1½ cups (375 ml/12 fl oz) milk
300 ml (10 fl oz) cream
½ cup (125 ml/4 fl oz) white wine
½ cup (50 g/1¾ oz) grated Parmesan
2 tablespoons chopped fresh flat-leaf parsley

Add the combined egg, oil and water gradually to the flour.

1 To make the pasta, sift the flour and salt into a bowl and make a well in the centre. Whisk the eggs, oil and 1 tablespoon water in a jug, then add gradually to the flour and mix to a firm dough. Gather into a ball.

2 Knead on a lightly floured surface for 5 minutes, or until smooth and elastic. Place in a lightly oiled bowl, cover with plastic wrap and set aside for 30 minutes.

3 To make the filling, mix together the butter, garlic, parsley, scallops and prawns. Set aside.

4 Roll out a quarter of the pasta dough at a time until very thin (each portion of dough should be roughly 10 cm/4 inches wide when rolled). Place 1 teaspoon of filling at 5 cm (2 inch) intervals down one side of each strip. Whisk the extra egg yolk with 3 tablespoons water. Brush along one side of the dough and between the filling. Fold the dough over the filling to meet the other side. Repeat with the remaining filling and dough. Press the edges of the dough together firmly to seal.

5 Cut between the mounds with a knife or a fluted pastry cutter. Cook in batches in a large pan of rapidly boiling water for 6 minutes each batch. Drain well and return to the pan to keep warm.

6 To make the sauce, melt the butter in a pan, add the flour and cook over low heat for 2 minutes. Remove from the heat and gradually stir in the combined milk, cream and white wine. Cook over low heat until the sauce begins to thicken, stirring constantly to prevent lumps forming. Bring to the boil and simmer gently for 5 minutes. Add the Parmesan and parsley and toss with the ravioli.

NUTRITION PER SERVE
Protein 30 g; Fat 40 g; Carbohydrate 57 g; Dietary Fibre 4 g; Cholesterol 322 mg; 3035 kJ (725 cal)

NOTE: We set the pasta dough aside for 30 minutes to let the gluten in the flour relax. If you don't do this, you run the risk of making tough pasta.

Baked Pasta

CLASSIC LASAGNE

Preparation time: 25 minutes
Total cooking time: 1 hour 15 minutes
Serves 4–6

250 g (8 oz) lasagne sheets
$1/2$ cup (75 g/$1^1/_2$ oz) grated mozzarella
$1/2$ cup (60 g/2 oz) grated Cheddar
$1/2$ cup (125 ml/4 fl oz) cream
3 tablespoons grated Parmesan

CHEESE SAUCE
60 g (2 oz) butter
$1/3$ cup (40 g/$1^1/_4$ oz) plain flour
2 cups (500 ml/16 fl oz) milk
1 cup (125 g/4 oz) grated Cheddar

MEAT SAUCE
1 tablespoon olive oil
1 onion, finely chopped
1 clove garlic, crushed
500 g (1 lb) beef mince
2 x 425 g (14 oz) cans tomatoes
$1/4$ cup (60 ml/2 fl oz) red wine
$1/2$ teaspoon ground oregano
$1/4$ teaspoon ground basil

1 Preheat the oven to moderate 180°C (350°F/Gas 4). Brush a shallow oven-proof dish (approximately 24 x 30 cm /10 x 12 inches) with melted butter or oil. Line with lasagne sheets, breaking them to fill any gaps, and set aside.
2 To make the cheese sauce, melt the butter in a pan. Add the flour and stir for 1 minute. Remove from the heat and slowly add the milk, stirring until smooth. Return to the heat and cook, stirring, over medium heat until the sauce

boils and thickens. Reduce the heat and simmer for 3 minutes. Stir in the cheese, season and set aside.
3 To make the meat sauce, heat the oil in a large pan. Add the onion and garlic and stir over low heat until the onion is tender. Add the mince and brown well, breaking up with a fork as it cooks. Stir in the tomatoes, wine, oregano, basil and salt and pepper. Bring to the boil, reduce the heat and simmer for 20 minutes.
4 Spoon one-third of the meat sauce over the lasagne sheets. Top with one-third of the cheese sauce. Arrange another layer of lasagne sheets over the top.
5 Continue layering, finishing with lasagne sheets. Sprinkle with the combined mozzarella and Cheddar cheeses. Pour the cream over the top. Sprinkle with Parmesan. Bake for 35–40 minutes or until golden.

NUTRITION PER SERVE (6)
Protein 41 g; Fat 58 g; Carbohydrate 45 g; Dietary Fibre 5 g; Cholesterol 170 mg; 3765 kJ (899 cal)

NOTE: Cheese sauce is a variation of Béchamel sauce that uses milk infused with flavorings such as bay leaf, cloves, peppercorns, parsley sprig and cinnamon stick. To do this, bring milk to boiling point with one or more of the flavorings and allow to stand for 10 minutes before straining for the flavors to infuse.

Finely chop the mushrooms in a food processor using the pulse button.

Cook the garlic and chopped mushrooms for 3 minutes, stirring constantly.

QUICK MUSHROOM AND RICOTTA CANNELLONI

Preparation time: 15 minutes
Total cooking time: 30 minutes
Serves 4

500 g (1 lb) button mushrooms
200 g (6½ oz) fresh lasagne sheets
2 tablespoons olive oil
3 cloves garlic, crushed
2 tablespoons lemon juice
400 g (13 oz) ricotta
3 tablespoons chopped fresh basil
425 g (14 oz) bottled tomato pasta sauce
1 cup (150 g/5 oz) grated mozzarella

1 Preheat the oven to moderate 180°C (350°F/Gas 4). Finely chop the mushrooms in a food processor. Cut the lasagne sheets into twelve 13 x 16 cm (5 x 6½ inch) rectangles.
2 Heat the oil in a large frying pan over medium heat. Add the garlic and mushrooms and cook, stirring, for 3 minutes. Add the lemon juice and cook for a further 2 minutes, or until softened. Transfer to a sieve over a bowl to collect the juices, pressing with a spoon to remove as much moisture as possible. Reserve.
3 Place the mushrooms in a bowl with the ricotta and basil. Add plenty of salt and black pepper and mix well. Take a lasagne sheet and place heaped tablespoons of the mixture along one long edge. Roll up and arrange in a single layer in a greased 2-litre shallow ovenproof dish. Repeat with the remaining mixture and lasagne sheets. Pour on the reserved mushroom cooking liquid then pour on the pasta sauce. Sprinkle with cheese and bake for 25 minutes, or until golden and bubbling.

NUTRITION PER SERVE
Protein 33 g; Fat 30 g; Carbohydrate 38 g; Dietary Fibre 6 g; Cholesterol 90 mg; 2290 kJ (545 cal)

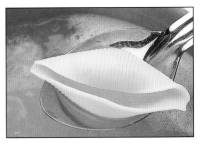

Cook the large pasta shells until they are tender, then drain.

Mix together the salmon, ricotta, parsley, chives, celery and Cheddar.

SALMON AND RICOTTA-STUFFED CONCHIGLIONE

Preparation time: 15 minutes
Total cooking time: 50 minutes
Serves 4

200 g (6½ oz) conchiglione (large pasta shells)
425 g (14 oz) can red salmon, drained, bones removed, flaked
500 g (1 lb) ricotta
1 tablespoon chopped fresh flat-leaf parsley
3 tablespoons chopped fresh chives
1½ celery stalks, finely chopped
¾ cup (90 g/3 oz) grated Cheddar
¾ cup (185 ml/6 fl oz) cream
¼ cup (30 g/1 oz) grated Parmesan

1 Preheat the oven to moderate 180°C (350°F/Gas 4). Cook the pasta in a large pan of rapidly boiling salted water until al dente. Drain and return to the pan to keep warm.
2 Combine the salmon, ricotta, parsley, chives, celery and Cheddar in a bowl and season to taste with salt and cracked black pepper.
3 Place 2 teaspoons of filling in each shell and arrange in a single layer in a 3-litre ovenproof dish. Pour on the cream and sprinkle with Parmesan. Cover with foil and bake for 20 minutes, then remove the foil and return to the oven for 15 minutes, or until golden brown. Serve with the sauce spooned over the shells.

NUTRITION PER SERVE
Protein 31 g; Fat 36 g; Carbohydrate 38 g; Dietary Fibre 3 g; Cholesterol 135 mg; 2470 kJ (590 cal)

SPINACH AND RICOTTA CANNELLONI

Preparation time: 1 hour
Total cooking time: 1 hour 15 minutes
Serves 4–6

375 g (12 oz) fresh lasagne sheets
2 tablespoons olive oil
1 large onion, finely chopped
1–2 cloves garlic, crushed
2 large bunches English spinach, finely
  chopped
650 g (1 lb 5 oz) ricotta, beaten
2 eggs, beaten
1/4 teaspoon freshly ground nutmeg
150 g (5 oz) grated mozzarella

TOMATO SAUCE
1 tablespoon olive oil
1 onion, chopped
2 cloves garlic, finely chopped
500 g (1 lb) ripe tomatoes, chopped
2 tablespoons tomato paste
1 teaspoon soft brown sugar

1 Cut the lasagne sheets into 15 even-sized pieces and trim lengthways so that they will fit neatly into a rectangular ovenproof dish when filled. Bring a large pan of water to a rapid boil. Cook 1–2 lasagne sheets at a time until just softened. This amount of time will differ depending on the type and brand of lasagne, but is usually about 2 minutes. Remove sheets carefully with two spatulas or wooden spoons and lay out flat on a clean damp tea towel. Do not use tongs to remove the sheets from the water as they might tear the sheets.
2 Heat the oil in a heavy-based frying pan. Cook the onion and garlic until golden, stirring regularly. Add the spinach and cook for 2 minutes, then cover with a tight-fitting lid and let the spinach steam for 5 minutes. Drain, removing as much liquid as possible. The spinach must be quite dry or the pasta will be soggy. Combine the spinach with the ricotta, eggs, nutmeg and season with salt and pepper. Mix well and set aside.
3 To make the tomato sauce, heat the oil in a frying pan and cook the onion and garlic for 10 minutes over low heat, stirring occasionally. Add the chopped tomatoes and their juice, tomato paste, sugar and 1/2 cup (125 ml/4 fl oz) water and season with salt and pepper. Bring the sauce to the boil, reduce the heat and simmer for 10 minutes. If you prefer a smooth sauce, purée it in a processor.
4 Preheat the oven to moderate 180°C (350°F/Gas 4) and lightly grease the ovenproof dish. Spread about one-third of the tomato sauce over the base of the dish. Working with one piece of the lasagne at a time, spoon 2 1/2 tablespoons of the spinach mixture down the centre of each sheet, leaving a border at each end. Roll up and lay seam-side-down in the dish. Trim the ends to fit evenly if necessary. Spoon the remaining tomato sauce over the cannelloni and scatter the cheese over the top. Bake for 30–35 minutes, or until golden. Set aside for 10 minutes before serving.

NUTRITION PER SERVE
Protein 28 g; Fat 30 g; Carbohydrate 50 g; Dietary Fibre 5 g; Cholesterol 128 mg; 2400 kJ (575 cal)

NOTE: You can use dried cannelloni tubes instead of fresh lasagne sheets. The texture of the pasta will be firmer.

Add the sliced prosciutto to the onion and garlic in a large pan.

Add the chicken mince and brown well, breaking it up with a fork as it cooks.

RICOTTA-STUFFED PASTA SHELLS WITH CHICKEN SAUCE

Preparation time: 30 minutes
Total cooking time: 1 hour 10 minutes
Serves 4

500 g (1 lb) conchiglie (large pasta shells)
2 tablespoons olive oil
1 onion, chopped
1 clove garlic, crushed
60 g (2 oz) prosciutto, sliced
125 g (4 oz) mushrooms, chopped
250 g (8 oz) chicken mince
2 tablespoons tomato paste
425 g (14 oz) can crushed tomatoes
1/2 cup (125 ml/4 fl oz) dry white wine
1 teaspoon dried oregano
250 g (8 oz) ricotta
220 g (7 oz) mozzarella, grated

1 teaspoon snipped chives
1 tablespoon chopped fresh parsley
3 tablespoons grated Parmesan

1 Cook the pasta in a large pan of rapidly boiling salted water until al dente. Drain and return to the pan to keep warm.
2 Meanwhile, heat the oil in a large frying pan. Add the onion and garlic, then stir over low heat until the onion is tender. Add the prosciutto and stir for 1 minute. Add the mushrooms and cook for 2 minutes. Add the chicken mince and brown well, breaking up any lumps with a fork as it cooks.
3 Stir in the tomato paste, tomatoes, wine and oregano and season to taste. Bring to the boil, reduce the heat and simmer for 20 minutes.
4 Preheat the oven to moderate 180°C (350°F/Gas 4). Combine the ricotta, mozzarella, chives, parsley and half the Parmesan. Spoon a little into each shell. Spoon some of the chicken sauce into the base of a casserole dish. Arrange

the conchiglie on top. Spread the remaining sauce over the top and sprinkle with the remaining Parmesan. Bake 25–30 minutes, or until golden.

NUTRITION PER SERVE

Protein 43 g; Fat 23 g; Carbohydrate 95 g; Dietary Fibre 9 g; Cholesterol 76 mg; 3282 kJ (785 cal)

Mix together the ricotta, pine nuts, basil, garlic and Parmesan.

Cook the pasta according to the packet instructions until al dente.

PUMPKIN, BASIL AND RICOTTA LASAGNE

Preparation time: 20 minutes
Total cooking time: 1 hour 25 minutes
Serves 4

650 g (1 lb 5 oz) pumpkin
2 tablespoons olive oil
500 g (1 lb) ricotta
⅓ cup (60 g/2 oz) pine nuts, toasted
¾ cup (35 g/1 oz) fresh basil
2 cloves garlic, crushed
⅓ cup (30 g/1 oz) grated Parmesan
125 g (4 oz) fresh lasagne sheets
1¼ cups (185 g/6 oz) grated mozzarella

1 Preheat the oven to moderate 180°C (350°F/Gas 4). Lightly grease a baking tray. Cut the pumpkin into thin slices and arrange in a single layer on the tray. Brush with oil and cook for 1 hour, or until softened, turning halfway through cooking.
2 Mix together the ricotta, pine nuts, basil, garlic and Parmesan.
3 Brush a square 20 cm (8 inch) ovenproof dish with oil. Cook the pasta according to the packet instructions. Arrange one-third of the pasta sheets over the base of the dish. Spread with the ricotta mixture. Top with half the remaining lasagne sheets.
4 Arrange the pumpkin evenly over the pasta with as few gaps as possible. Season with salt and cracked black pepper and top with the final layer of pasta sheets. Sprinkle with mozzarella. Bake for 20–25 minutes, or until the cheese is golden. Leave for 10 minutes, then cut into squares.

NUTRITION PER SERVE
Protein 24 g; Fat 32 g; Carbohydrate 33 g; Dietary Fibre 4.5 g; Cholesterol 37 mg; 2166 kJ (517 cal)

NOTE: If the pasta has no cooking instructions, blanch the sheets one at a time.

Cook the pasta in a large pan of rapidly boiling water until it is tender.

Mix together the soup, sour cream and curry powder to make the sauce.

SPEEDY CHICKEN AND PASTA BAKE

Preparation time: 15 minutes
Total cooking time: 45 minutes
Serves 4

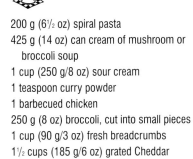

200 g (6½ oz) spiral pasta
425 g (14 oz) can cream of mushroom or broccoli soup
1 cup (250 g/8 oz) sour cream
1 teaspoon curry powder
1 barbecued chicken
250 g (8 oz) broccoli, cut into small pieces
1 cup (90 g/3 oz) fresh breadcrumbs
1½ cups (185 g/6 oz) grated Cheddar

1 Preheat the oven to moderate 180°C (350°F/Gas 4). Cook the pasta in a large pan of rapidly boiling salted water until al dente. Drain and return to the pan to keep warm.
2 Combine the soup, sour cream and curry powder and season to taste with freshly ground black pepper.
3 Remove the meat from the chicken and roughly chop. Combine the chicken with the pasta, broccoli and soup mixture. Spoon into four lightly greased 2-cup (500 ml/16 fl oz) ovenproof dishes and sprinkle with the combined breadcrumbs and cheese. Bake for 25–30 minutes, or until the cheese melts.

NUTRITION PER SERVE
Protein 67 g; Fat 47 g; Carbohydrate 55 g; Dietary Fibre 8 g; Cholesterol 254 mg; 3812 kJ (911 cal)

VARIATION: This recipe can be made in a 2-litre ovenproof dish and baked for 40 minutes, or until the cheese has melted.

Cook the onion in the butter over medium heat until softened.

MACARONI CHEESE

Preparation time: 15 minutes
Total cooking time: 35 minutes
Serves 4

225 g (7 oz) macaroni
90 g (3 oz) butter
1 onion, finely chopped
3 tablespoons plain flour
2 cups (500 ml/16 fl oz) milk
2 teaspoons wholegrain mustard
150 g (5 oz) mature Cheddar, grated
100 g (3½ oz) Cheddar, grated
30 g (1 oz) fresh breadcrumbs

1 Cook the pasta in a large pan of rapidly boiling salted water until al dente. Drain and return to the pan.

2 Preheat the oven to moderate 180°C (350°F/Gas 4) and grease a 1.5 litre ovenproof dish.

3 Melt the butter in a large pan over low heat, add the onion and cook for 5 minutes, or until softened. Stir in the flour and cook for 1 minute, or until pale and foaming. Remove from the heat and gradually stir in the milk. Return to the heat and stir constantly until the sauce boils and thickens. Reduce the heat and simmer for 2 minutes. Stir in the mustard and about three-quarters of the combined cheeses. Season to taste. Add the cooked pasta to the pan and stir until coated in the mixture. Spoon into the dish and smooth the surface.

4 Combine the breadcrumbs and remaining cheese and scatter over the top. Bake for about 15 minutes, or until golden brown and bubbling.

NUTRITION PER SERVE
Protein 30 g; Fat 45 g; Carbohydrate 60 g; Dietary Fibre 4 g; Cholesterol 130 mg; 3087 kJ (737 cal)

Cut the fish fillets into even-sized pieces with a sharp knife.

Stir the sauce over low heat until it comes to the boil and thickens.

SEAFOOD LASAGNE

Preparation time: 15 minutes
Total cooking time: 50 minutes
Serves 6

250 g (8 oz) fresh lasagne sheets
1 tablespoon olive oil
30 g (1 oz) butter
1 onion, finely chopped
2 cloves garlic, crushed
400 g (13 oz) raw prawns, peeled and
   deveined
500 g (1 lb) skinless firm white fish fillets
   (see NOTE), chopped
250 g (8 oz) scallops with roe, membrane
   removed
750 g (1½ lb) bottled tomato pasta sauce
1 tablespoon tomato paste
1 teaspoon soft brown sugar
½ cup (60 g/2 oz) grated Cheddar
¼ cup (30 g/1 oz) grated Parmesan

CHEESE SAUCE
120 g (4 oz) butter
⅔ cup (90 g/3 oz) plain flour
1.5 litres milk
2 cups (250 g/8 oz) grated Cheddar
1 cup (100 g/3½ oz) grated Parmesan

1 Preheat the oven to moderate 180°C (350°F/Gas 4). Lightly grease a 2.5-litre ovenproof dish and line with the lasagne sheets.
2 Heat the oil and butter in a large saucepan. Add the onion and cook for 2–3 minutes, or until softened. Add the garlic and cook for 30 seconds. Cook the prawns and fish pieces for 2 minutes, then add the scallops and cook for 1 minute. Stir in the pasta sauce, tomato paste and sugar and simmer for 5 minutes.
3 For the cheese sauce, melt the butter over low heat in a saucepan, stir in the flour and cook for 1 minute, or until pale and foaming. Remove from the heat and gradually stir in the milk. Return to the heat and stir until the sauce boils and thickens. Reduce the heat, simmer for 2 minutes, then stir in the cheeses. Season, to taste.

4 Spoon one-third of the seafood sauce over the lasagne sheets. Top with one third of the cheese sauce. Arrange lasagne sheets over the top. Repeat to make three layers. Sprinkle with the combined cheeses and bake for 30 minutes or until golden. Leave for 10 minutes before slicing.

NUTRITION PER SERVE
Protein 70.5 g; Fat 63 g; Carbohydrate 50 g; Dietary Fibre 4.6 g; Cholesterol 332 mg; 4321 kJ (1033 cal)

NOTE: We suggest using, hake, snapper, flake, gemfish or ling.

LOW-FAT LASAGNE

Preparation time: 40 minutes
Total cooking time: 1 hour 35 minutes
Serves 8

2 teaspoons olive oil
1 large onion, chopped
2 carrots, finely chopped
2 celery stalks, finely chopped
2 zucchini, finely chopped
2 cloves garlic, crushed
500 g (1 lb) lean beef mince
2 x 400 g (13 oz) cans crushed tomatoes
1/2 cup (125 ml/4 fl oz) beef stock
2 tablespoons tomato paste
2 teaspoons dried oregano
375 g (12 oz) lasagne sheets

CHEESE SAUCE
3 cups (750 ml/24 fl oz) skim milk
1/3 cup (40 g/1 1/4 oz) cornflour
100 g (3 1/2 oz) reduced-fat cheese, grated

1 Heat the olive oil in a large non-stick frying pan. Add the onion and cook for 5 minutes, until soft. Add the carrot, celery and zucchini and cook, stirring constantly, for 5 minutes, or until the vegetables are soft. Add the crushed garlic and cook for another minute. Add the beef mince and cook over high heat, stirring, until well browned. Break up any lumps of meat with a wooden spoon.

Chop the garlic and crush using the flat side of a large knife.

2 Add the crushed tomato, beef stock, tomato paste and dried oregano to the pan and stir to thoroughly combine. Bring the mixture to the boil, then reduce the heat and simmer gently, partially covered, for 20 minutes, stirring occasionally to prevent the mixture sticking to the pan.

3 Preheat the oven to moderate 180°C (350°F/Gas 4). Spread a little of the meat sauce into the base of a 23 x 30 cm (9 x 12 inch) ovenproof dish. Arrange a layer of lasagne sheets in the dish, breaking some of the sheets, if necessary, to fit in neatly.

4 Spread half the meat sauce over the top to cover evenly. Cover with another layer of lasagne sheets, a layer of meat sauce, then a final layer of lasagne sheets.

5 To make the cheese sauce, blend a little of the milk with the cornflour, to form a smooth paste, in a small pan. Gradually blend in the remaining milk and stir constantly over low heat until the mixture boils and thickens. Remove from the heat and stir in the grated cheese until melted. Spread evenly over the top of the lasagne and bake for 1 hour.

6 Check the lasagne after 25 minutes. If the top is browning too quickly, cover loosely with non-stick baking paper or foil. Take care when removing the baking paper or foil that the topping does not come away with the paper. For serving, cut the lasagne into eight portions and garnish with fresh herbs.

NUTRITION PER SERVE

Protein 15 g; Fat 12 g; Carbohydrate 50 g; Dietary Fibre 5 g; Cholesterol 10 mg; 1885 kJ (450 cal)

STORAGE: Can be frozen for up to 2–3 months. When required, thaw overnight in the refrigerator, then reheat, covered with foil, for about 30 minutes in a moderate oven.

When the mince has browned, add the passata, water and oregano.

Cook, stirring, until the sauce thickens, then add the nutmeg and Cheddar.

RICH BEEF AND MUSHROOM LASAGNE

Preparation time: 30 minutes
Total cooking time: 2 hours
Serves 8

1 tablespoon olive oil
2 cloves garlic, crushed
1 onion, chopped
1 carrot, grated
1 celery stalk, diced
125 g (4 oz) mushrooms, chopped
600 g (1¼ lb) minced beef
2½ cups (600 ml/20 fl oz) Italian tomato
    passata
1 teaspoon dried oregano leaves
300 g (10 oz) instant lasagne sheets
1 cup (100 g/3½ oz) grated Parmesan

CHEESE SAUCE
60 g (2 oz) butter
⅓ cup (40 g/1¼ oz) plain flour
1 litre milk
½ teaspoon ground nutmeg
1 cup (125 g/4 oz) grated Cheddar

1 Heat the oil in a large heavy-based pan. Add the garlic, onion, carrot, celery and mushroom. Cook, stirring, over medium heat for 2–3 minutes, or until the onion has softened. Increase the heat, add the mince and stir for a further 3–4 minutes, or until the mince has browned and is well broken up.
2 Add the tomato passata, oregano and 2 cups (500 ml/16 fl oz) water. Bring to the boil, stirring, then lower the heat and simmer for 1 hour, or until the mixture has thickened. Stir occasionally.
3 To make the cheese sauce, melt the butter in a heavy-based pan. Add the flour and cook, stirring, for 1 minute until pale and foaming. Remove from the heat, gradually add the milk and stir until smooth. Return to the heat and stir

continuously for 3–4 minutes, or until the sauce boils and thickens. Cook over low heat for 1 minute. Stir in the nutmeg and Cheddar. Season.
4 To assemble, preheat the oven to moderate 180°C (350°F/Gas 4). Grease a 2.5 litre baking dish. Arrange four lasagne sheets over the base of the baking dish. Spread one-third of the meat mixture over the sheets, then pour over about ¾ cup (185 ml/ 6 fl oz) of the cheese sauce. Repeat with two more layers of each. Top with the four remaining lasagne sheets, then with the remaining sauce and finish with the Parmesan. Bake for 45 minutes, or until golden. Leave to stand for 5 minutes before serving.

NUTRITION PER SERVE
Protein 35 g; Fat 30 g; Carbohydrate 45 g; Dietary Fibre 5 g; Cholesterol 110 mg; 2560 kJ (610 cal)

Add the semolina to the milk and stir over the heat until very stiff.

Refrigerate the semolina in the tin for an hour and then cut out with a floured cutter.

GNOCCHI ALLA ROMANA

Preparation time: 15 minutes + 1 hour refrigeration
Total cooking time: 40 minutes
Serves 4

3 cups (750 ml/24 fl oz) milk
¹/₂ teaspoon ground nutmeg
²/₃ cup (90 g/3 oz) semolina
1 egg, beaten
1¹/₂ cups (150 g/5 oz) grated Parmesan
60 g (2 oz) butter, melted
¹/₂ cup (125 ml/4 fl oz) cream
¹/₂ cup (75 g/2¹/₂ oz) grated mozzarella

1 Line a deep 30 x 20 cm (12 x 8 inch) swiss roll tin with baking paper. Put the milk and half the nutmeg in a pan and season. Bring to the boil. Reduce the heat and gradually stir in the semolina. Cook, stirring occasionally, for 5–10 minutes or until very stiff. Remove from the heat. Add the egg and 1 cup (90 g/3 oz) Parmesan and stir well. Spread in the tin and refrigerate for 1 hour or until firm.

2 Preheat the oven to moderate 180°C (350°F/Gas 4). Cut the semolina into rounds using a small floured biscuit cutter. Arrange in a greased shallow casserole dish.

3 Pour the melted butter over the gnocchi, followed by the cream. Sprinkle with the remaining Parmesan, mozzarella and nutmeg. Bake for 20–25 minutes or until golden.

NUTRITION PER SERVE
Protein 34 g; Fat 53 g; Carbohydrate 32 g; Dietary Fibre 1 g; Cholesterol 170 mg; 3077 kJ (735 cal)

VEGETARIAN LASAGNE

Preparation time: 1 hour
Total cooking time: 1 hour 30 minutes
Serves 8

500 g (1 lb) fresh spinach lasagne sheets
1/2 cup (30 g/1 oz) fresh basil leaves,
    coarsely chopped
2 tablespoons fresh breadcrumbs
3 tablespoons pine nuts
2 teaspoons paprika
1 tablespoon grated Parmesan

RICOTTA FILLING
750 g (1 1/2 lb) ricotta
1/2 cup (50 g/1 3/4 oz) grated Parmesan
pinch of nutmeg

TOMATO SAUCE
1 tablespoon olive oil
2 onions, chopped
2 cloves garlic, crushed
800 g (1 lb 10 oz) can crushed tomatoes
1 tablespoon tomato paste

BECHAMEL SAUCE
60 g (2 oz) butter
1/2 cup (60 g/2 oz) plain flour
2 cups (500 ml/16 fl oz) milk
2 eggs, lightly beaten
1/3 cup (30 g/1 oz) grated Parmesan

1 Lightly grease a 25 x 32 cm (10 x 13 inch) baking dish. Cut the pasta sheets into large pieces and cook, a couple at a time, in boiling water for 3 minutes. Drain and spread on damp tea towels until needed.

2 To make the ricotta filling, put the ricotta and Parmesan cheeses and nutmeg in a bowl and mix together well. Season with black pepper and set aside.

3 To make the tomato sauce, heat the oil in a frying pan, add the onion and cook for about 10 minutes, stirring occasionally, until very soft. Add the garlic and cook for 1 more minute. Add the tomato and tomato paste and stir until well combined. Stir until the mixture comes to the boil. Reduce the heat and simmer uncovered for 15 minutes, or until thickened, stirring occasionally.

4 To make the Béchamel sauce, heat the butter in a small pan. When starting to foam, add the flour and stir for 3 minutes, or until just colored. Remove from the heat; add the milk gradually, stirring after each addition, then return to the heat and stir until the sauce boils and thickens. Remove from the heat and stir in the eggs. Return to moderate heat and stir until almost boiling, but do not boil. Add the cheese and season to taste. Put plastic wrap onto the surface to prevent a skin forming. Preheat the oven to 200°C (400°F/Gas 6).

5 Put a layer of lasagne sheets in the dish. Spread with a third of the ricotta filling, sprinkle with basil, then top with a third of the tomato sauce. Repeat the layers, finishing with pasta.

6 Pour over the Béchamel sauce, spread until smooth, then sprinkle with the combined breadcrumbs, pine nuts, paprika and Parmesan. Bake for 45 minutes, or until browned. Leave to stand for 10 minutes before serving.

NUTRITION PER SERVE
Protein 22 g; Fat 30 g; Carbohydrate 16 g; Dietary Fibre 14 g; Cholesterol 130 mg; 1750 kJ (416 cal)

Cook the lasagne in a large pan of boiling water, a couple of sheets at a time.

Cut the eggplant lengthways into slices and then fry in batches.

Add the tomato to the sauce and cook until pulpy and the liquid has evaporated.

RICOTTA, EGGPLANT AND PASTA TIMBALES

Preparation time: 15 minutes
Total cooking time: 45 minutes
Makes 4

¹/₂ cup (125 ml/4 fl oz) light olive oil
1 large eggplant, cut lengthways into thin slices
200 g (6¹/₂ oz) macaroni
1 small onion, finely chopped
2 cloves garlic, crushed
400 g (13 oz) can diced tomatoes
400 g (13 oz) ricotta
1 cup (90 g/3 oz) roughly grated Parmesan
¹/₂ cup (15 g/¹/₂ oz) shredded fresh basil

1 Preheat the oven to moderate 180°C (350°F/Gas 4). Heat 2 tablespoons of the oil in a large, non-stick frying pan and cook the eggplant in three batches over medium heat for 2–3 minutes each side, or until golden, adding 2 tablespoons of the oil with each batch. Remove from the pan and drain on crumpled paper towels. Meanwhile, cook the pasta in a large pan of rapidly boiling salted water until al dente. Drain and return to the pan to keep warm.
2 Add the onion and garlic to the frying pan and cook over medium heat for 2–3 minutes, or until just golden. Add the tomato and cook for 5 minutes, or until the sauce is pulpy and most of the liquid has evaporated. Season, then remove from the heat.

3 Combine the ricotta, Parmesan and basil in a large bowl, then mix in the pasta. Line four 1¹/₂ cup (375 ml/12 fl oz) ramekins with eggplant, trimming to fit the base and sides. Top with half the pasta mix, pressing down firmly. Spoon on the tomato sauce, then cover with the remaining pasta mix. Bake for 10–15 minutes, or until heated through and golden on top. Leave for 5 minutes, then run a knife around the ramekin to loosen the timbale before turning out.

NUTRITION PER TIMBALE
Protein 26 g; Fat 40 g; Carbohydrate 43 g; Dietary Fibre 6 g; Cholesterol 67 mg; 2645 kJ (630 cal)

Cook the spring onion and the zucchini in the butter until soft.

Spoon the pasta into four greased individual ovenproof dishes.

ZUCCHINI PASTA BAKE

Preparation time: 15 minutes
Total cooking time: 45 minutes
Serves 4

200 g (6½ oz) risoni
40 g (1¼ oz) butter
4 spring onions, thinly sliced
400 g (13 oz) zucchini, grated
4 eggs
½ cup (125 ml/4 fl oz) cream
100 g (3½ oz) ricotta (see Note)
⅔ cup (100 g/3½ oz) grated mozzarella
¾ cup (75 g/2½ oz) grated Parmesan

1 Preheat the oven to moderate 180°C (350°F/Gas 4). Cook the pasta in a large pan of rapidly boiling salted water until al dente. Drain and return to the pan to keep warm. Meanwhile, heat the butter in a frying pan, add the spring onion and cook for 1 minute, then add the zucchini and cook for 4 minutes, or until soft. Cool slightly.
2 Place the eggs, cream, ricotta, mozzarella, risoni and half of the Parmesan in a bowl and mix together well. Stir in the zucchini mixture, then season with salt and pepper. Spoon the mixture into four 2-cup (500 ml/16 fl oz) greased ovenproof dishes, but do not fill to the brim. Sprinkle with the remaining Parmesan and cook for 25–30 minutes until firm and golden.

NUTRITION PER SERVE

Protein 29g; Fat 41 g; Carbohydrate 39 g; Dietary Fibre 5 g; Cholesterol 311 mg; 2635 kJ (630 cal)

NOTE: With such simple flavors, it is important to use good-quality fresh ricotta from the delicatessen or the deli section of your local supermarket.

PASTICCIO

Preparation time: 25 minutes + 15 minutes resting
Total cooking time: 2 hours
Serves 4–6

¼ cup (60 ml/2 fl oz) olive oil
1 onion, finely chopped
2 cloves garlic, crushed
90 g (3 oz) pancetta, finely chopped
500 g (1 lb) beef mince
1 teaspoon chopped fresh oregano
60 g (2 oz) button mushrooms, sliced
120 g (4 oz) chicken livers, trimmed and
    finely chopped
¼ teaspoon ground nutmeg
pinch of cayenne pepper
¼ cup (60 ml/2 fl oz) dry white wine
2 tablespoons tomato paste
1½ cups (375 ml/12 fl oz) beef stock
2 tablespoons grated Parmesan
1 egg, beaten
150 g (5 oz) macaroni
100 g (3½ oz) ricotta
2 tablespoons milk
pinch of cayenne pepper, extra
pinch of ground nutmeg, extra
1 egg, beaten, extra
1 cup (100 g/3½ oz) grated Parmesan, extra

BECHAMEL SAUCE
40 g (1¼ oz) butter
1½ tablespoons plain flour
pinch of ground nutmeg
300 ml (10 fl oz) milk
1 small bay leaf

1 Preheat the oven to moderate 180°C (350°F/Gas 4). Lightly grease a 1.5 litre ovenproof dish. Heat the oil in a large frying pan over medium heat and cook the onion, garlic and pancetta, stirring, for 5–6 minutes, or until the onion is golden. Add the beef, increase the heat and stir for 5 minutes, or until the meat is browned.

2 Add the oregano, mushrooms, chicken livers, nutmeg and cayenne, season and cook for 2 minutes, or until the livers change color. Add the wine and cook over high heat for 1 minute to evaporate. Stir in the tomato paste and stock. Reduce the heat and simmer for 45 minutes, or until thickened. Beat the Parmesan and egg together and quickly stir through.

3 Cook the pasta in a large pan of rapidly boiling salted water until al dente. Drain and return to the pan to keep warm. Meanwhile, blend the ricotta, milk, extra cayenne, extra nutmeg, extra egg and a quarter of the extra Parmesan. Season. Drain the macaroni, add to the ricotta mixture and mix well.

4 To make the Béchamel sauce, melt the butter in a small saucepan. Stir in the flour and cook over low heat until beginning to turn golden, then stir in the nutmeg. Remove from the heat and gradually stir in the milk. Add the bay leaf and season. Return to low heat and simmer, stirring, until thickened. Discard the bay leaf.

5 Spread half the meat sauce in the dish, layer half the pasta over the top and sprinkle with half the remaining Parmesan. Layer with the remaining meat sauce and pasta. Press down firmly with the back of a spoon. Spread the Béchamel over the top and sprinkle with the remaining Parmesan. Bake for 45–50 minutes until golden. Rest for 15 minutes before serving.

NUTRITION PER SERVE (6)
Protein 43 g; Fat 40 g; Carbohydrate 27 g; Dietary Fibre 2.5 g; Cholesterol 192 mg; 2670 kJ (638 cal)

Cook the spinach until wilted, then season well and stir into the orzo.

Cook the sauce, stirring constantly, until it boils and thickens.

ORZO AND GREEK CHEESE BAKE

Preparation time: 15 minutes
Total cooking time: 40 minutes
Serves 6

2 cups (415 g/13 oz) orzo
60 g (2 oz) butter
6 spring onions, chopped
450 g (14 oz) English spinach, trimmed and
    chopped
2 tablespoons plain flour
1.25 litres milk
250 g (8 oz) kefalotyri cheese, grated (see
    Note)
250 g (8 oz) marinated feta, drained
3 tablespoons chopped fresh dill

1 Preheat the oven to moderately hot 190°C (375°F/Gas 5). Cook the pasta in a large pan of rapidly boiling salted water until al dente. Drain well and return to the pan keep warm. Heat 1 tablespoon of the butter in a large saucepan over high heat and cook the spring onion for 30 seconds. Add the spinach and stir for 1 minute, or until wilted. Season and stir into the pasta.
2 Put the remaining butter in the saucepan in which the spinach was cooked. Melt over low heat, then stir in the flour and cook for 1 minute, or until pale and foaming. Remove from the heat and gradually stir in the milk. Return to the heat and stir constantly for 5 minutes, or until the sauce boils and thickens. Add two-thirds of the kefalotyri and all of the feta and stir for 2 minutes until melted. Remove from the heat and stir in the dill.
3 Combine the pasta mixture with the cheese sauce, season to taste and pour into a lightly greased 2.5-litre oven-proof dish. Sprinkle the remaining cheese on top and bake for 15 minutes, or until golden.

NUTRITION PER SERVE

Protein 31 g; Fat 34 g; Carbohydrate 63 g; Dietary Fibre 6 g; Cholesterol 103 mg; 2835 kJ (680 cal)

NOTE: Kefalotyri is a hard Greek sheep's milk cheese; it is similar to Parmesan.

When the cream is just coming to the boil, add the four cheeses and stir until melted.

Add the pasta to the cheese sauce and then spoon into the dish.

FOUR-CHEESE MACARONI

Preparation time: 15 minutes
Total cooking time: 40 minutes
Serves 4

450 g (14 oz) elbow macaroni
2 tablespoons butter
300 ml (10 fl oz) cream
125 g (4 oz) fontina cheese, sliced
125 g (4 oz) provolone cheese, grated
100 g (3^1/$_2$ oz) Gruyère cheese, grated
125 g (4 oz) blue castello cheese, crumbled
^{1}/$_2$ cup (40 g/1^1/$_4$ oz) fresh white
    breadcrumbs
^{1}/$_4$ cup (30 g/1 oz) grated Parmesan

1 Preheat the oven to moderate 180°C (350°F/Gas 4). Cook the pasta in a large pan of rapidly boiling salted water until al dente. Drain well and return to the pan to keep warm. Melt half the butter in a large saucepan. Add the cream and, when just coming to the boil, add the fontina, provolone, Gruyère and blue castello cheeses, stirring constantly over low heat for 3 minutes, or until melted. Season with salt and white pepper. Add the pasta to the cheese mixture and mix well.

2 Spoon the mixture into a lightly greased shallow 2-litre ovenproof dish. Sprinkle with the breadcrumbs mixed with the Parmesan, dot with the remaining cubed butter and bake for 25 minutes, or until the top is golden and crisp.

NUTRITION PER SERVE

Protein 49 g; Fat 81 g; Carbohydrate 89 g; Dietary Fibre 6 g; Cholesterol 260 mg; 5330 kJ (1275 cal)

Mix together the soup, eggs, mayonnaise, mustard and half the cheese.

Cook the chicken in a lightly greased non-stick frying pan.

CHICKEN, BROCCOLI AND PASTA BAKE

Preparation time: 15 minutes
Total cooking time: 35 minutes
Serves 6–8

300 g (10 oz) pasta
425 g (14 oz) can cream of mushroom soup
2 eggs
³/₄ cup (185 g/6 oz) mayonnaise
1 tablespoon Dijon mustard
1²/₃ cups (200 g/6¹/₂ oz) grated Cheddar
600 g (1¹/₄ lb) chicken breast fillets, thinly sliced
400 g (13 oz) frozen broccoli pieces, thawed
¹/₂ cup (40 g/1¹/₄ oz) fresh breadcrumbs

1 Preheat the oven to moderate 180°C (350°F/Gas 4). Cook the pasta in a large pan of rapidly boiling salted water until al dente. Drain well and return to the pan to keep warm. Combine the soup, eggs, mayonnaise, mustard and half the cheese in a bowl.
2 Heat a lightly greased non-stick frying pan over medium heat, add the chicken and cook for 5–6 minutes, or until cooked through. Season with salt and pepper, then set aside to cool.
3 Add the chicken and broccoli to the pasta, pour the soup mixture over the top and stir until well combined. Transfer the mixture to a 3-litre ovenproof dish. Sprinkle with the combined breadcrumbs and remaining cheese. Bake for 20 minutes, or until the top becomes golden brown.

NUTRITION PER SERVE (8)
Protein 34 g; Fat 33 g; Carbohydrate 33 g; Dietary Fibre 4.5 g; Cholesterol 143 mg; 2340 kJ (560 cal)

Spread the mixture of pasta, artichokes, oil, cream, thyme, garlic and cheese into the dish.

Arrange the sliced tomatoes in an overlapping layer over the pasta.

PASTA, TOMATO AND ARTICHOKE GRILL

Preparation time: 15 minutes
Total cooking time: 20 minutes
Serves 4

350 g (12 oz) pasta
285 g (9 oz) jar marinated artichoke hearts, drained and chopped
2 tablespoons olive oil
1 cup (250 ml/8 fl oz) thick cream
2 tablespoons chopped fresh thyme
2 cloves garlic, crushed
3/4 cup (75 g/2 1/2 oz) grated Parmesan
1 2/3 cups (200 g/6 1/2 oz) grated Cheddar
1 kg (2 lb) tomatoes, thinly sliced

1 Cook the pasta in a large pan of rapidly boiling salted water until al dente. Drain well. Grease a 23 x 30 cm (9 x 12 inch) ovenproof dish. Stir the artichokes, olive oil, cream, thyme, garlic, half the Parmesan and 1 1/4 cups (150 g/5 oz) of the Cheddar through the hot pasta and season well. Spread evenly into the prepared dish.
2 Arrange the tomatoes over the top, overlapping. Season and sprinkle with the remaining Cheddar and Parmesan. Grill for 6 minutes to brown the top.

NUTRITION PER SERVE
Protein 33 g; Fat 56 g; Carbohydrate 69 g; Dietary Fibre 9 g; Cholesterol 137 mg; 3800 kJ (910 cal)

Cook the mince until browned, breaking up any lumps with a spoon.

Cook the sauce, stirring, until it comes to the boil and thickens.

BEEF VERMICELLI CAKE

Preparation time: 10 minutes + 10 minutes standing
Total cooking time: 50 minutes
Serves 4–6

90 g (3 oz) butter
1 onion, chopped
500 g (1 lb) beef mince
800 g (1 lb 10 oz) bottled tomato pasta sauce
2 tablespoons tomato paste
250 g (8 oz) vermicelli
1/4 cup (30 g/1 oz) plain flour
1 1/4 cups (315 ml/10 oz) milk
1 1/4 cups (150 g/5 oz) grated Cheddar

1 Preheat the oven to moderate 180°C (350°F/Gas 4). Lightly grease a 24 cm (10 inch) round deep springform tin. Melt a tablespoon of the butter in a large deep frying pan and cook the onion over medium heat for 2–3 minutes, or until soft. Add the beef mince, breaking up any lumps with the back of a spoon, and cook for 4–5 minutes, or until browned. Stir in the pasta sauce and tomato paste, reduce the heat and simmer for 20–25 minutes. Season well.
2 Cook the pasta in a large pan of rapidly boiling salted water until al dente. Drain well and rinse. Meanwhile, melt the remaining butter in a saucepan over low heat. Stir in the flour and cook for 1 minute, or until pale and foaming. Remove from the heat and gradually stir in the milk. Return to the heat and stir constantly until the sauce boils and thickens. Reduce the heat and simmer for 2 minutes.

3 Spread half the pasta over the base of the tin, then cover with half the meat sauce. Cover with the remaining pasta, pressing down with the palm of your hand. Spoon on the remaining meat sauce and then pour on the white sauce. Sprinkle with cheese and cook for 15 minutes. Leave to stand for 10 minutes before removing from the tin. Cut into wedges to serve.

NUTRITION PER SERVE (6)
Protein 34 g; Fat 32 g; Carbohydrate 47 g; Dietary Fibre 6 g; Cholesterol 121 mg; 2535 kJ (605 cal)

Top with half the bocconcini and spinach, then drizzle with cream and sprinkle with prosciutto.

Mix together the mozzarella and Parmesan and sprinkle over the lasagne.

BOCCONCINI, PROSCIUTTO AND SPINACH LASAGNE

Preparation time: 15 minutes + 10 minutes standing
Total cooking time: 25 minutes
Serves 4–6

600 g (1¼ lb) bottled tomato pasta sauce
250 g (8 oz) fresh lasagne sheets
400 g (13 oz) bocconcini, thinly sliced
500 g (1 lb) English spinach, trimmed
½ cup (125 ml/4 fl oz) cream
10 thin slices prosciutto, chopped
1 cup (150 g/5 oz) grated mozzarella
½ cup (60 g/2 oz) grated Parmesan

1 Preheat the oven to moderate 180°C (350°F/Gas 4). Lightly grease a shallow 3-litre ovenproof dish. Spread half of the tomato pasta sauce over the base of the dish. Cover with a third of the lasagne sheets. Top with half of the bocconcini and half of the spinach. Drizzle on half of the cream and sprinkle with half of the prosciutto. Season well. Repeat to give two layers, starting with half of the remaining lasagne sheets.

2 Lay the final layer of lasagne over the top and spread with the remaining pasta sauce. Sprinkle with the mozzarella and Parmesan. Bake for 25 minutes, or until cooked. Leave to stand for 10 minutes before serving for the lasagne to firm up.

NUTRITION PER SERVE (6)
Protein 35 g; Fat 30 g; Carbohydrate 31 g; Dietary Fibre 4.5 g; Cholesterol 120.5 mg; 2200 kJ (525 Cal)

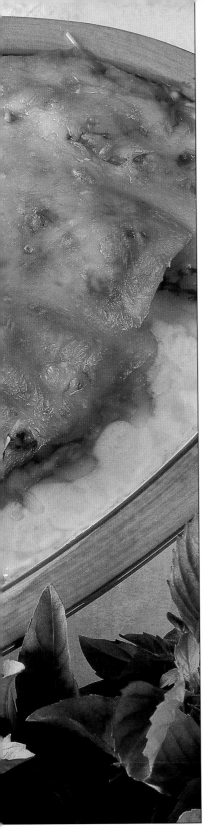

BEEF AND SPINACH CANNELLONI

Preparation time: 35 minutes
Total cooking time: 1 hour 10 minutes
Serves 4–6

FILLING
1 tablespoon olive oil
1 onion, chopped
1 clove garlic, crushed
500 g (1 lb) beef mince
250 g (8 oz) frozen spinach, thawed
3 tablespoons tomato paste
1/2 cup (125 g/4 oz) ricotta
1 egg
1/2 teaspoon ground oregano

BECHAMEL SAUCE
1 cup (250 ml/8 fl oz) milk
1 sprig fresh parsley
5 peppercorns
30 g (1 oz) butter
1 tablespoon plain flour
1/2 cup (125 ml/4 fl oz) cream

TOMATO SAUCE
425 g (14 oz) can tomato purée
2 tablespoons chopped fresh basil
1 clove garlic, crushed
1/2 teaspoon sugar

12–15 instant cannelloni tubes
1 cup (150 g/5 oz) grated mozzarella
1/2 cup (60 g/2 oz) grated Parmesan

1 Preheat the oven to moderate 180°C (350°F/Gas 4). Lightly oil a large shallow ovenproof dish. To make the filling, heat the oil in a frying pan. Add the onion and garlic and stir over low heat until the onion is tender. Add the mince and brown well, breaking up any lumps with a fork as it cooks. Add the spinach and tomato paste. Cook, stirring, for 1 minute. Remove from the heat. Mix together the ricotta, egg, oregano and some salt and pepper. Add to the mince mixture and stir well.

2 To make the Béchamel sauce, put the milk, parsley and peppercorns in a small pan. Bring to the boil. Remove from the heat and cool for 10 minutes. Strain, discarding the flavorings. Melt the butter in a small pan and stir in the flour. Cook, stirring, for 1 minute. Remove from the heat. Gradually blend in the strained milk, stirring until smooth. Return to the heat and cook, stirring constantly over medium heat, until the sauce boils and thickens. Reduce the heat and simmer for 3 minutes. Add the cream and season with salt and pepper.

3 To make the tomato sauce, put all the ingredients in a pan and bring to the boil. Reduce the heat and simmer for 5 minutes.

4 Spoon the filling into a piping bag and fill the cannelloni tubes (or fill with a teaspoon).

5 Spoon a little of the tomato sauce in the base of the dish. Arrange the cannelloni on top.

6 Pour Béchamel sauce over the cannelloni, followed by the remaining tomato sauce. Sprinkle the combined cheeses over the top. Bake for 30–35 minutes or until golden.

NUTRITION PER SERVE (6)
Protein 40 g; Fat 30 g; Carbohydrate 68 g; Dietary Fibre 9 g; Cholesterol 120 mg; 3010 kJ (720 Cal)

Cook the mushrooms in the butter over low heat for 2–3 minutes.

Stir in the ham and frozen peas and then remove from the heat to cool slightly.

BAKED SPAGHETTI FRITTATA

Preparation time: 15 minutes
Total cooking time: 35 minutes
Serves 4

30 g (1 oz) butter
125 g (4 oz) mushrooms, sliced
1 capsicum, seeded and chopped
125 g (4 oz) ham, sliced
1/2 cup (90 g/3 oz) frozen peas
6 eggs
1 cup (250 ml/8 fl oz) cream or milk
100 g (3 1/2 oz) cooked spaghetti, chopped
2 tablespoons chopped fresh parsley
3 tablespoons grated Parmesan

1 Preheat the oven to moderate 180°C (350°F/Gas 4). Grease a 23 cm (9 inch) flan dish. Melt the butter in a frying pan and add the mushrooms. Cook over low heat for 2–3 minutes.

2 Add the capsicum and cook for 1 minute. Stir in the ham and peas. Remove from the heat to cool slightly.

3 Whisk together the eggs and cream and some salt and pepper. Add the spaghetti, parsley and mushroom mixture and stir. Pour into the dish and sprinkle with Parmesan cheese. Bake for 25–30 minutes.

NUTRITION PER SERVE
Protein 23 g; Fat 38 g; Carbohydrate 23 g; Dietary Fibre 4 g; Cholesterol 110 mg; 2170 kJ (518 cal)

Cut the fish and scallops into bite-sized pieces and chop the prawns.

Slowly stir in the wine and milk and stir until the sauce is smooth.

BAKED SEAFOOD PASTA

Preparation time: 15 minutes
Total cooking time: 45 minutes
Serves 4–6

250 g (8 oz) lasagne sheets
500 g (1 lb) boneless fish fillets
125 g (4 oz) scallops, cleaned
500 g (1 lb) raw prawns, peeled and
  deveined
125 g (4 oz) butter
1 leek, sliced
²/₃ cup (90 g/3 oz) plain flour
2 cups (500 ml/16 fl oz) milk
2 cups (500 ml/16 fl oz) dry white wine
1 cup (125 g/4 oz) grated Cheddar
¹/₂ cup (125 ml/4 fl oz) cream
¹/₂ cup (60 g/2 oz) grated Parmesan
2 tablespoons chopped fresh parsley

1 Preheat the oven to moderate 180°C (350°F/Gas 4). Line a greased shallow 24 x 30 cm (10 x 12 inch) ovenproof dish with lasagne sheets, breaking them to fill any gaps. Chop the fish and scallops into even-sized pieces. Chop the prawns.

2 Melt the butter in a large pan and cook the leek, stirring, for 1 minute. Add the flour and cook, stirring, for 1 minute. Remove from the heat and slowly stir in the milk and wine until smooth. Return to medium heat and stir constantly until the sauce boils and thickens. Reduce the heat and simmer for 3 minutes. Stir in the cheese and seafood, season and simmer for 1 minute.

3 Spoon half the seafood sauce over the lasagne sheets. Top with another layer of lasagne sheets. Continue layering, finishing with lasagne sheets.

4 Pour the cream over the top. Sprinkle with the combined Parmesan and parsley and bake for 30 minutes or until bubbling and golden.

NUTRITION PER SERVE (6)

Protein 57 g; Fat 28 g; Carbohydrate 45 g; Dietary Fibre 3 g; Cholesterol 264 mg; 3000 kJ (720 cal)

Cook the mince until browned before adding the tomato, wine, stock, tomato paste and herbs.

Cook the pasta until al dente then mix with the eggs. Press into the dish.

PASTITSIO

Preparation time: 1 hour
Total cooking time: 1 hour 25 minutes
Serves 8

2 tablespoons olive oil
4 cloves garlic, crushed
3 onions, chopped
1 kg (2 lb) lamb mince
800 g (1 lb 10 oz) can crushed tomatoes
1 cup (250 ml/8 fl oz) red wine
1 cup (250 ml/8 fl oz) chicken stock
3 tablespoons tomato paste
2 tablespoons fresh oregano leaves
2 bay leaves
350 g (11 oz) ziti or spaghetti
2 eggs, lightly beaten
750 g (1½ lb) Greek-style yoghurt
3 eggs, extra, lightly beaten
200 g (6½ oz) kefalotyri or manchego
   cheese, grated (see NOTE)
½ teaspoon ground nutmeg

½ cup (50 g/1¾ oz) grated Parmesan
1 cup (80 g/2¾ oz) fresh breadcrumbs

1 Preheat the oven to moderately hot 200°C (400°F/Gas 6). To make the meat sauce, heat the oil in a large heavy-based pan and cook the garlic and onion over low heat for 10 minutes, or until the onion is soft and golden.
2 Add the mince and cook over high heat until browned, stirring constantly and breaking up any lumps. Add the tomato, wine, stock, tomato paste, oregano and bay leaves. Bring to the boil, reduce the heat and simmer, covered, for 15 minutes. Remove the lid and cook for 30 minutes. Season with salt and pepper.
3 While the meat is cooking, cook the pasta in a large pan of rapidly boiling salted water until al dente. Drain well. Transfer to a bowl and stir the eggs through. Spoon into a lightly greased 4-litre capacity ovenproof dish. Top with the meat sauce.

4 Whisk the yoghurt, extra eggs, cheese and nutmeg in a jug to combine and pour the mixture over the meat sauce. Sprinkle with the combined Parmesan and breadcrumbs. Bake for 30–35 minutes, or until the top is crisp and golden. Leave for 20 minutes before slicing.

NUTRITION PER SERVE:
Protein 50 g; Fat 40 g; Carbohydrate 45 g; Dietary Fibre 5 g; Cholesterol 250 mg; 3275 kJ (780 cal)

NOTE: Kefalotyri and manchego are firm, grating cheeses. Use Parmesan if they are unavailable.

Melt the butter in a pan and cook the onion over low heat until tender.

Add the fettucine and sour cream to the pan and simmer until well coated.

BAKED FETTUCINE

Preparation time: 20 minutes
Total cooking time: 25 minutes
Serves 4

500 g (1 lb) spinach fettucine
60 g (2 oz) butter
1 onion, finely chopped
300 g (10 oz) sour cream
1 cup (250 ml/8 fl oz) cream
1/4 teaspoon ground nutmeg
1/2 cup (60 g/2 oz) grated Parmesan
1 cup (150 g/5 oz) grated mozzarella

1 Preheat the oven to moderate 180°C (350°F/Gas 4). Cook the pasta in a large pan of rapidly boiling salted water until al dente. Drain well.
2 Meanwhile, melt the butter in a large pan and cook the onion over low heat until tender. Add the pasta. Add the sour cream and toss well. Simmer, stirring, until the pasta is well coated.
3 Stir in the cream, nutmeg and half the Parmesan and season well. Pour into a greased ovenproof dish. Sprinkle with the combined mozzarella and remaining Parmesan. Bake for 15 minutes or until golden.

NUTRITION PER SERVE (6)
Protein 30 g; Fat 55 g; Carbohydrate 92 g; Dietary Fibre 7 g; Cholesterol 133 mg; 4120 kJ (990 cal)

CHICKEN AND PUMPKIN CANNELLONI

Preparation time: 1 hour
Total cooking time: 2 hours
Serves 6

CHICKEN AND PUMPKIN FILLING
500 g (1 lb) butternut pumpkin, with skin and
    seeds
30 g (1 oz) butter
100 g (3½ oz) pancetta, roughly chopped
2 teaspoons olive oil
2 garlic cloves, crushed
500 g (1 lb) chicken thigh fillets, minced
½ teaspoon garam masala
2 tablespoons fresh flat-leaf parsley,
    chopped
150 g (5 oz) goats cheese
50 g (1¾ oz) ricotta
375 g (12 oz) fresh lasagne sheets
1 cup (100 g/3½ oz) grated Parmesan

TOMATO SAUCE
30 g (1 oz) butter
1 garlic clove, crushed
2 x 425 g (14 oz) cans crushed tomatoes
¼ cup (7 g/¼ oz) fresh flat-leaf parsley,
    chopped
¼ cup (60 ml/2 fl oz) white wine

1 Preheat the oven to hot 220°C (425°F/Gas 7).
Brush the pumpkin with 10 g (¼ oz) of the

Roughly chop the pancetta with a large knife. If you
can't find pancetta, use bacon.

butter and bake on an oven tray for 1 hour, or
until tender. When the pumpkin has cooked and
while it is still hot, remove the seeds. Scrape
out the flesh and mash it with a fork. Set aside
to cool.
2 Add another 10 g (¼ oz) of the butter to a
heavy-based frying pan and cook the pancetta
over medium heat for 2–3 minutes. Remove
from the pan and drain on paper towels.
3 In the same pan, heat the remaining butter
and olive oil. Add the garlic and stir for 30
seconds. Add the chicken in small batches and
brown, making sure the chicken is cooked
through. Set aside to cool on paper towels.
Reduce the oven temperature to moderately hot
200°C (400°F/Gas 6).
4 Combine the pumpkin with the pancetta and
chicken in a bowl. Mix in the garam marsala,
parsley, goats cheese, ricotta and some salt and
black pepper. Cut the lasagne sheets into rough
15 cm (6 inch) squares. Place 3 tablespoons of
the filling at one end of each square and roll up.
Repeat with the rest of the lasagne sheets and
filling.
5 To make the tomato sauce, melt the butter in
a heavy-based pan and add the garlic. Cook for
1 minute, add the tomatoes and simmer over
medium heat for 1 minute. Add the parsley and
white wine and simmer gently for another 5
minutes. Season, to taste.
6 Spread a little of the tomato sauce in a 3-litre
ovenproof dish and arrange the cannelloni on
top in a single layer. Spoon the remaining
tomato sauce over the cannelloni and sprinkle
with Parmesan. Bake for 20–25 minutes, or until
the cheese is golden.

NUTRITION PER SERVE (6)
Protein 44 g; Fat 26 g; Carbohydrate 55 g;
Dietary Fibre 7 g; Cholesterol 115 mg; 2670 kJ
(650 cal)

NOTE: You can use instant cannelloni tubes
instead of lasagne. Stand the tubes on end on a
chopping board and spoon in the filling.

Chop the onion and capsicum into quite small pieces and slice the zucchini.

Cover the red lentil mixture with a layer of lasagne sheets.

RED LENTIL AND RICOTTA LASAGNE

Preparation time: 30 minutes + soaking
Total cooking time: 2 hours 10 minutes
Serves 6

¹/₂ cup (125 g/4 oz) red lentils
2 teaspoons olive oil
2–3 cloves garlic, crushed
1 large onion, chopped
1 small red capsicum, chopped
2 zucchini, sliced
1 celery stalk, sliced
2 x 425 g (14 oz) cans chopped tomatoes
2 tablespoons tomato paste
1 teaspoon dried oregano
350 g (12 oz) ricotta
12 lasagne sheets
60 g (2 oz) Cheddar, grated

WHITE SAUCE
¹/₃ cup (40 g/1¹/₄ oz) cornflour
3 cups (750 ml/24 fl oz) skim milk
¹/₄ onion
¹/₂ teaspoon ground nutmeg

1 Soak the lentils in boiling water to cover, for at least 30 minutes, then drain. Meanwhile, heat the oil in a large pan, add the garlic and onion and cook for 2 minutes. Add the capsicum, zucchini and celery and cook for 2–3 minutes.
2 Add the lentils, tomato, tomato paste, oregano and 1¹/₂ cups (375 ml/ 12 fl oz) water. Bring slowly to the boil, reduce the heat and simmer for 30 minutes, or until the lentils are tender. Stir occasionally.
3 To make the white sauce, blend the cornflour with 2 tablespoons of the milk until smooth. Pour the remaining milk into the pan, add the onion and stir over low heat until the mixture boils and thickens. Add the nutmeg and pepper, then cook over low heat for 5 minutes. Remove the onion.

4 Beat the ricotta with about ¹/₂ cup (125 ml/4 fl oz) of the white sauce. Preheat the oven to moderate 180°C (350°F/Gas 4). Spread one-third of the lentil mixture over the base of a 3-litre ovenproof dish. Cover with a layer of lasagne sheets. Spread another third of the lentil mixture over the pasta, then spread the ricotta evenly over the top. Follow with another layer of lasagne, then the remaining lentils. Pour the white sauce evenly over the top and sprinkle with the grated cheese. Bake for 1 hour, covering loosely with foil if the top starts to brown too much. Leave for 5 minutes before serving.

NUTRITION PER SERVE

Protein 25 g; Fat 10 g; Carbohydrate 65 g; Dietary Fibre 9 g; Cholesterol 40 mg; 1995 kJ (475 cal)

Cook the onion and garlic until tender, then add the bacon and cook until crisp.

Spoon the risoni and cheese mixture into the capsicum halves.

PASTA-FILLED CAPSICUMS

Preparation time: 20 minutes
Total cooking time: 45 minutes
Serves 4–6

1 tablespoon olive oil
1 onion, finely chopped
1 clove garlic, crushed
3 rashers bacon, finely chopped
150 g (5 oz) risoni, cooked
1 cup (150 g/5 oz) grated mozzarella cheese
1/2 cup (60 g/2 oz) grated Parmesan
2 tablespoons chopped fresh parsley
4 large red capsicums, halved lengthways, seeds removed
425 g (14 oz) can crushed tomatoes
1/2 cup (125 ml/4 fl oz) dry white wine
1 tablespoon tomato paste
1/2 teaspoon ground oregano
2 tablespoons chopped fresh basil

1 Preheat the oven to moderate 180°C (350°F/Gas 4). Lightly grease a large shallow ovenproof dish. Heat the oil in a pan and cook the onion and garlic over low heat until tender. Add the bacon and stir until crisp.
2 Transfer to a large bowl and add the risoni, cheeses and parsley. Spoon into the capsicum halves and arrange in the dish.
3 Combine the tomatoes, wine, tomato paste and oregano. Season and spoon over the risoni mixture. Sprinkle with basil. Bake for 35–40 minutes.

NUTRITION PER SERVE (6)
Protein 18 g; Fat 13 g; Carbohydrate 24 g; Dietary Fibre 4 g; Cholesterol 32 mg; 1250 kJ (300 cal)

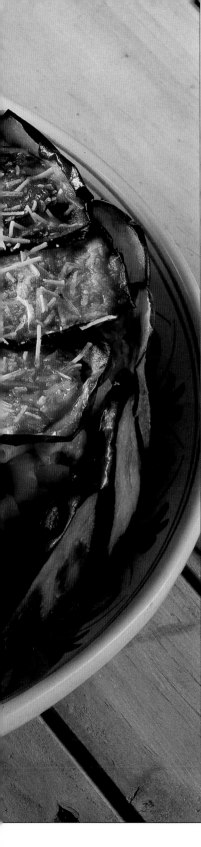

MACARONI EGGPLANT BAKE

**Preparation time: 30 minutes +
    20 minutes resting**
Total cooking time: 1 hour
Serves 4–6

125 g (4 oz) macaroni
2–3 eggplants, sliced thinly lengthways
salt
olive oil
1 onion, chopped
1 clove garlic, crushed
500 g (1 lb) pork, beef or chicken mince
425 g (14 oz) can crushed tomatoes
2 tablespoons tomato paste
1/2 cup (150 g/5 oz) frozen peas
1 cup (150 g/5 oz) grated mozzarella
1/2 cup (60 g/2 oz) grated Cheddar
1 egg, beaten
1/2 cup (60 g/2 oz) grated Parmesan

1 Grease and line a deep 23 cm (9 inch) round springform tin. Cook the pasta in a large pan of rapidly boiling salted water until al dente. Drain well and return to the pan to keep warm. Arrange the eggplant in a large colander and sprinkle generously with salt. Leave for 20 minutes, then rinse well. Pat dry with paper towels. Heat 2 tablespoons of the oil in a frying pan and fry the eggplant in batches in a single layer until golden on each side. Add more oil as required. Drain on paper towels.

2 Add the onion and garlic to the same pan and stir over low heat until tender. Add the mince and cook, breaking up any lumps with a spoon or fork, until browned. Add the tomatoes, tomato paste and salt and pepper and stir well. Bring to the boil. Reduce the heat and simmer for 15–20 minutes, then set aside.

3 Mix together the peas, macaroni, mozzarella and Cheddar cheeses, egg and half the Parmesan.

4 Preheat the oven to moderate 180°C (350°F/Gas 4). Place a slice of eggplant in the centre of the tin. Arrange three-quarters of the remaining eggplant in an overlapping pattern to completely cover the base and side of the tin. Sprinkle with half the remaining Parmesan cheese.

5 Combine the mince with the macaroni mixture. Carefully spoon filling into the eggplant shell, packing down well. Arrange the remaining eggplant slices, overlapping, over the filling. Sprinkle with the remaining Parmesan cheese.

6 Bake for 25–30 minutes or until golden. Leave for 5 minutes before unmoulding onto a serving plate.

NUTRITION PER SERVE (6)

Protein 40 g; Fat 22 g; Carbohydrate 20 g; Dietary Fibre 5 g; Cholesterol 120 mg; 1866 kJ (446 cal)

VARIATIONS: If preferred, omit the mince and add chopped cooked Italian sausage and chopped cooked chicken to the tomato mixture.

Salt the eggplant to draw out any bitterness, then fry in a single layer until golden.

Brown the mince and then add the crushed tomatoes and tomato paste.

Let the mixture cool for a while before you add the eggs and cream.

Make a water bath by putting the moulds in a roasting tin of boiling water.

PASTA AND SPINACH TIMBALES

Preparation time: 15 minutes
Total cooking time: 40 minutes
Serves 6

30 g (1 oz) butter
1 tablespoon olive oil
1 onion, chopped
500 g (1 lb) English spinach, cooked
8 eggs, beaten
1 cup (250 ml/8 fl oz) cream
100 g (3½ oz) spaghetti, cooked
½ cup (60 g/2 oz) grated Cheddar
½ cup (60 g/2 oz) grated Parmesan

1 Preheat the oven to moderate 180°C (350°F/Gas 4). Brush six 1-cup (250 ml/8 fl oz) moulds with melted butter or oil. Line the bases with baking paper. Heat the butter and oil together in a frying pan. Add the onion and stir over low heat until tender. Add the well-drained spinach and cook for 1 minute. Remove from the heat and allow to cool. Whisk in the eggs and cream. Stir in the spaghetti, grated cheeses and salt and pepper; stir well. Spoon into the moulds.

2 Place the moulds in a roasting tin. Pour boiling water into the tin to come halfway up the sides of the moulds. Bake for 30–35 minutes or until set. Halfway through cooking, you may need to cover with a sheet of foil to prevent overbrowning. Near the end of cooking time, test the timbales with the point of a knife—the knife should come out clean.

3 Allow the timbales to rest for 15 minutes, then run the point of a knife around the edge of each mould and unmould onto serving plates.

NUTRITION PER SERVE

Protein 16 g; Fat 20 g; Carbohydrate 13 g; Dietary Fibre 2 g; Cholesterol 260 mg; 1280 kJ (300 cal)

Cook the pasta and drain well, then spread in the ovenproof dish.

Cook the onion and pancetta in the oil and then add the ham.

PASTA PIE

Preparation time: 15 minutes
Total cooking time: 55 minutes
Serves 4

250 g (8 oz) macaroni
1 tablespoon olive oil
1 onion, sliced
125 g (4 oz) pancetta, chopped
125 g (4 oz) ham, chopped
4 eggs
1 cup (250 ml/8 fl oz) milk
1 cup (250 ml/8 fl oz) cream
2 tablespoons snipped chives
1 cup (120 g/4 oz) grated Cheddar
125 g (4 oz) bocconcini, chopped

1 Preheat the oven to moderate 180°C (350°F/Gas 4). Cook the pasta in a large pan of rapidly boiling salted water until al dente. Drain well. Spread evenly in the base of a deep ovenproof dish.

2 Heat the oil in a large pan and cook the onion over low heat until tender. Add the pancetta and cook for 2 minutes. Add the ham and stir well. Remove from the heat to cool.

3 Whisk together the eggs, milk, cream, chives and some salt and pepper. Add the Cheddar cheese, chopped bocconcini and the pancetta mixture and stir well. Spread evenly over the macaroni. Bake for 35–40 minutes or until set.

NUTRITION PER SERVE
Protein 50 g; Fat 70 g; Carbohydrate 50 g; Dietary Fibre 4 g; Cholesterol 386 mg; 4300 kJ (1027 Cal)

HINT: Serve with slices of egg tomato.

LOW-FAT CHICKEN AND VEGETABLE LASAGNE

Preparation time: 45 minutes
Total cooking time: 1 hour 20 minutes
Serves 8

500 g (1 lb) chicken breast fillets
cooking oil spray
2 cloves garlic, crushed
1 onion, chopped
2 zucchini, chopped
2 celery stalks, chopped
2 carrots, chopped
300 g (10 oz) pumpkin, diced
2 x 400 g (13 oz) cans crushed tomatoes
2 sprigs fresh thyme
2 bay leaves
$\frac{1}{2}$ cup (125 ml/4 fl oz) white wine
2 tablespoons tomato paste
2 tablespoons chopped fresh basil
500 g (1 lb) English spinach
500 g (1 lb) cottage cheese
450 g (14 oz) ricotta
$\frac{1}{4}$ cup (60 ml/2 fl oz) skim milk
$\frac{1}{2}$ teaspoon ground nutmeg
$\frac{1}{3}$ cup (35 g/1$\frac{1}{4}$ oz) grated Parmesan
300 g (10 oz) lasagne sheets

1 Preheat the oven to moderate 180°C (350°F/Gas 4). Trim any excess fat from the chicken breasts, then finely mince in a food processor. Heat a large, deep, non-stick frying pan, spray lightly with oil and cook the chicken mince in batches until browned. Remove and set aside.

2 Add the garlic and onion to the pan and cook until softened. Return the chicken to the pan and add the zucchini, celery, carrot, pumpkin, tomato, thyme, bay leaves, wine and tomato paste. Simmer, covered, for 20 minutes. Remove the bay leaves and thyme, stir in the fresh basil and set aside.

3 Shred the spinach and set aside. Mix the cottage cheese, ricotta, skim milk, nutmeg and half the Parmesan.

4 Spoon a little of the tomato mixture over the base of a casserole dish and top with a single layer of pasta. Top with half the remaining tomato mixture, then the spinach and spoon over half the cottage cheese mixture. Continue with another layer of pasta, the remaining tomato and another layer of pasta. Spread the remaining cottage cheese mixture on top and sprinkle with Parmesan. Bake for 40–50 minutes, or until golden. The top may puff up slightly but will settle on standing.

NUTRITION PER SERVE
Protein 40 g; Fat 10 g; Carbohydrate 35 g; Dietary Fibre 7 g; Cholesterol 70 mg; 1790 kJ (430 cal)

Finely mince the trimmed chicken fillets in a food processor.

Add the vegetables with the bay leaves, thyme, wine and tomato paste to the pan.

Add the milk to the sauce slowly, stirring until smooth before returning to the heat.

Spoon the pasta, egg and cheese into the dishes and then sprinkle with cheese.

BAKED MACARONI WITH BUTTER SAUCE

Preparation time: 15 minutes + 5 minutes resting
Total cooking time: 40 minutes
Serves 4

200 g (6¹/₂ oz) macaroni
150 g (5 oz) butter
¹/₄ cup (30 g/1 oz) plain flour
2¹/₂ cups (600 ml/20 fl oz) milk
1 egg, lightly beaten
1¹/₂ cups (185 g/6 oz) grated Cheddar
2 cloves garlic, crushed
2 ripe tomatoes, seeded and diced

1 Preheat the oven to moderate 180°C (350°F/Gas 4). Lightly grease four shallow 1-cup (250 ml/8 fl oz) ovenproof dishes. Cook the pasta in a large pan of rapidly boiling salted water until al dente. Drain well and return to the pan to keep warm. Meanwhile, melt 60 g (2 oz) of the butter in a large saucepan, add the flour and cook, stirring, over low heat for 1 minute. Remove from the heat and gradually add the milk, stirring until smooth. Return to the heat and cook, stirring, over medium heat for 4 minutes, or until the mixture boils and thickens. Reduce the heat and simmer for 1 minute. Remove from the heat and season well.

2 Add the pasta, egg and two-thirds of the cheese and stir until well combined. Spoon into the dishes and sprinkle with the remaining cheese. Place in a roasting tin and pour enough boiling water into the tin to come halfway up the sides of the dishes. Bake for 25 minutes, or until set. Remove from the roasting tin and leave to rest for 5 minutes.

3 To make the sauce, melt the remaining butter in a frying pan. Add the garlic and tomato and stir over medium heat for 2 minutes. Unmould the baked macaroni onto plates and spoon the warm sauce around the outside. Serve immediately.

NUTRITION PER SERVE

Protein 26 g; Fat 57 g; Carbohydrate 50 g; Dietary Fibre 4 g; Cholesterol 215 mg; 3385 kJ (810 cal)

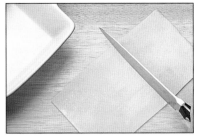

Cut the lasagne sheets to fit the bases of the pre-pared dishes.

Drizzle the tomato and mushrooms with the oil and thyme and bake until soft.

INDIVIDUAL SPINACH AND LEEK LASAGNES

Preparation time: 20 minutes
Total cooking time: 45 minutes
Serves 4

8 fresh lasagne sheets
8 Roma tomatoes, halved
4 large field mushrooms, stalks removed
¹/₃ cup (80 ml/2³/₄ fl oz) olive oil
1 tablespoon chopped fresh thyme
60 g (2 oz) butter
2 large leeks, finely sliced
2 cloves garlic, crushed
500 g (1 lb) packet frozen chopped English
    spinach, thawed
1 cup (250 g/8 oz) light sour cream
1 cup (250 g/8 oz) light cream
600 g (1¹/₄ lb) ricotta
1 egg, lightly beaten
1 cup (125 g/4 oz) grated Cheddar

1 Preheat the oven to moderately hot 200°C (400°F/Gas 6). Lightly grease four 2-cup (500 ml/16 fl oz) ovenproof dishes. Cut half the lasagne sheets to fit the bases of the dishes.
2 Place the tomatoes and mushrooms face down in a baking dish. Mix together the oil and thyme and drizzle over the tomato and mushroom. Season. Bake for 15 minutes, then turn over and bake for another 10 minutes, or until softened. Roughly chop.
3 Heat the butter in a frying pan, add the leek and garlic and cook over medium heat for 2–3 minutes, or until soft. Squeeze the liquid from the spinach and add to the leek mixture with the sour cream and cream. Stir well, bring to the boil and cook for 5 minutes, or until reduced slightly. Stir in the tomato and mushroom.
4 Spoon half the spinach and leek mixture into the dishes. Cover with the remaining lasagne sheets and repeat with the remaining mixture. Spread with the combined ricotta and egg and sprinkle with Cheddar. Bake for 20 minutes, or until golden.

NUTRITION PER SERVE
Protein 60 g; Fat 20 g; Carbohydrate 60 g; Dietary Fibre 23 g; Cholesterol 435 mg; 5833 kJ (1393 cal)

Finely chop the prosciutto, chives and basil in a food processor.

Melt the butter in a large frying pan and cook the prosciutto mixture for 5 minutes.

BAKED SHELLS WITH RICOTTA AND PROSCIUTTO

Preparation time: 15 minutes
Total cooking time: 45 minutes
Serves 4–6

24 conchiglione (large pasta shells)
200 g (6¹/₂ oz) prosciutto, roughly chopped
2 tablespoons chopped chives
1 cup (60 g/2 oz) chopped fresh basil
90 g (3 oz) butter
500 g (1 lb) ricotta
1 cup (150 g/5 oz) chopped sun-dried
  capsicum
1 cup (100 g/3¹/₂ oz) grated Parmesan
3 cups (750 g/1¹/₂ lb) bottled tomato pasta
  sauce

1 Preheat the oven to moderate 180°C (350°F/Gas 4). Cook the pasta in a large pan of rapidly boiling salted water until al dente. Drain well and return to the pan to keep warm. Place the prosciutto, chives and basil in a food processor or blender and pulse until chopped.
2 Melt the butter in a large frying pan over medium heat. Add the prosciutto mixture and cook for about 5 minutes, or until the prosciutto is golden and crisp. Transfer the mixture to a bowl, add the ricotta, capsicum and a quarter of the Parmesan. Stir well and season to taste.
3 Pour the pasta sauce into a 3-litre ovenproof dish. Spoon the ricotta mixture into the pasta shells and place in the dish. Sprinkle the remaining Parmesan over the shells and bake for 25–30 minutes, or until golden. Spoon the sauce over the shells and serve.

NUTRITION PER SERVE (6)
Protein 27 g; Fat 28 g; Carbohydrate 32 g; Dietary Fibre 4.5 g; Cholesterol 107 mg; 2040 kJ (485 cal)

Use a teaspoon to fill the cannelloni tubes with the mince mixture.

Cook the tomato sauce for 15 minutes before adding the chopped basil.

BAKED CANNELLONI MILANESE

Preparation time: 20 minutes
Total cooking time: 1 hour 50 minutes
Serves 4

500 g (1 lb) pork and veal mince
1/2 cup (60 g/2 oz) dry breadcrumbs
1 cup (120 g/4 oz) grated Parmesan
2 eggs, beaten
1 teaspoon dried oregano
12–15 cannelloni tubes
375 g (12 oz) ricotta
1/2 cup (60 g/2 oz) grated Cheddar

TOMATO SAUCE
425 g (14 oz) can crushed tomatoes
425 g (14 oz) can tomatoes
2 cloves garlic, crushed
1/4 cup (15 g/1/2 oz) chopped fresh basil

1 Preheat the oven to moderate 180°C (350°F/Gas 4). Lightly grease a shallow ovenproof dish. Mix together the mince, breadcrumbs, half the Parmesan cheese, the beaten egg, oregano and some salt and pepper. Use a teaspoon to stuff the mixture into the cannelloni tubes.
2 To make the tomato sauce, put the tomatoes and garlic in a pan and bring to the boil. Reduce the heat and simmer for 15 minutes. Add the basil and some black pepper and stir well.
3 Spoon half the sauce over the base of the dish.
4 Arrange the cannelloni tubes on top of the sauce. Cover with the remaining sauce. Spread with the ricotta and sprinkle with the Cheddar and remaining Parmesan. Bake, covered with foil, for 1 hour. Uncover and bake for another 15 minutes or until golden. Cut into squares for serving.

NUTRITION PER SERVE
Protein 80 g; Fat 38 g; Carbohydrate 100 g; Dietary Fibre 10 g; Cholesterol 250 mg; 4540 kJ (1084 cal)

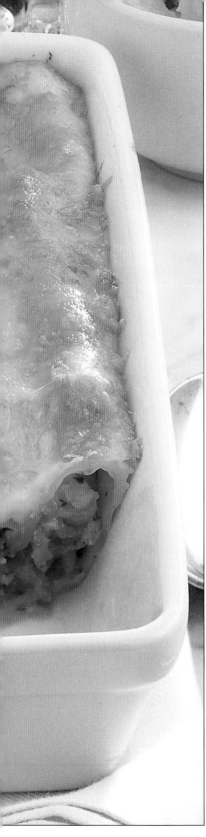

SEAFOOD CANNELLONI

Preparation time: 30 minutes
Total cooking time: 1 hour 55 minutes
Serves 6

1 onion, sliced
1 carrot, sliced
1 celery stalk, cut in half
1 bouquet garni
1 cup (250 ml/8 fl oz) white wine
4 whole black peppercorns
300 g (10 oz) scallops
500 g (1 lb) raw prawns
300 g (10 oz) skinless fish fillets (e.g.
    flathead, flake, hake, ling, cod), boned and
    chopped
60 g (2 oz) butter
1 onion, finely chopped
200 g (6½ oz) button mushrooms, finely
    chopped
2 x 400 g (13 oz) cans crushed tomatoes
2 tablespoons chopped fresh parsley
2 tablespoons chopped fresh basil
2 tablespoons cream
15 cannelloni tubes
125 g (4 oz) Cheddar, grated

BECHAMEL SAUCE
60 g (2 oz) butter
2 tablespoons plain flour
3 cups (750 ml/24 fl oz) milk

Cut all the seafood into pieces small enough to fit
in the cannelloni tubes.

1 Preheat the oven to moderate 180°C
(350°F/Gas 4). Combine the onion, carrot,
celery, bouquet garni and 2 cups (500 ml/16 fl
oz) water in a large pan and bring to the boil.
Reduce the heat and simmer for 15 minutes.
Add the wine and peppercorns and simmer for
15 minutes. Strain, discard the vegetables and
reserve the liquid.

2 Meanwhile, slice or pull off any vein,
membrane or hard white muscle from the
scallops, leaving any roe attached. Dice the
scallops. Peel the prawns and gently pull out the
dark vein from each prawn back, starting at the
head end, and roughly dice the prawn meat. Cut
the seafood small enough to fit in the cannelloni
tubes.

3 Put the reserved liquid in a clean pan and
bring to the boil. Add the seafood. Reduce the
heat and simmer for 3 minutes, or until tender.
Strain and reserve the liquid.

4 Melt the butter in a large frying pan, add the
onion and cook over medium heat until golden
brown. Add the mushrooms and cook until
tender. Add ¼ cup (60 ml/2 fl oz) of the
reserved liquid, the tomato and herbs and bring
to the boil. Reduce the heat and simmer for 30
minutes, or until the sauce thickens slightly. Stir
in the seafood and cream and season with salt
and pepper to taste.

5 For the Béchamel sauce, melt the butter in a
saucepan, add the flour and stir for 1 minute, or
until pale and foaming. Remove from the heat
and gradually stir in the milk. Return to the heat
and stir until the sauce comes to the boil and
thickens.

6 Spoon the seafood mixture into the
cannelloni tubes and place in a greased 3-litre
ovenproof dish. Pour the sauce over the top and
sprinkle with the grated cheese. Bake for 40
minutes, or until the cannelloni tubes are tender.

NUTRITION PER SERVE
Protein 56 g; Fat 35 g; Carbohydrate 76 g;
Dietary Fibre 8 g; Cholesterol 274 mg; 3638 kJ
(869 cal)

Make a collar for the soufflé dish by tying a strip of foil around the outside.

Add the macaroni, salmon, parsley, lemon rind and some salt and pepper.

PASTA SOUFFLE

Preparation time: 20 minutes
Total cooking time: 55 minutes
Serves 4

2 tablespoons grated Parmesan
60 g (2 oz) butter
1 small onion, finely chopped
2 tablespoons plain flour
2 cups (500 ml/16 fl oz) milk
1/2 cup (125 ml/4 fl oz) chicken stock
3 eggs, separated
125 g (4 oz) small macaroni, cooked
210 g (7 oz) can salmon, drained and flaked
1 tablespoon chopped fresh parsley
grated rind of 1 lemon

1 Preheat the oven to hot 210°C (415°F/Gas 6–7). Brush a round 18 cm (7 inch) soufflé dish with oil. Coat the base and sides with Parmesan, shaking off the excess. Make a collar for the dish by cutting a piece of aluminium foil or greaseproof paper a little longer than the circumference of the dish. Fold the foil in half lengthways and wrap around the outside of the dish so that it extends 5 cm (2 inches) above the rim. Secure with string.

2 Heat the butter in a large pan and cook the onion over low heat until tender. Add the flour. Stir for 2 minutes or until lightly golden. Remove from heat and gradually stir in the milk and stock until smooth. Return to the heat and stir constantly until the mixture boils and thickens. Reduce the heat and simmer for 3 minutes. Add the egg yolks and whisk until smooth. Add the macaroni, salmon, parsley, lemon rind and some salt and pepper. Stir well and transfer to a bowl to cool.

3 Beat the egg whites in a small dry bowl until stiff peaks form. Using a metal spoon, fold gently into the salmon mixture. Spoon into the soufflé dish. Bake for 40–45 minutes or until well risen. Serve immediately.

NUTRITION PER SERVE
Protein 27 g; Fat 26 g; Carbohydrate 34 g; Dietary Fibre 2 g; Cholesterol 200 mg; 1994 kJ (476 cal)

STORAGE: Hot soufflés should be served immediately as they will collapse very quickly after removal from the oven. The base mixture can be prepared, up to the end of Step 2, well in advance. Soften the mixture before folding in beaten egg whites. The whites should be folded into the mixture just before cooking so they don't lose their volume.

Form heaped teaspoons of the mixture into small meatballs.

Fry the meatballs until they are well browned, then drain on paper towels.

BAKED MEATBALLS AND PASTA

Preparation time: 25 minutes
Total cooking time: 1 hour
Serves 4

100 g (3½ oz) macaroni
500 g (1 lb) beef mince
1 onion, finely chopped
2 tablespoons grated Parmesan
1 tablespoon chopped fresh basil
1 egg, beaten
1 cup (90 g/3 oz) fresh breadcrumbs
2 tablespoons olive oil
1 cup (150 g/5 oz) grated mozzarella

SAUCE
1 onion, sliced
1 clove garlic, crushed
1 capsicum, seeded and sliced
125 g (4 oz) mushrooms, sliced
3 tablespoons tomato paste
½ cup (125 ml/4 fl oz) red wine

1 Cook the pasta in a large pan of rapidly boiling salted water until al dente. Drain well and return to the pan to keep warm. Mix together the mince, onion, Parmesan, basil, egg and half the breadcrumbs. Form heaped teaspoons of the mixture into balls.
2 Heat the oil in a frying pan and cook the meatballs until well browned. Drain on paper towels. Transfer to an ovenproof dish. Preheat the oven to moderate 180°C (350°F/Gas 4).

3 To make the sauce, add the onion and garlic to the same pan and stir over low heat until tender. Add the capsicum and mushrooms and cook for 2 minutes. Stir in the tomato paste. Add 1 cup (250 ml/8 fl oz) water and the wine and bring to the boil. Mix in the macaroni and salt and pepper. Pour over the meatballs.
4 Bake for 30–35 minutes. Sprinkle with the mozzarella cheese and remaining breadcrumbs. Bake for another 10 minutes or until golden.

NUTRITION PER SERVE
Protein 44 g; Fat 34 g; Carbohydrate 38 g; Dietary Fibre 4 g; Cholesterol 150 mg; 2740 kJ (650 cal)

238

Pasta Salads

FARFALLE SALAD WITH SUN-DRIED TOMATOES AND SPINACH

Preparation time: 20 minutes
Total cooking time: 15 minutes
Serves 4–6

500 g (1 lb) farfalle or spiral pasta
3 spring onions
60 g (2 oz) sun-dried tomatoes, cut into
    strips
500 g (1 lb) English spinach, trimmed and
    shredded
1/3 cup (50 g/1 3/4 oz) pine nuts, toasted
1 tablespoon chopped fresh oregano

DRESSING
3 tablespoons olive oil
1 teaspoon fresh chopped chilli
1 clove garlic, crushed

1 Cook the pasta in a large pan of rapidly boiling salted water until al dente. Drain well and rinse under cold water. Transfer to a large salad bowl. Trim the spring onions and chop finely. Add to the pasta with the tomato, spinach, pine nuts and fresh oregano.
2 To make the dressing, put the oil, chilli and garlic in a small screw-top jar and add salt and pepper to taste. Shake well.
3 Pour the dressing over the salad, toss well and serve immediately.

NUTRITION PER SERVE (6)
Protein 12 g; Fat 8 g; Carbohydrate 60 g; Dietary Fibre 6 g; Cholesterol 0 mg; 1490 kJ (357 cal)

Put the dressing ingredients in a screw-top jar so you can mix them together by shaking.

Pour the dressing over the salad and then toss together before serving.

Slice the chargrilled red capsicum into very thin strips.

Process all the dressing ingredients together until well blended and smooth.

ITALIAN-STYLE PRAWN AND PASTA SALAD

Preparation time: 15 minutes
Total cooking time: 15 minutes
Serves 4

DRESSING
1/3 cup (80 ml/2 3/4 fl oz) olive oil
1 1/2 tablespoons white wine vinegar
1 1/2 tablespoons pine nuts, toasted
1 tablespoon roughly chopped fresh basil
1 tablespoon roughly chopped fresh flat-leaf
  parsley
1 clove garlic
1 tablespoon grated Parmesan
pinch of sugar

400 g (13 oz) large pasta shells
1 tablespoon olive oil, extra
500 g (1 lb) small cooked prawns
100 g (3 1/2 oz) bocconcini, thinly sliced
125 g (4 oz) chargrilled red capsicum, cut
  into thin strips
125 g (4 oz) cherry tomatoes, halved
fresh basil leaves, to garnish

1 For the dressing, process all the ingredients together in a blender or food processor until smooth.
2 Cook the pasta in a large pan of rapidly boiling salted water until al dente. Drain well, return to the pan and toss with the extra olive oil. Allow to cool.
3 Peel the prawns and gently pull out the dark vein from each prawn back, starting at the head end.
4 Put the pasta, prawns, bocconcini, capsicum and tomatoes in a serving bowl and pour on the dressing. Toss together well and garnish with basil leaves to serve.

NUTRITION PER SERVE
Protein 51 g; Fat 35 g; Carbohydrate 73 g; Dietary Fibre 7 g; Cholesterol 257 mg; 3420 kJ (815 cal)

Use two wooden spoons to toss the pesto through the drained pasta.

Fry the drained capers in the hot oil, stirring occasionally, until crisp.

WARM PESTO AND PRAWN SALAD

Preparation time: 15 minutes
Total cooking time: 20 minutes
Serves 4

PESTO
2 cloves garlic, crushed
1 teaspoon salt
¼ cup (40 g/1¼ oz) pine nuts, toasted
2 cups (60 g/2 oz) fresh basil
½ cup (60 g/2 oz) grated Parmesan
¼ cup (60 ml/2 fl oz) extra virgin olive oil

500 g (1 lb) pasta
150 g (5 oz) jar capers in brine
3 tablespoons olive oil
2 tablespoons extra virgin olive oil
2 cloves garlic, chopped
2 tomatoes, seeded and diced
150 g (5 oz) thin asparagus, trimmed, halved and blanched

2 tablespoons balsamic vinegar
150 g (5 oz) rocket
20 cooked prawns, peeled, tails intact
shaved Parmesan, to garnish

1 For the pesto, blend the garlic, salt, pine nuts, fresh basil leaves and grated Parmesan in a food processor or blender until thoroughly combined. With the motor running, add the oil in a thin steady stream and process until the pesto is smooth.
2 Cook the pasta in a large pan of rapidly boiling salted water until al dente. Drain well, transfer to a large bowl and toss the pesto through.
3 Pat the drained capers dry with paper towels, then heat the olive oil in a frying pan and fry the capers for 4–5 minutes, stirring occasionally, until crisp. Drain on paper towels.
4 Heat the extra virgin olive oil in a deep frying pan over medium heat and add the garlic, tomatoes and asparagus. Toss continuously for 1–2 minutes, or until warmed through. Stir in the balsamic vinegar.

5 When the pasta is just warm, not hot (or it will wilt the rocket), toss the tomato mixture, rocket and prawns with the pasta and season with salt and pepper, to taste. Serve sprinkled with capers and shaved Parmesan.

NUTRITION PER SERVE
Protein 42 g; Fat 52 g; Carbohydrate 92 g; Dietary Fibre 10 g; Cholesterol 163 mg; 4195 kJ (1000 cal)

When the capsicum has cooled, peel away the skin and dice the flesh.

Cook the steak in a non-stick frying pan until it is medium-rare.

PESTO BEEF SALAD

Preparation time: 30 minutes
Total cooking time: 25 minutes
Serves 4

100 g (3½ oz) button mushrooms
1 large yellow capsicum
1 large red capsicum
cooking oil spray
100 g (3½ oz) lean fillet steak
1½ cups (125 g/4 oz) penne

PESTO
1 cup (50 g/1¾ oz) tightly packed fresh basil
   leaves
2 cloves garlic, chopped
2 tablespoons pepitas (pumpkin seeds)
1 tablespoon olive oil
2 tablespoons orange juice
1 tablespoon lemon juice

1 Cut the mushrooms into quarters. Cut the capsicums into quarters, discarding the seeds and membrane. Grill the capsicum, skin-side-up, until the skins blacken and blister. Cool under a damp tea towel, then peel and dice the flesh.

2 Spray a non-stick frying pan with oil and cook the steak over high heat for 3–4 minutes each side. Remove and leave for 5 minutes before cutting into thin slices. Season with a little salt.

3 To make the pesto, finely chop the basil leaves, garlic and pepitas in a food processor. With the motor running, add the oil, orange and lemon juice. Season well.

4 Meanwhile, cook the pasta in a large pan of rapidly boiling salted water until al dente. Drain well and toss with the pesto in a large bowl.

5 Add the capsicum pieces, steak slices and mushroom quarters to the penne and toss to distribute evenly. Serve immediately.

NUTRITION PER SERVE
Protein 15 g; Fat 10 g; Carbohydrate 30 g; Dietary Fibre 4 g; Cholesterol 15 mg; 1330 kJ (270 cal)

Add the spinach and mushrooms to the leek and capsicum and cook until the spinach wilts.

Gradually whisk the oil into the combined garlic, cumin, coriander and vinegar.

PASTA AND BEAN SALAD WITH CUMIN AND CORIANDER DRESSING

Preparation time: 25 minutes
Total cooking time: 15 minutes
Serves 6

300 g (10 oz) spiral pasta
2 tablespoons sunflower oil
1 leek, sliced
1 red capsicum, seeded and diced
2 cups (125 g/4 oz) finely shredded English
  spinach
150 g (5 oz) button mushrooms, halved
300 g (10 oz) can red kidney beans, rinsed
  and drained
300 g (10 oz) can butter beans, rinsed and
  drained
2 tablespoons snipped chives
1/2 teaspoon coarsely ground black pepper
60 g (2 oz) sunflower seeds, toasted

CUMIN AND CORIANDER DRESSING
2 cloves garlic, crushed
1/2 teaspoon ground cumin
1/2 teaspoon ground coriander
2 tablespoons cider vinegar
1/2 cup (125 ml/4 fl oz) olive oil

1 Cook the pasta in a large pan of rapidly boiling salted water until al dente. Drain well.
2 Heat the oil in a large pan, add the leek and capsicum and stir-fry over medium heat for 2–3 minutes. Add the spinach and mushrooms and toss together for about 1 minute, or until the spinach just wilts.
3 To make the dressing, mix the garlic, cumin, coriander and vinegar together. Gradually add the olive oil and whisk to combine.
4 Toss together the pasta, vegetables, beans, chives and black pepper. Toss with the dressing and sprinkle with the sunflower seeds to serve.

NUTRITION PER SERVE

Protein 15 g; Fat 30 g; Carbohydrate 45 g; Dietary Fibre 10 g; Cholesterol 0 mg; 2215 kJ (525 cal)

Drain the cooked pasta and spread on a tray to dry and cool.

Remove the seeds and white membrane from the capsicums and cut into large pieces.

MEDITERRANEAN PASTA SALAD WITH BLACK OLIVE DRESSING

Preparation time: 30 minutes
Total cooking time: 25 minutes
Serves 4

250 g (8 oz) spiral pasta
1 red capsicum
1 yellow or green capsicum
1 tablespoon sunflower oil
2 tablespoons olive oil
2 cloves garlic, crushed
1 eggplant, cubed
2 zucchini, thickly sliced
2 large ripe tomatoes, peeled, seeded and
    chopped (see NOTE)
¼ cup (7 g/¼ oz) chopped fresh flat-leaf
    parsley
1 teaspoon seasoned pepper
150 g (5 oz) feta cheese, crumbled

BLACK OLIVE DRESSING
6 large marinated black olives, pitted
½ cup (125 ml/4 fl oz) olive oil
2 tablespoons balsamic vinegar

1 Cook the pasta in a large pan of rapidly boiling salted water until al dente. Drain well, spread in a single layer on a baking tray to dry, then refrigerate, uncovered, until chilled.
2 Cut the red and yellow capsicum into large pieces, removing the seeds and membrane. Place, skin-side-up, under a hot grill until the skin blackens and blisters. Leave under a tea towel to cool, then peel away the skin. Slice the flesh into thick strips.
3 Heat the sunflower and olive oil in a frying pan. Add the garlic and eggplant and fry quickly, tossing, until lightly browned. Remove from the heat and place in a large bowl. Steam the zucchini for 1–2 minutes, or until just tender. Rinse under cold water, drain and add to the eggplant.

4 To make the dressing, process the olives in a food processor until finely chopped. Gradually add the olive oil, processing until thoroughly combined after each addition. Add the vinegar, season and process to combine.
5 Combine the pasta, capsicum, eggplant, zucchini, tomato, parsley and pepper in a large bowl. Top with the feta and drizzle with the dressing.

NUTRITION PER SERVE
Protein 15 g; Fat 55 g; Carbohydrate 50 g; Dietary Fibre 8 g; Cholesterol 25 mg; 3220 kJ (765 cal)

NOTE: To peel tomatoes, score a cross in the base of each tomato. Leave in a pan of boiling water for 1 minute, then plunge into cold water. Peel the skin away from the cross. To remove the seeds, cut the tomato in half and scoop out the seeds with a teaspoon.

Grate the cheese, chop the asparagus and finely slice the spring onion.

Pour the stock over the chicken and poach over low heat, turning regularly.

CHICKEN AND PASTA SALAD

Preparation time: 30 minutes
Total cooking time: 25 minutes
Serves 4

250 g (8 oz) chicken breast fillet
1½ cups (375 ml/12 fl oz) chicken stock
350 g (11 oz) spiral pasta
150 g (5 oz) asparagus, cut into short
   lengths
150 g (5 oz) Gruyère cheese, grated
2 spring onions, finely sliced

DRESSING
¼ cup (60 ml/2 fl oz) olive oil
¼ cup (60 ml/2 fl oz) lemon juice
½ teaspoon sugar

1 Put the chicken and stock in a frying pan. Bring to the boil, reduce the heat and poach gently, turning regularly, for 8 minutes, or until tender. Remove, cool and slice thinly.
2 Cook the pasta in a large pan of rapidly boiling salted water until al dente. Drain well and cool.
3 Cook the asparagus in boiling water for 2 minutes. Drain and place in a bowl of iced water. Drain again. Combine with the chicken, pasta and cheese in a large bowl.
4 To make the dressing, whisk the ingredients together. Season with salt and pepper. Add to the salad and toss well. Transfer to a serving bowl and scatter with the spring onions.

NUTRITION PER SERVE
Protein 40 g; Fat 30 g; Carbohydrate 60 g; Dietary Fibre 5 g; Cholesterol 70 mg; 2785 kJ (665 cal)

Cut the broccoli into small florets and the other vegetables into strips.

Cook the carrot, broccoli and capsicum in boiling water for 30 seconds.

TOMATO PASTA SALAD WITH THAI-STYLE VEGETABLES

Preparation time: 20 minutes
Total cooking time: 20 minutes
Serves 4–6

350 g (11 oz) tomato fettucine or plain
    fettucine
100 g (3½ oz) fresh baby corn, halved
    lengthways
1 carrot, cut into julienne strips (see Note)
200 g (6½ oz) broccoli, cut into small florets
½ red capsicum, cut into julienne strips
2 teaspoons sesame seeds
3 spring onions, chopped

DRESSING
¼ cup (60 ml/2 fl oz) sweet chilli sauce
2 teaspoons fish sauce
¼ cup (90 g/3 oz) honey

1 Cook the pasta in a large pan of rapidly boiling salted water until al dente. Drain well and cool.

2 Cook the corn in boiling water for 1 minute. Remove and plunge into a bowl of iced water. Cook the carrot, broccoli and capsicum in boiling water for 30 seconds, then drain and add to the iced water to cool. Drain the vegetables and add to the pasta.

3 To make the dressing, whisk the ingredients together, drizzle over the salad and toss well. Sprinkle with the sesame seeds and spring onions.

NUTRITION PER SERVE (6)
Protein 10 g; Fat 1 g; Carbohydrate 60 g; Dietary Fibre 6 g; Cholesterol 0 mg; 1260 kJ (300 cal)

NOTE: Julienne strips are even-sized strips of vegetables, cut to the size and shape of matchsticks.

Use a sharp knife to halve the fennel and then cut into slices.

Cut the salami into strips and add to the bowl along with the chopped parsley.

SALAMI PASTA SALAD

Preparation time: 20 minutes
Total cooking time: 15 minutes
Serves 8

1 red capsicum, cut into strips
1 green capsicum, cut into strips
4 celery stalks, sliced
1 fennel bulb, trimmed and sliced
1 red onion, sliced
200 g (6^1/$_2$ oz) salami, thickly sliced and
    then cut into strips
^{1}/$_2$ cup (15 g/^{1}/$_2$ oz) chopped fresh flat-leaf
    parsley
300 g (10 oz) fettucine

DRESSING
^{1}/$_2$ cup (125 ml/4 fl oz) olive oil
3 tablespoons lemon juice
2^1/$_2$ tablespoons Dijon mustard
1 teaspoon sugar
1 clove garlic, crushed

1 Mix together the red and green capsicum, celery, fennel, onion, salami and parsley in a large bowl.
2 Cook the pasta in a large pan of rapidly boiling salted water until al dente. Drain well and rinse under cold water. Add to the bowl and toss with the vegetables and salami.
3 To make the dressing, combine the olive oil, lemon juice, mustard, sugar and crushed garlic and season to taste. Pour over the salad and toss well.

NUTRITION PER SERVE
Protein 10 g; Fat 25 g; Carbohydrate 30 g; Dietary Fibre 2.5 g; Cholesterol 26 mg; 1599 kJ (380 cal)

Cut the red onion in half and then use a sharp knife to finely chop.

Remvoe the seeds and membrane from the capsicum before grilling.

GRILLED CAPSICUM AND ANCHOVY SALAD

Preparation time: 15 minutes
Total cooking time: 25 minutes
Serves 4–6

500 g (1 lb) penne or spiral pasta
2 large red capsicums
1 small red onion, finely chopped
1 cup (30 g/1 oz) fresh flat-leaf parsley
    leaves
2 anchovies, whole or chopped
3 tablespoons olive oil
2 tablespoons lemon juice

1 Cook the pasta in a large pan of rapidly boiling salted water until al dente. Drain and rinse under cold water.

2 Cut the capsicum into large pieces, removing the seeds and membrane. Place cut-side-down under a hot grill and cook for 8 minutes or until the skin is blistered and black. Cover with a tea towel and leave to cool, then peel away the skin and cut the flesh into thin strips.

3 Toss together the pasta, capsicum, onion, parsley, anchovies, oil, lemon juice and some salt and pepper. Serve immediately.

NUTRITION PER SERVE (6)
Protein 11 g; Fat 11 g; Carbohydrate 62 g; Dietary Fibre 7 g; Cholesterol 0 mg; 1640 kJ (400 cal)

HINT: The capsicum can be peeled a day in advance, covered well and then refrigerated. Removing the skin in this way results in a much sweeter taste.

Chop the basil leaves just before you are ready to use them as the cut edges turn black.

Mix together the basil, tomato, garlic, olives, oil and vinegar and leave to stand.

SPAGHETTI TOMATO SALAD

Preparation time: 25 minutes
Total cooking time: 15 minutes
Serves 4–6

500 g (1 lb) spaghetti
1 cup (30 g/1 oz) fresh basil leaves
250 g (8 oz) cherry tomatoes, halved
1 clove garlic, crushed
1/2 cup (60 g/2 oz) chopped black olives
3 tablespoons olive oil
1 tablespoon balsamic vinegar
1/2 cup (60 g/2 oz) grated Parmesan

1 Cook the pasta in a large pan of rapidly boiling salted water until al dente. Drain well and rinse under cold water. Using a sharp knife, chop the basil leaves into fine strips.
2 Mix together the basil, tomato, garlic, olives, oil and vinegar. Leave for 15 minutes. Toss with the pasta.
3 Add the Parmesan and some salt and pepper. Toss well to serve.

NUTRITION PER SERVE (6)
Protein 14 g; Fat 15 g; Carbohydrate 65 g; Dietary Fibre 14 g; Cholesterol 10 mg; 1866 kJ (446 cal)

Put the tomatoes cut-side-up on a baking tray and roast until soft.

Cook the pasta in rapidly boiling water until it is just tender.

GREEK PASTA SALAD

Preparation time: 10 minutes
Total cooking time: 45 minutes
Serves 4

4 Roma tomatoes, quartered
1 tablespoon chopped fresh oregano
500 g (1 lb) rigatoni
250 g (8 oz) marinated soft feta
1 red onion, sliced
1 tablespoon capers in salt, rinsed and
   patted dry (see Note)
2 tablespoons red wine vinegar
$\frac{1}{2}$ cup (15 g/$\frac{1}{2}$ oz) chopped fresh flat-leaf
   parsley
2 tablespoons ready-made olive tapenade

1 Preheat the oven to moderate 180°C (350°F/Gas 4). Place the tomatoes cut-side-up on a baking tray, sprinkle with 1 teaspoon of the oregano and season well. Roast for 30–40 minutes, or until soft and caramelized.
2 Cook the pasta in a large pan of rapidly boiling salted water until al dente. Drain well and return to the pan to keep warm.
3 Drain and crumble the feta, reserving the oil and herbs. Heat 2 teaspoons of the reserved oil in a small frying pan, add the onion and cook over medium heat for 2–3 minutes, or until soft, then add the capers and cook for a further minute. Combine the rest of the reserved oil with the vinegar and stir into the pan. Remove from the heat and stir through the pasta, adding the remaining oregano and the parsley. Top with the tomato, feta and the tapenade to serve.

NUTRITION PER SERVE

Protein 27 g; Fat 16 g; Carbohydrate 89 g; Dietary Fibre 6 g; Cholesterol 43 mg; 2570 kJ (615 cal)

NOTE: You can buy capers in salt from delicatessens—they are smaller than normal capers and are kept in salt rather than brine. If you want to use capers in brine, buy baby capers and drain them before use.

Spread the walnuts on a baking tray and toast for 10 minutes.

Remove the rind from one-third of the cheese and cut the rest into cubes.

WARM SWEET POTATO, WALNUT AND PASTA SALAD

Preparation time: 15 minutes
Total cooking time: 30 minutes
Serves 4

800 g (1 lb 10 oz) orange sweet potato, cut into small cubes
150 ml (5 fl oz) olive oil
1 cup (125 g/4 oz) walnut pieces
350 g (11 oz) pasta
150 g (5 oz) white castello cheese
2 cloves garlic, crushed
2 teaspoons lemon juice
1/2 teaspoon sugar
100 g (3 1/2 oz) rocket

1 Preheat the oven to moderately hot 200°C (400°F/Gas 6). Toss the orange sweet potato in 2 tablespoons of the oil and place in a single layer on a baking tray lined with baking paper. Season with salt and pepper. Cook, turning halfway through, for 30 minutes, or until golden and cooked through. Spread the walnuts onto a separate baking tray and add to the oven for the last 10 minutes, or until crisp and golden.
2 Meanwhile, cook the pasta in a large pan of rapidly boiling salted water until al dente. Drain well and return to the pan to keep warm. Remove the rind from one-third of the cheese and cut the rest into cubes. Finely chop 2 tablespoons of the toasted walnuts and place in a jar with the garlic, lemon juice, sugar, remaining oil and rindless cheese and season. Shake the jar until well combined. You may need to break the cheese up with a fork to help mix it through if it is too firm.
3 Toss the pasta, sweet potato, rocket, cubed cheese and remaining walnuts in a bowl, drizzle with the dressing and toss together. Divide among four serving bowls and season to taste with salt and black pepper.

NUTRITION PER SERVE
Protein 27 g; Fat 69 g; Carbohydrate 92 g; Dietary Fibre 11 g; Cholesterol 38 mg; 4570 kJ (1090 cal)

USEFUL INFORMATION

The recipes in this book were developed using a tablespoon measure of 20 ml. In some other countries the tablespoon is 15 ml. For most recipes this difference will not be noticeable but, for recipes using baking powder, gelatine, bicarbonate of soda, small amounts of flour and cornflour, we suggest that, if you are using the smaller tablespoon, you add an extra teaspoon for each tablespoon.

The recipes in this book are written using convenient cup measurements. You can buy special measuring cups in the supermarket or use an ordinary household cup: first you need to check it holds 250 ml (8 fl oz) by filling it with water and measuring the water (pour it into a measuring jug or even an empty yoghurt carton). This cup can then be used for both liquid and dry cup measurements.

Liquid cup measures

1/4 cup	60 ml	2 fluid oz
1/3 cup	80 ml	2 1/2 fluid oz
1/2 cup	125 ml	4 fluid oz
3/4 cup	180 ml	6 fluid oz
1 cup	250 ml	8 fluid oz

Spoon measures

1/4 teaspoon	1.25 ml
1/2 teaspoon	2.5 ml
1 teaspoon	5 ml
1 tablespoon	20 ml

Nutritional information

The nutritional information given for each recipe does not include any garnishes or accompaniments, such as rice or pasta, unless they are included in specific quantities in the ingredients list. The nutritional values are approximations and can be affected by biological and seasonal variations in foods, the unknown composition of some manufactured foods and uncertainty in the dietary database. Nutrient data given are derived primarily from the NUTTAB95 database produced by the Australian New Zealand Food Authority.

Oven Temperatures
You may find cooking times vary depending on the oven you are using. For fan-forced ovens, as a general rule, set oven temperature to 20°C lower than indicated in the recipe.

Note: Those who might be at risk from the effects of salmonella food poisoning (the elderly, pregnant women, young children and those suffering from immune deficiency diseases) should consult their GP with any concerns about eating raw eggs.

Alternative names

bicarbonate of soda	—	baking soda
capsicum	—	red or green (bell) pepper
chickpeas	—	garbanzo beans
cornflour	—	cornstarch
fresh coriander	—	cilantro
cream	—	single cream
eggplant	—	aubergine
flat-leaf parsley	—	Italian parsley
hazelnut	—	filbert
plain flour	—	all-purpose flour
prawns	—	shrimp
sambal oelek	—	chilli paste
snow pea	—	mange tout
spring onion	—	scallion
thick cream	—	double/heavy cream
tomato paste (US/Aus.)	—	tomato purée (UK)
kettle barbecue	—	Kettle grill/Covered barbecue
zucchini	—	courgette

Weight

10 g	1/4 oz	220 g	7 oz	425 g	14 oz
30 g	1 oz	250 g	8 oz	475 g	15 oz
60 g	2 oz	275 g	9 oz	500 g	1 lb
90 g	3 oz	300 g	10 oz	600 g	1 1/4 lb
125 g	4 oz	330 g	11 oz	650 g	1 lb 5 oz
150 g	5 oz	375 g	12 oz	750 g	1 1/2 lb
185 g	6 oz	400 g	13 oz	1 kg	2 lb

© 2006 Text, design and photography by Murdoch Books Pty Ltd.

This 2006 edition published by Metro Books, by arrangement with Murdoch Books Pty Ltd.

Metro Books
122 Fifth Avenue
New York, NY 10011

ISBN-13: 978-0-7607-8296-5

Printed and bound in China

3 5 7 9 10 8 6 4 2